BERLIOZ

Series edited by Stanley Sadie

The Master Musicians

Titles available in paperback

Berlioz *Hugh Macdonald*
Brahms *Malcolm MacDonald*
Britten *Michael Kennedy*
Bruckner *Derek Watson*
Chopin *Jim Samson*
Grieg *John Horton*
Handel *Donald Burrows*
Liszt *Derek Watson*
Mahler *Michael Kennedy*
Mendelssohn *Philip Radcliffe*
Monteverdi *Denis Arnold*
Purcell *J.A. Westrup*

Rachmaninoff *Geoffrey Norris*
Rossini *Richard Osborne*
Schoenberg *Malcolm MacDonald*
Schubert *John Reed*
Sibelius *Robert Layton*
Richard Strauss *Michael Kennedy*
Tchaikovsky *Edward Garden*
Vaughan Williams *James Day*
Verdi *Julian Budden*
Vivaldi *Michael Talbot*
Wagner *Barry Millington*

Titles available in hardback

Bach *Malcolm Boyd*
Beethoven *Barry Cooper*
Chopin *Jim Samson*
Elgar *Robert Anderson*
Handel *Donald Burrows*

Schubert *John Reed*
Schumann *Eric Frederick Jensen*
Schütz *Basil Smallman*
Richard Strauss *Michael Kennedy*
Stravinsky *Paul Griffiths*

In preparation

Bartók *Malcolm Gillies*
Dvořák *Jan Smaczny*

Musorgsky *David Brown*
Puccini *Julian Budden*

BERLIOZ

Hugh Macdonald

OXFORD
UNIVERSITY PRESS

OXFORD
UNIVERSITY PRESS
Great Clarendon Street, Oxford OX2 6DP

Oxford University Press is a department of the University of Oxford.
It furthers the University's objective of excellence in research, scholarship,
and education by publishing worldwide in

Oxford New York

Athens Auckland Bangkok Bogotá Buenos Aires Calcutta
Cape Town Chennai Dar es Salaam Delhi Florence Hong Kong Istanbul
Karachi Kuala Lumpur Madrid Melbourne Mexico City Mumbai
Nairobi Paris São Paulo Singapore Taipei Tokyo Toronto Warsaw

and associated companies in Berlin Ibadan

Oxford is a registered trade mark of Oxford University Press
in the UK and in certain other countries

Published in the United States
by Oxford University Press Inc., New York

First published 1982, followed by the first paperback edition 1991,
by J.M. Dent & Sons Ltd

First published in paperback by Oxford University Press 2000

The moral rights of the author have been asserted

Database right Oxford University Press (maker)

British Library Cataloguing in Publication Data

Data available

Library of Congress Cataloging in Publication Data
Macdonald, Hugh, 1940–
Berlioz / Hugh Macdonald.
p. cm.—(The master musicians)
Includes bibliographical references (p.) and index.
1. Berlioz, Hector, 1803–1869. 2. Composers—France—Biography.
I. Title. II. Master musicians series.
ML410.B5 M13 2000 780'.92—dc21 00–040065
ISBN 0-19-816483-1

1 3 5 7 9 8 6 4 2

**Printed in the United States of America
on acid-free paper**

Note on the paperback edition

I have taken the opportunity of a new edition to correct a number of errors in the text and to bring the bibliography up to date.

St Louis, 1990   H.J.M.

Acknowledgments

In the writing of this book I have incurred three especial debts: to David Cairns, whose unequalled knowledge of Berlioz's life and character saved me from many an error in the biographical sections; to Kern Holoman, on whose monumental *Catalogue* (still in preparation) and vast command of Berlioz's life and works I have freely drawn; and to my wife, Beth, who has nursed, typed and indexed the book; many of her ideas lie unacknowledged in the text.

Glasgow, 1981   H.J.M.

Contents

Illustrations

1

1803–1830

The Berlioz family had been settled in the region between Lyons and Grenoble, the Isère *département* of France, since the beginning of the seventeenth century, if not before, and from being tanners in earlier generations they had risen to the respectable professions of law and medicine. Most of Berlioz's paternal relatives were lawyers or doctors, and he considered entering both professions himself, however briefly. His grandfather, Louis-Joseph Berlioz (1747–1815) was a lawyer in Grenoble and his father, also Louis-Joseph (1776–1848), was a doctor in the small town La Côte-St-André, about thirty miles north-west, not far from the main road north to Lyons. In this community Berlioz's father was a prominent well-to-do citizen, briefly mayor in 1817, holding clear authority and responsibilities and giving himself energetically to them. His wife, Marie-Antoinette-Joséphine, *née* Marmion (1784–1838), was brought up at Meylan, a few miles east of Grenoble.

The composer was their eldest child, born on 11th December 1803 and baptized Louis-Hector. Five more children were born in the succeeding seventeen years of whom only two survived to maturity, Berlioz's sisters Nanci (1806–50) and Adèle (1814–60); an intermediate sister, Louise, died at the age of seven. The family house (now a museum) provided a spacious, elegant home, and the town's position overlooking a broad landscape with the foot-hills of the Alps in the distance and snowy peaks beyond made a striking impression on the child Berlioz, as it does on the visitor today. Berlioz spent his working life in Paris and showed little interest in rural pursuits and less in folksong, but he always spoke of La Côte-St-André with affection, and all his life kept in touch with friends and relatives from the region. The family was knit by deep bonds of mutual affection; Berlioz's attachment to his two sisters grew with every passing year, and all his remarks about his father show a devotion based on filial admiration and shared attitudes which surmounted the prolonged difficulties occasioned by Berlioz's choice of profession and his marriage. Despite these great impediments Berlioz saw his father to be a humane, unprejudiced, sensitive man of liberal outlook and broad intelligence, well read in Latin and French classical literature and devoted to his work and his fellow-creatures. It was fortunate that he should have taken on Berlioz's education himself, apart from a brief period spent at a local infant seminary, for he showed wide intellectual interests (he published some important work on chronic diseases, hydrotherapy and other topics) and taught his son the rudiments of music. Later on, after their intermittent estrangements, Berlioz showed deepened affection and no trace of bitterness, while his father acknowledged that he had been proved wrong about his son's career: though he lived to 1848 he never heard any of his music.

His mother was a Catholic of narrower outlook and more dogmatic temperament, even less able than her husband to comprehend Hector's constant enthusiasms. For this distinctive element of Berlioz's personality manifested itself early: first (according to the *Memoirs*) it was a short-lived religious devotion, and then, through the experience of hearing a tune from one of Dalayrac's opérascomiques at his First Communion, the mystical equivalence of music and religious ecstasy; then he discovered books of travel, tales of the South Seas and the Pacific Isles, including Captain Cook's *Voyages*. Then Virgil; after an initial distaste for memorizing lines of Latin verse, the dramatic impact of Dido's sufferings (a scene later to be recreated in the final act of *Les Troyens*) drew tears from the boy's eyes; his father 'pretending not to have noticed anything, rose abruptly and shut the book. "That will do, my boy," he said, "I'm tired." '[1] Next came the impact of sentimental passion when he was twelve and Estelle Dubœuf, the object of his adoration, was eighteen. He called her his *Stella montis*, associating her with the mountains behind Meylan, his maternal grandfather's village, where she lived, and with Florian's *Estelle et Némorin* which he had already 'read and re-read a hundred times'. He was teased about his infatuation, but it proved to be deeper than anyone suspected. As was to happen many times again in later life, the emotional experience triggered his creativity; he at once wished to express his response in music.

At that stage he had mastered a flageolet, found at the bottom of a drawer, and learned to play the flute, purchased and instructed by his father (Némorin, who loved Estelle, also played the flute). He used Devienne's flute *Method* and practised Drouet's flute concertos; he was also able to sight-sing with ease. So his father joined other families in La Côte and engaged a music teacher, Imbert, to continue this instruction. Berlioz was thirteen, already anxious to compose and still infatuated with Estelle. For a local string quartet, who played every Sunday after mass, Imbert's son (a horn player) and himself as flautist, he wrote a sextet on Italian airs, applying what he could learn of harmony from reading Rameau's and Catel's treatises and from listening to Pleyel's quartets. There appears to have been no piano at La Côte and he never studied the instrument. For reasons we know nothing of, Imbert's son committed suicide, so the group became a quintet for which Berlioz composed his next two pieces. Both were later destroyed, although one melody was preserved as the lilting second subject of the *Francs-juges* overture:

Ex. 1

Thus his beginnings as a composer were in the realm of chamber music for which he wrote nothing at all in later years. Imbert's successor as music-teacher, Dorant, gave lessons on the guitar (among other instruments), and Berlioz rapidly learned this instrument too. He wrote guitar accompaniments for fashionable romances by Dalayrac, Berton, Boieldieu and others, and composed a number of songs on pastoral and sentimental verses. This suited his adolescent taste for the sentimental, now developing into a more ardent inclination to passionate expression which was to be the hallmark of the mature composer. By the age of fifteen Berlioz had the confidence to write to a number of Paris publishers (two letters have survived;[2] there must have been many more) offering them the sextet and some romances with piano accompaniment. At least one publisher replied favourably, and thus the romance, *Le dépit de la bergère*, appeared in print shortly afterwards. Its melody came back to Berlioz forty-two years later and found its place (in the minor mode) as the *Sicilienne* in *Béatrice et Bénédict*, his last work:

Ex. 2

(a)

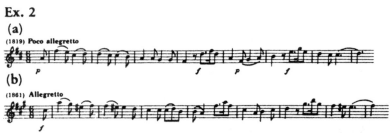

(b)

He set some of the poems from Florian's pastoral and charming *Estelle et Némorin* and, though he says he burned them before he left home in 1821, he reworked them into an opera in 1823 and preserved one of the melodies as the opening passage of the *Symphonie fantastique* in 1830. Music had seized his adolescent soul, and he quickly exhausted the narrow musical resources of La Côte. He felt irresistibly drawn even before he had heard a note of music by any composer greater than Pleyel or Boieldieu. Yet he dimly grasped the potential of expressive dramatic music and recounts how his first sight of 24-stave manuscript paper excited him by the imaginary concept of splendid orchestral and vocal music to be written upon it.

Dr Berlioz's encouragement of his son's musical gifts declined when he foresaw the conflict to which a choice of careers would lead. Berlioz never showed much inclination towards medicine, yet his father's wish that he should pursue the same career prevailed. Berlioz in fact had little choice and he may well have been spurred to complying with his father's wishes by the new world of music which he knew he would encounter in Paris, where he was to attend medical school.

His medical studies commenced at home, and he obtained his bachelor's degree in Grenoble in March 1821. By the time he left for Paris in October of that year, he displayed all the imbalance between aspiration and experience that a provincial upbringing inevitably led to in those days. His knowledge of distant lands was gleaned from books, his longing for exotic shores hopelessly unfulfilled. His knowledge of human nature and of emotional conflict derived more from reading La Fontaine, Bernardin de St Pierre and Chateaubriand than from his own admittedly precocious experience. His awareness of politics in those restless years stemmed more from his dashing uncle Félix Marmion's exploits in Napoleon's army in Spain, Russia and at Waterloo, than from the immediate impact of war, which was not very considerable; La Côte was occupied by foreign troops for brief periods in 1814 and 1815. Such vicarious experience in such an ardent mind produced a thirst for the wider world which only a decisive move away could slake, and since these feelings were reinforced by urgent musical appetites, we can imagine that Berlioz's feelings as he left home for Paris were keen in anticipation. We have an official record of the external man at this time: 'Height 1.63 metres [just over 5 feet 4 inches], hair fair, forehead normal, eyelashes fair, eyes grey, nose good, mouth moderate, beard incipient, chin round, face oval, complexion fair, distinguishing marks none.'[3]

Berlioz shared lodgings on the left bank with his cousin Alphonse Robert, also a medical student devoted to music, who took his studies much more seriously than Berlioz. The latter's early determination to study medicine seriously quickly evaporated when Robert took him to the dissecting room:

> At the sight of that terrible charnel-house – the fragments of limbs, the grinning faces and gaping skulls, the bloody quagmire underfoot and the atrocious smell it gave off, the swarms of sparrows wrangling over scraps of lung, the rats in their corner gnawing the bleeding vertebrae – such a feeling of revulsion possessed me that I leapt through the window of the dissecting-room and fled for home as though Death and all his hideous train were at my heels.[4]

The capital proved an enticing distraction. Berlioz attended classes in physics, chemistry, French history and literature, and went to balls, which he disliked. The great revelation was the Opéra which the two cousins attended as soon and as often as they could. There is some contradiction between the *Memoirs* and the correspondence as to which operas Berlioz heard first, but none as to the impact they had upon him. The works he saw were Salieri's *Danaïdes*, Méhul's *Stratonice* and Gluck's *Iphigénie en Tauride*, none of it very recent or modern. From the first he felt an instinctive admiration for Gluck, and being thus exposed to his greatest work sung by the great tenor Nourrit, he developed an intense enthusiasm for his music never displaced by his later awareness of Beethoven or other more modern composers. He saw all Gluck's major works in the next four years, an opportunity he would not have had later when newer fashions in opera displaced Gluck from the repertory. As instinctively as he felt drawn to Gluck and Spontini, he felt antipathy to Rossini's music when he heard it in 1824. Thus his musical tastes were polarized between his faith in the French classical tradition and his opposition to Italian opera, the music of the 'dilettanti'. In 1822 he discovered that the Conservatoire library was open to the public and there he was able to study and copy Gluck's scores, including those that he had not heard.

He was already having some success as a composer. Six romances for one or two voices with piano appeared in print during his first year and a half in Paris, and by the end of 1822 he sought and obtained an introduction to Lesueur, a senior, somewhat eccentric figure among French composers and the recipient of Napoleon's favours for his opera *Ossian ou les bardes* in 1804. Neither this work nor his monumental *La mort d'Adam* were still in the repertory, yet Berlioz studied the scores, and after showing Lesueur his first orchestral work, a cantata on Millevoye's poem *Le cheval arabe*, now lost, was accepted as a private pupil. One effect of Lesueur's teaching was that Berlioz published no more romances, in fact no more music at all, for about six years; the other was that his disinclination to pursue medicine became stronger than ever since his master expressed early confidence that he, Berlioz, had real talent as a composer. The switch from medicine to music was dramatic, but not quite so abrupt as the *Memoirs* suggest, for he sustained his medical studies for over two years, at least until his 'baccalauréat ès sciences physiques', which he took in January 1824. Relations with his family were immediately strained by these plans. His visit home in the autumn of 1822 seems to have passed off without incident, but the following March he returned home to face stern efforts to persuade him to renounce a musical career. His father held a deep belief that music offered an unstable and unworthy future and had a horror of second-rate artists, while his mother shared the widespread view that artists and musicians made disreputable company and that Berlioz was 'setting his feet on the broad road that leads to disgrace in this world and damnation in the next'.[5] Medicine, in their view, was an honourable profession with none of the instability which Berlioz was indeed to experience for himself as a musician. It was not simply his father's allowance that was at stake, but also his parents' moral support for what he knew to be his calling.

We have little music from his first years as Lesueur's pupil by which we might judge how Berlioz so certainly trusted his own genius: there was clearly a powerful inner force that told him he could and would prove himself in due course. Three important works from this period (1823–4) are wholly lost: an opera *Estelle et Némorin*, based on his favourite Florian, an oratorio, *Le passage de la mer rouge*, and a dramatic scena *Beverley ou le joueur*. None of these were performed. On a yet larger scale, the *Mass*, of which one of the nine movements does, happily, survive, was composed for St-Roch church, but when it was rehearsed on 28th December 1824 it was such a fiasco that the performance was cancelled.

News of this, his first attempt to organize a public performance of his own music, reached La Côte-St-André and was regarded by his father as clear indication of his failure as a composer. 'Enthusiasm', wrote his father, 'destroys every quality of the heart and renders those who are possessed by it weak, immoral, egotistical and despicable',[6] and to back this up he cut off the allowance. This was the beginning of several years of hardship for Berlioz; we do not need to suppose that he was starving in a garret – although the *Memoirs* paint a picture of his left-bank life with Antoine Charbonnel which is close to an idealized *vie de Bohème* – for by borrowing, giving lessons, writing occasional articles in *Le corsaire*, and later singing in a theatre chorus, he maintained what he regarded as the essentials of life; attending the opera, studying with Lesueur, later attending Conservatoire classes and performing his own works.

In early 1825 his first preoccupation was to perform the *Mass* and prove to himself and his family that a successful performance was possible. With tremendous audacity he had already asked Chateaubriand for the 1,200 francs he needed to perform the *Mass* and received a courteous and sympathetic refusal, but he was successful in borrowing the same sum from a wealthy young fellow-Gluckist, Augustin de Pons, and the performance thus took place, on 10th July 1825, a day of triumph and revelation for the composer. To have presented his work to the Paris public for the first time and to have stirred them was satisfaction enough, but Berlioz was perhaps more fired by his own response:

> When I heard the crescendo at the end of the Kyrie my breast swelled like the orchestra, my heart-beats followed the strokes of the timpani. I don't know what I was saying but at the end of the piece, Valentino [the conductor] said: 'Try to keep quiet, my friend, if you don't want me to lose my head.' In the 'Iterum venturus' after the proclamation of the coming of the Last Judgement by all the trumpets and trombones in the world, the chorus of human voices unfolded, recoiling in terror. O God! I was swimming in this tempestuous sea, I drank in those waves of frightening vibrations.[7]

Seven newspapers carried notices of the performance; furthermore his much-loved and much-respected teacher was unequivocally stirred: 'Let me embrace you. Believe me, you will be neither a doctor nor an apothecary, but a great composer; you have genius, I tell you because it's true.'[8] But his parents were unmoved, and though his allowance seems to have been intermittently resumed at a modest fifty francs a month, their attitude was unbending. Chapter 10 of the *Memoirs* describes a harrowing scene at La Côte (probably in October 1825) when his mother, on her knees, implored him to abandon music and then, when he refused, disowned him with a malediction that rang in his ears.

Of his group of Parisian friends at this period, the most enduring was Humbert Ferrand; Berlioz's letters to him, collected in the volume *Lettres intimes* in 1882, stretch from 1824 to 1867; he was often cast as Horatio in Berlioz's self-dramatization as Hamlet. He was then studying law but was more preoccupied with poetry and drama and he wrote two, and possibly more, texts for Berlioz to set. The first was a cantata for chorus and orchestra on a topical subject dear to all fervent spirits of the day, the *Révolution grecque*, composed in the winter of 1825, and the second was an opera, *Les francs-juges*, on which Berlioz worked energetically during the summer of 1826. It had a romantic medieval setting and a story of tyranny, heroism and rescue, truly in the tradition of the French Revolutionary operas of Cherubini and Méhul, enlivened by the spirit of Weber's *Der Freischütz*, a recent success in Paris. Berlioz's eyes were ambitiously set on the prestige of the operatic stage, having as yet little conception of concert music (then almost unknown in France) and little taste for fashionable domestic music-making for the piano, the guitar and the harp. Opera, above all, allowed him to express situations and feelings in music, as Gluck and Spontini had done, and it was against these composers that he ventured to match himself. A plan to compose an opera on Walter Scott's *Talisman*, entitled *Richard en Palestine*, came to nothing, despite lengthy correspondence with the librettist, but *Les francs-juges* was completed, including its stirring overture, the only part of the opera Berlioz did not reject and the piece he was to acknowledge as his first orchestral work. The opera itself was rejected by the Odéon theatre, then the Opéra, then the Nouveautés, then the German Theatre; plans to mount it in Karlsruhe failed. Berlioz revised it in 1829 and again in 1833 but still failed to secure a performance, except for individual solos and duets, which he inserted in his own concert programmes. So eventually he destroyed it piecemeal, adapting movements for later works, publishing the overture as a concert piece, and ending up with a bundle of fragments.

Discouragement on a serious scale was still far off, however, and he persisted with operatic projects of every kind for many years, very few of which passed the stage of outline ideas. In France at this time the art of music meant either the opera or the salon, and it was the former which Berlioz knew to be his own. It was also the usual avenue to acceptance as a composer. Another was through the corridors of the Conservatoire, that pioneering institution which came out of the ferment of revolution with the highest ideals for the propagation of art for the people but which rapidly retreated into academic sterility as the century progressed. It was the only musical institution of standing in the country and it counted notable musicians on its staff, including the redoubtable Cherubini at its head. Despite admiration for his dramatic music, Berlioz quickly alienated Cherubini and thus lost the chance of influential support, even though his studies progressed intensively in the next few years. He enrolled in August 1826 and continued, now officially, in Lesueur's class and also attended Antonin Reicha's class in composition and fugue. Born in Bohemia and having lived for a period in Bonn, where he knew Beethoven, Reicha was a strange mixture of Germanic orthodoxy and impulsive eccentricity, whose passion for calculation and precision ran counter to Berlioz's feeling for expression. But he commanded Berlioz's respect and instilled in him a flexible and very personal fugal technique. This had already been tested, with or without prior study, earlier in 1826 when Berlioz presented himself for the preliminary round of the Prix de Rome, the prestigious and valuable prize awarded every year by the Institute enabling artists and musicians to study at the Villa Medici in Rome. The Prix de Rome was an enlightened scheme that offered much to painters and sculptors since the richest sources of their art were to be found in Italy, but for musicians, as Berlioz and many other laureates were later to discover, the advantages were more questionable. At this stage, however, Berlioz had his eye more on the five-year pension and the prestige, and for the next four years the Prix was the focus of his ambitions. At his first attempt Berlioz's modest fugue (which survives) failed the *concours d'essai*, causing dismay at La Côte. Increasingly pressed for funds, Berlioz considered emigration, offering to play the flute 'in an orchestra in New York, Mexico, Sydney or Calcutta'.[9] He went to see the Brazilian consul, lured, like the engineer Robert Stephenson, by the promised wealth of the New World. Lesueur offered to lend him money, counselling him not to audition for the Opéra chorus. But he did audition for a chorus job at the Théatre des Nouveautés – a scene of high comedy as described in the *Memoirs* – and succeeded. So for some months he crept stealthily off to sing works like *The Little Beggar Girl*, keeping his employment secret even from Charbonnel, with whom he shared rooms, for fear that the news would filter back to La Côte. The secret of Berlioz's 'disgrace' working in a vaudeville theatre was indeed disclosed over ten years later, to the renewed anguish of his family.

But he still found time and money to attend his Conservatoire classes, to learn Italian (expecting to win the Prix de Rome in due course), to buy a piano (expecting to rehearse his singers for *Les francs-juges*), and to buy translations of Walter Scott and Fenimore Cooper, which he read with consuming fervour. He bought an alarm clock in order to get up early and copy parts for his opera, and as soon as *Les francs-juges* was completed he began another overture, *Waverley*, already sensing his powers as an orchestral composer and avidly studying every aspect of instrumentation at the Opéra, where he had procured a free pass. In 1827 he again entered the Prix de Rome and this time passed the preliminary test, going on to compose the prescribed cantata *en loge*, that is, confined within the Institut for a period of three weeks as the regulation laid down. The obligatory text was *La mort d'Orphée* which Berlioz set with all the orchestral resource at his command. As a result the pianist required to play the candidates' scores to the adjudicating panel of composers failed miserably and the work was declared 'unplayable'. Berlioz was disqualified, or, more specifically, asked to withdraw. Berton, a composer of modest achievement and sixty years, one of the judges, told him:

> It's a chimera, my dear boy, there's no such thing as *novelty* in music; the great masters accepted certain musical forms which you do not wish to adopt. Why try to improve on the great masters? Then I know you have great admiration for a man who is certainly not without talent, not without genius . . . Spontini . . . Let me tell you, my dear boy, in the eyes of true connoisseurs Spontini does not enjoy very great esteem.[10]

Nothing could be better calculated to fire Berlioz's desire to do something new in music than to hear his adored Spontini belittled by the very men who sat in judgment on his cantata. His letters take on a new determination and speak of new ideas teeming in his head. Parental opposition, academic rejection and the frustration of having an opera composed but unperformed; these combined with Berlioz's naturally volcanic temperament and acute sensitivity to powerful external stimulus so that he seemed like a coiled spring or a primed charge. The three years that follow, from 1827 to 1830, mark the first detonation of these explosive forces, the first release of the spring. Not only were the circumstances of Berlioz's life and temperament poised to project him far beyond the achievements of his friends and fellows (Ferrand, Gounet and Guiraud, for instance), but he was also miraculously in tune with the tenor of the times. The increasing reaction of Restoration France was generating a group of rebellious voices in the press and the theatre, chief of them Victor Hugo with his superhuman energy and romantic bravura. The bastions of French classicism were stormed, first in the famous preface to *Cromwell* in 1827 and then in 1830, with the fiery action of *Hernani*. German romantic theatre crossed the Rhine: the world of dreams and fantasy, and a new sensitivity to art, above all to the power of music, made itself felt. The macabre and the grotesque were no longer unacceptably ugly; they had their own new fascination. Géricault painted his self-portrait alongside a skull; the hunchback Quasimodo excited sympathy, not abhorrence.

These widening horizons were not new to Berlioz; he already knew Chateaubriand, Weber and Walter Scott, and had responded keenly to their unmistakably romantic evocation. But the great revelations were yet to come and his total submission to their impact epitomizes the intensity of feeling which the romantic soul cultivated with such ardour. The three hammer-blows which descended on him in quick succession were Shakespeare, Beethoven and Goethe, coupled with the experience of passionate, unrequited love: a weaker constitution might have succumbed to passive inactivity under this attack, but in Berlioz it produced a creative fervour whose momentum lasted over thirty years. So much that had been ill-defined in his outlook came into focus and the somewhat archaic element in his musical make-up, going back to Gluck, became uncompromisingly modern. As usual with Berlioz the new worlds of experience were literary as well as musical, affecting both feeling and technique.

'I come now to the supreme drama of my life', wrote Berlioz at the head of the chapter of the *Memoirs* which recounts the revelation of Shakespeare. On 11th September 1827 he attended a performance of *Hamlet* at the Odéon Theatre given by an English company, with Charles Kemble as Hamlet and Harriet Smithson as Ophelia.

> Shakespeare, coming upon me unawares, struck me like a thunderbolt. The lightning flash of that discovery revealed to me at a stroke the whole heaven of art, illuminating it to its remotest corners. I recognised the meaning of grandeur, beauty, dramatic truth.[11]

Four days later he saw *Romeo and Juliet* and was again so overwhelmed that he resolved to stay away from the theatre thereafter for fear of another such ordeal. Kemble and Smithson were again in the main roles, and the combination of her beauty and the dramatic power of the poetry reduced Berlioz to a state of emotional torpor. He knew no English, yet the force of the drama was plain, accentuated by the strongly realistic style cultivated by the company. Harriet Smithson's real tears in Ophelia's mad scene would have crossed any language barrier. When Kean and Macready joined the company later in the season, Kean's Shylock and Macready's Macbeth shocked and terrified the French by their naturalistic power. Berlioz says he stayed away, but in the eleven months of that first season it seems improbable that he did not see *Othello, King Lear, The Merchant of Venice, Richard III*, or the two non-Shakespearean plays, Rowe's *Jane Shore* and Knowles's *Virginius*, in which Harriet Smithson had further triumphs. It was in fact she who sustained the company with her personal success as an actress, for the impact of Shakespeare, though considerable, was evidently more confined to the literary figures who were to borrow so liberally from Shakespeare in the development of French romantic drama: Hugo, Dumas, de Vigny, Deschamps, de Musset, and (in painting) Delacroix. All applauded Harriet Smithson vociferously: at her benefit performance on 3rd March 1828, a thousand people were turned away at the door and the stage lay buried in flowers.

Berlioz's letters of adoration were doubtless not the only ones she never answered. He succumbed to a deep lassitude of spirit, overwhelmed by *Hamlet* and poor Ophelia's mimed despair. He roamed the streets of Paris, he tells us, aimless and sleepless. For the first time he seems to have been unable to compose. He gave a second performance of his *Mass* (on 22nd November 1827), venturing to conduct the work himself, but otherwise his activities of the winter, if any, are obscure. Shakespeare was eventually to inspire him nobly, in a whole series of works in every medium, but at first his inspiration lay dormant. Harriet Smithson's continued success inspired Berlioz with the idea of giving a concert of his own music, to prove to her that he too was an artist, and doubtless to prove to his teachers, his parents and the public that he had a future as a composer. The concert was on 26th May 1828, conducted by Bloc, and despite every possible administrative hurdle thrown in Berlioz's way, it included the first performances of *Les francs-juges* and *Waverley* overtures, the *Révolution grecque*, parts of the opera *Les francs-juges* and a *Marche religieuse des mages* (now lost), and it was a portentous event as the first of innumerable concerts which Berlioz was to give all over Europe in the next thirty-five years. No other composer in France had ever sought to give concerts as a means of extending his audience and, as he vainly hoped, of making money.

The concert was also inspired by the recent creation of the 'Société des Concerts du Conservatoire', the brainchild of Habeneck, an able violinist and conductor who was already the most influential musician in Paris and was eventually to be in charge of the Opéra as well as of all concerts at the Conservatoire. Habeneck was the first of Beethoven's admirers in France and had tried through the *Eroica* with a student orchestra many years before he finally brought it to performance at the Conservatoire on 9th March 1828, and again two weeks later, followed by the Fifth Symphony on 13th April. Berlioz was undoubtedly present. 'The shock was almost as great as that of Shakespeare had been. Beethoven opened before me a new world of music, as Shakespeare had revealed a new universe of poetry.'[12] The new world was the world of concert music and symphony, previously neglected in France. The Société des Concerts was a tardy imitation of Vienna's Gesellschaft der Musikfreunde and London's Philharmonic Society, both of which based their repertory on the modern Viennese classics, Haydn, Mozart and Beethoven, usually interspersed with solos and vocal numbers of every kind. For Berlioz it was not simply a shift of balance between favouring symphonic rather than operatic music, it was the perception of a more powerful form of expression, *without* resorting to words, already plainly within Berlioz's natural powers, as the overture to *Les francs-juges* had demonstrated. Berlioz's faith in opera did not diminish, but he saw at once, amid the emotional impact of Beethoven's music, that he could himself promote and direct concerts of symphonic music whereas the doors of all opera-houses were firmly closed. Ironically his early reputation as an audacious modern symphonist made acceptance at the Opéra all the harder to win. He wrote many years later:

> If a composer begins by writing a symphony and if that symphony causes a sensation, then he is classified and marked: he's a symphonist, he must only write symphonies, he must keep away from the theatre for which he is not fitted, he cannot know how to write for the voice, etc. . . . He would escape this difficulty if his first symphony passes unnoticed, or if it's worthless. He would even find theatre managers prejudiced in his favour: 'He has failed in symphonic music, he is bound to succeed in the theatre. He does not know how to orchestrate, he is sure to write beautifully for the voice. He knows no harmony, he must be overflowing with melody . . .'[13]

Beethoven, like Shakespeare, lay dormant as a creative stimulus for a year or two. Goethe, on the other hand, triggered composition at once. Gérard de Nerval's translation of *Faust*, Part I, appeared in December 1827 and it seems that Berlioz discovered it the following summer. 'The marvellous book fascinated me from the first. I could not put it down, I read it incessantly, at meals, at the theatre, in the street.'[14] In a letter of September 1828 he wrote to Ferrand, from Grenoble, urging him to join him at La Côte:

> We will read *Hamlet* and *Faust* together. Shakespeare and Goethe! The silent confidants of my torments, they hold the key to my life. Come, oh come! no one here understands their raging genius. The sun blinds them. They just find it bizarre. Two days ago I wrote, in a carriage, the 'Ballad of the King of Thule', in gothic style; I will give it to you to put in your *Faust*, if you have one.[15]

The *Ballad*, which now lies at the heart of *La damnation de Faust*, was thus an impromptu response to reading Nerval's translation, and it seems as if Berlioz had no more ambitious plans than that. Yet he soon added to it a number of other settings of the verse parts of the translation, eight in all. For a while it seemed as if he might secure a commission to compose a *Faust* ballet, but when this fell through, he had his *Huit scènes de Faust* engraved at his own expense and issued by the publisher Schlesinger as his opus 1 in April 1829. He sent a copy proudly to Goethe, who, unable to read music, sought the opinion of his friend Zelter. 'Certain people', replied Zelter, 'can show their capabilities only by coughs, snorts, croaks and expectorations; Herr Hector Berlioz seems to be among them'; he went on to describe the work as 'an abortion arising from loathsome incest'.[16] So Goethe felt no compulsion to acknowledge the score and Berlioz merely smarted at the silence, mercifully unaware of Zelter's judgment. The *Huit scènes*, being all for different combinations of instruments, were not designed as a single concert work, and only one, the *Concert de sylphes*, was performed, at Berlioz's second Paris concert on 1st November 1829. Something in the performance undermined his faith in the work and he withdrew it, destroying as many scores as he could lay hands on. By any standards it was a remarkable opus 1, teeming with ideas, not to mention quotations from Shakespeare; but dimly perhaps he saw that the music deserved a more elaborate and artful setting, as it was to get seventeen years later in *La damnation de Faust*.

The La Côte visit of September 1828 was the first for three years, and Berlioz, with his obsession with Shakespeare and Goethe, Weber and Beethoven, must have seemed more irretrievably committed to the artist's life than ever. On the subject of Harriet Smithson he was doubtless silent. His letters to his sister Nanci are hereafter more searching and personal, and he found the little Adèle, now fourteen, lively and charming. The following winter was much more productive than the last. No sooner were the *Faust* pieces composed than he found Thomas Moore's *Irish Melodies* and wrote rapturously of them to his friends. His desire to speak a little English sharpened and he took some lessons. But the published French translation of Moore and some verse translations by a friend, Thomas Gounet, provided him with texts for nine Moore settings, for various voices and piano, and these pieces, bridging the chasm between the older type of romance and the newest dramatic style, were published at the end of 1829. A little piece of *diablerie*, a setting of a Herder poem in translation, *Le ballet des ombres*, also appeared in 1829 but was quickly withdrawn, like the *Huit scènes de Faust*.

A regular source of income at this time came from giving guitar lessons and he even published some variations on Mozart's *Là ci darem* for guitar solo, now lost. Of this side to his life he later wrote:

> In 1829 I had the honour to teach the guitar (I have always been attracted to terrible instruments) in a well-known school for young ladies in the Marais. Three times a week I would emerge from my garret in the Rue de Richelieu and wend my weary way along endless boulevards to near the Place de la Bastille to teach Carulli's *Divertissements*. My pupils were scarcely more than children,

almost all as shy as lambs and as intelligent as guinea-fowl. I was in a wretched state and would have perished altogether if two or three older girls had not decided to join my class one day begging me to drop the guitar lessons and have, instead of bright and lively conversation, a little music. 'Sing us something', they would say . . . and from that moment the guitar lessons became quite bearable music lessons; and my pupils made progress. One day, I remember, I was singing Orpheus' romance

> Objet de mon amour
> Je te demande au jour
> Avant l'aurore.

when one of the young ladies cried out: 'Who wrote that, Monsieur?' 'It's by Gluck.' 'Oh. Never heard of him. But it's very nice. It's even better than that last romance by Romagnesi. Is there a quadrille on *Orphée*?' 'Not yet.' 'But do tell me when there is; I'll buy it!'

Young and old thus acquired a knowledge of music which guitar arpeggios alone would never have given them, and I would not be surprised if any of them had become a prima donna and had her carriage drawn daily by her fans in Sydney or Hobart.[17]

After many years Berlioz's memory of those days was sardonic and detached, but at the time his feelings dominated his whole life. In January 1829 he wrote to Edouard Rocher:

> Oh! If only I did not suffer so! . . . What a ferment of musical ideas there is in me! . . . Now that I have broken the chains of routine I see an immense plain laid out before me which academic rules once forbade me to enter. Now that I have heard that awe-inspiring giant, Beethoven, I know where the art of music now stands, now I have to take it to that point and then push it yet further . . . no, not further, that is impossible, he has reached the limits of art, but equally far in another direction. There are new things to be done and plenty of them, I sense this with intense energy, and I will do them, you may be sure, if I live. Oh! Must my whole destiny be swallowed up by this overwhelming passion? Yet if it works out well, everything I have suffered would serve to amplify my musical ideas, I would work with such ardour, my resources would be tripled, a whole musical world would be thrust forth fully armed from my brain, or rather from my heart, to conquer that which an artist holds most dear, the approval of those who are capable of appreciating him.
>
> Time is on my side, and I am still living; with life and time great events can be born.[18]

Prophetic words! Berlioz felt the genius within him more powerfully than ever, and in particular he felt the *Symphonie fantastique* within him, of that there can be no doubt. Beethoven showed him the power and the expression of the symphony, Shakespeare and Goethe opened up new worlds of feeling. Somehow 'great events' were to be fashioned from these experiences. A *Faust* symphony was the obvious step, but though Berlioz spoke of such a thing and may have made sketches, it never materialized.

Throughout all this there was his 'overwhelming passion' for the Irish actress who reappeared in Paris from time to time, and whose attention he vainly sought to attract. In February 1829 she was lodging across the street and they even shared the same bill, for the *Waverley* overture was played as a curtain-raiser at the Opéra-comique for her appearance in scenes from *Romeo and Juliet*. But he did not risk staying to hear her and she refused to reply to his letters, even when he wrote in English. Intensity of feeling built up inexorably through 1829, occasionally emitting blasts of passionate music, such as *Cleopâtre* (written for the Prix de Rome) or the *Élégie* (the last of the Moore settings), but the full explosion did not come until February of 1830 at the height of a crescendo traceable in his correspondence for at least two years. He described his condition to his father (19th February 1830):

> Sometimes I can scarcely endure this moral or physical pain (I cannot distinguish the two), especially on fine summer days when I'm in an open space like the Tuileries gardens, alone. Then I could believe a violent *expansive force* to be within me; I see the wide horizon and the sun, and I suffer so much, *so much*, that if I did not make an effort to restrain myself I would cry out and roll on the ground. I have only ever found one way of satisfying this enormous appetite for emotion, and that is music. Without it I am certain I could not go on living.[19]

Then he sat down to compose the *Symphonie fantastique*, and in two months it was done. He had stepped into the 'immense plain' that Beethoven had pointed to by combining the framework of a Beethoven symphony not with Shakespeare nor with Goethe, but with his own bitter experience of an unremitting passion that won no response. The symphony was unashamedly autobiographical, as no symphony had ever been before, and it told of the 'vague des passions', the ill-defined longing that had afflicted him since childhood, leading to the appearance of the beloved and the turbulent states of mind the artist falls into. The twist which made the form of the symphony possible was despair. The artist realizes that his love is hopeless; he dreams he has killed her and is executed, and the last movement is the nightmare of hell's vengeance.

The composition of the *Symphonie fantastique* was a momentous event in Berlioz's career, his first full-scale masterpiece, and equally momentous in the history of music as the first unequivocal declaration of romantic ideas in style and musical language, and its echo has pervaded all music of passion and personal experience to this day. Many would prefer to hear the work as a musical utterance on its own terms, but for Berlioz himself it signified a prolonged personal experience to which his letters, his memoirs and the symphony's programme give the key. Of Harriet Smithson's identity as the 'beloved', portrayed by an 'idée fixe' in the form of an obsessive theme that recurs in all the movements, there can be no question. What cannot be established is whether his love turned sour before or after the symphony was written, relating the artist's ultimate despair. For in the very same letter (to Ferrand, written on 16th April 1830) which reports setting down the last note of the symphony, Berlioz relates that

> horrible truths, revealed beyond the possibility of doubt, have set me on the way to recovery, and I think it will be as complete as my obstinate nature will permit. I have just sealed my resolution with a work with which I am completely satisfied . . . The immense mental effort of writing my work has fatigued my imagination, and I want to sleep and rest all the time . . .[20]

The 'horrible truths', we later learn, were revealed to him by an eighteen-year-old pianist, Camille Moke, half Belgian and half German, who was teaching the piano at the school where Berlioz was teaching the guitar. Although attached to Berlioz's friend Ferdinand Hiller (who gave the first Paris performance of the Emperor Concerto in Berlioz's concert of November 1829), she transferred her attentions to Berlioz and rapidly won his heart. She is first mentioned in a letter to Hiller of 3rd March; on 16th April Berlioz reports the 'horrible truths', and on 5th June he writes to his father seeking his permission for them to marry. Without doubt Camille was exceedingly attractive and vivacious and her very real presence easily swamped Berlioz's bitter awareness of the absent and unattainable Harriet. Camille hastened her pursuit with fabrications about the 'malheureuse' Harriet. There is perhaps no great sensation or import in the replacement of an idealized passion by an immediate, physical one (she and Berlioz slipped away to Vincennes for a night on 6th

June), but it is tantalizingly difficult to establish whether or not Camille played any part in the composition of the *Symphonie fantastique*. The *Memoirs* say that they met 'during the summer'. This could be the previous summer, since Berlioz knew her by March 1830 and was certainly seeing Hiller often before that. It is just possible that she had brought Berlioz's mind to bitter conclusions about Harriet at the very moment when the symphony, so long gestating in his mind, needed its dramatic resolution as a bad dream. Previously it may have been planned to end optimistically, like a Beethoven symphony, but once he had 'sealed his resolution' to turn his back on Harriet, the vision of murdering his beloved and its concomitant nightmare became a musical reality.

Much of the pent up emotional energy of the previous two years expended itself in the symphony, and much of it was given to planning his new life with Camille. His father had already begun to write in more sympathetic and encouraging tones than ever before, and her mother gave her consent in June, cautiously naming the day a year or two ahead, having first pressed the claim of Pleyel, an insistent suitor whose wealth and standing considerably outclassed Berlioz's. Camille's preference was plain, and it only remained for Berlioz to win the Prix de Rome and the financial security her mother demanded.

After the failure of his 1827 attempt at the Prix de Rome, he had won the Second Prize in 1828 with the cantata *Herminie*, after an extraordinary debate by the jury (described in Chapter 23 of the *Memoirs*). All seemed set for a First Prize in 1829, when the given text, on the death of Cleopatra, inspired from Berlioz a setting of striking originality and dramatic power. Yet no First Prize was awarded, a decision explained by Boieldieu (one of the judges) in a fashion similar to that of Berton two years before, that Berlioz had no business to introduce novel harmonies and rhythms into his work as if he were attempting to insult his seniors. So in 1830, with two First Prizes to be awarded, Berlioz felt more confident of success, and he had resolved to ease his path by writing in a tamer, more conventional style rather than risk offending the greybeards whose duty it was to award the prize. Indeed he did win, with a cantata on the death of Sardanapalus, another melodramatic subject. Ashamed of the music, Berlioz destroyed it later, although part of the Conflagration which he added to enliven its official performance at the Conservatoire has survived.

As he emerged from confinement in the Institut on 29th July 1830 he found the streets of Paris lined with barricades and bullets flying as the spirit of revolution seized the city. The king fled and Lafayette proclaimed Louis-Philippe 'as the best of all possible republics', a notion which touched Berlioz's sense of patriotism sufficiently to occasion a stirring arrangement of the *Marseillaise* for chorus and orchestra, although republicanism came later to ring very hollow in his ears. He then began an overture on *The Tempest*, but unlike *Waverley* and any Beethoven overture it included a part for chorus, singing in Italian. Learning Italian again, now with a firm prospect of going to Italy, he invoked Ariel, Miranda and Caliban in phrasebook language. It also had an orchestral part for piano, four hands, an instrumental innovation which had not been tried before and which was not tried again, either for solo or for duet, until Mussorgsky's *Boris Godunov*. *La tempête* was his first piece of Shakespearean music. He selected neither *Hamlet* nor *Romeo and Juliet* (the plays he had seen and lived passionately with but identified too closely with Harriet) but one he had only read. Its personal significance was that Camille was his 'Ariel', the spirit of air.

In the few months left before his departure for Italy Berlioz thus had three new works to perform, not to mention *Les francs-juges* for which he still entertained hopes of a production. On 30th October the official prize-giving session of the Institute was held, to hear the laureates' cantatas. Despite a successful rehearsal the performance of *Sardanapale* failed miserably since an incompetent conductor missed entries in the wind and ruined the Conflagration on which the entire effect depended. Berlioz in a rage threw his score at the players (newspapers confirm the *Memoirs'* account). He was in any case disappointed that neither his parents, nor Camille and her mother (who was wavering in her faith in Berlioz as a son-in-law) nor Lesueur were there, and at the same time enraged that Spontini, who *was* there, should have heard such a travesty of his work. A week later *La tempête* was performed at a benefit night at the Opéra under Habeneck, the first of many Berlioz first performances he was to give. Once again a promising rehearsal was followed by a disappointing performance, this time due not to incompetence but to misfortune, since a real tempest fell upon Paris that evening and only a handful of people were present.

The third concert was a different matter altogether. It was given at the Conservatoire at 2 p.m. on 5th December 1830 with

Habeneck again conducting. The programme included the *Francs-juges* overture, the *Sardanapale* cantata with its Conflagration – which caught fire properly this time – and the first performance of the *Symphonie fantastique*, his three boldest works presented to an audience that included Camille and her mother, Meyerbeer, Fétis, Spontini, and the nineteen-year-old Liszt, who was quickly to become one of Berlioz's closest friends and one of the very small group outside his family whom he addressed as the familiar 'tu'. The *Marche au supplice* was encored, and no one was left in any doubt of the force and invention of this new music. Spontini sent Berlioz a score of his *Olympie*, Fétis professed warm admiration in his notice. Berlioz was most of all relieved to learn that Mme Moke was sufficiently impressed to stop wavering and confirm her approval; he was obsessed with his Ariel and quite unmindful of Harriet Smithson whom everyone in Paris knew to be the subject of the symphony and who was that very night playing the part of the dumb girl in Auber's *La muette de Portici* a few streets away at the Opéra.

His career had taken an unmistakably decisive step forward, for the successes of the year and the optimism of a new, more liberal régime made Paris the focus of all his musical interests. He now had many friends in the musical fraternity, many of them foreign, like Schlösser, Pixis, Hiller and Liszt; he had won the admiration of Spontini and Fétis; he had won the Prix de Rome and placated his parents. His creative impulse was intensely active. He had a widening circle of literary friends. He needed above all to remain in Paris to exploit his success, to win access to the Opéra and to remain with Camille. Yet the regulations of the Institute insisted on attendance at their school in Rome to be followed by a stay in Germany and no amount of reasoning or pleading would permit this rule to be waived. In October Berlioz wrote to the Minister of the Interior claiming that the expectation of performances in Paris obliged him to remain and that his health had been undermined. He appended a doctor's note, certifying that he suffered from nervous complaints and cerebral congestion and should keep away from a hot climate. Fétis, Spontini, Meyerbeer and Lesueur supported the application, yet the ministerial decision, over a month later, was a curt refusal. The medical certificate was not mere manoeuvring: his letters report ill-health surprisingly frequently in these years, usually referring to nervous disorders which we may reasonably relate to the emotional and spiritual intensity of his life. An attack of quinsy in 1827 and an abscess in his throat which he lanced himself preceded periodic bouts of ill-health which resemble and may even relate to his long final intestinal illness.

On the very day he left Paris, 30th December 1830, he spoke of an 'immense project' in his mind, probably *Le dernier jour du monde,* an idea which recurs in the next few years but which was never realized. Had he stayed in Paris he might have composed it, and the momentum of 1830 might have thrust him forward into the strongholds of Parisian music. He might have staged *Les francs-juges* and he might have married Camille. Instead he spent nearly two years in Italy, stemming the headlong course of his career and the mental ferment of the previous three years. He achieved some tranquillity of mind and his music developed in countless subtle ways, but we may well speculate that he thereby lost the chance of worldly success which was to elude him for the rest of his life.

2
1831–1848

Berlioz left Paris on 30th December 1830 and went to his home in La Côte-St-André for a month. His health was not good and the separation from Camille irked him: his exchange of letters with Hiller, in Paris, touched on her easy-going acceptance of his departure and on 'mysteries' which he felt unable to reveal. His parents were welcoming, and proud of his success, but leaving Paris weighed heavily on him. He took the boat down the Rhône from Lyons and stayed in Marseilles a few days, awaiting a crossing to Italy. This was his first sight of the sea, the 'sublime monster', as he called it, and it evoked his childhood dreams of travel and distant lands; he discovered the pleasures of clambering around the rocks. Eventually he secured a passage on a Sardinian boat crossing to Leghorn with a bunch of Italian revolutionaries, one of whom enticingly claimed to have known Byron. The voyage began to resemble a Byronic adventure when the ship was caught in a sudden storm and the foolhardy captain ran them close to disaster. The onslaught of the elements, which he survived without being sea-sick, brought a realistic note to his idealized view of the sea. He may have had this experience still in mind many years later when he tested his son's wish to join the navy and when, in *Les Troyens*, Aeneas's soldiers grumble about the hardships of sea life.

He arrived in Italy strongly prejudiced against Italian music, and seeing Bellini's *I Montecchi ed i Capuletti* in Florence, based loosely on his adored *Romeo and Juliet*, angered him greatly. 'Ignoble, ridiculous, feeble, worthless', he called it. Even before reaching Rome he called the city a 'musical sewer'. But when he arrived there, early in March, the view of the Eternal City from the hills and the beautiful situation of the Villa Medici, where he was to lodge in the French Academy, captured his heart. Turning his back on the music of the capital he felt drawn to the outdoor life, to the world of brigands and mountains, and longed to taste these Byronic delights for himself. The Villa Medici provided old and new friends, as well as a tranquil milieu for composition, had he wished it. The unpopularity of the French at that time brought the constant threat of Italian insurgents, so their movements were prudently restricted. He met Mendelssohn and delighted in his company, mocking his Lutheran orthodoxy but admiring his unequalled musical fluency. But peace of mind was out of reach: he found no letters in Rome from his family or from Camille, and within three weeks impatience got the better of him (he must have been tedious company at the Villa) and he told Horace Vernet, the gentle and sympathetic director of the Academy, that he was returning to France and risking his scholarship. He left on 1st April 1831. In Florence he suffered another attack of quinsy and waited a week or more in case letters might be forwarded from Rome, filling in time by revising the *Symphonie fantastique*, musing on Dante and Michelangelo and devouring Shakespeare on the banks of the Arno; he read *King Lear* for the first time and was horribly moved. He chanced to follow the funeral procession of a young wife who had died in childbirth from the Duomo to the mortuary, and there, at midnight, he was able to gaze on the girl's pallid face and kiss her dead hand. His vivid and touching account is a mixture of a medical student's examination and a romantic artist's obsession with death, at last enacting Romeo's despair in Juliet's vault. The following day he attended the burial service for Napoleon's nephew, Napoléon-Louis, in Santo Spirito.

Death was all around him when eventually a letter came, not from Camille, but from her mother, informing him that Camille was to be married to Pleyel, that she had never been promised to Berlioz and requesting him not to kill himself. This touched a violent nerve in his already stormy condition, and there followed the extraordinary and well-known escapade with his immediate decision to dispose of mother, daughter, *futur* and finally himself in a grand dramatic *scena*, operatic, we might call it. He purchased a lady's maid's outfit as a disguise, grasped the two double-barrelled pistols provided for fighting off marauders at the Villa Medici, and set off for Paris. His resolution lasted two or three days, but then in Genoa some kind of crisis intervened and he wavered. He describes himself as stretched like a dead salmon beneath the city ramparts; he was desperately hungry, since he had had only oranges to eat, and he had lost the maid's costume. He could still laugh at himself, but what it amounted to was no less than a mortal conflict between life and death. Having first resolved upon death, he began again to feel the

Caricature of Berlioz by Horace Vernet, *c.* 1831

lure of survival. At Diano, a little further along the coast, he wrote to Vernet begging him to continue his scholarship and promising not to leave Italy. 'But at least I am alive, I must live for two sisters whose death would be brought about by my own, and I must live for my art.'[1] High above the breaking waves on the Corniche the urgency and beauty of living seized him, and arriving at Nice (still at that time a part of Italy) he felt wholly cured.

The crisis thus surmounted led to a period of intense happiness and creativity. His murderous and suicidal resolution had been real enough for a few days, but he also needed the proximity and sympathy of his family and may have been running home as much as running to Paris. Just as his release from Harriet Smithson had unleashed the composition of the *Symphonie fantastique* a year before, the process of ridding his mind of Camille now set in motion the composition of *Le retour à la vie* (later entitled *Lélio*)[2] which begins with the words 'God! I am still alive . . .' and describes the artist's recovery from a disastrous infatuation through the healing power of music. The work was eventually coupled with the *Symphonie fantastique* and the beloved again identified with Harriet, but its origin lay in that moment when he dismissed Camille from his mind, and fled from the prospect of death.

He fell in love with Nice, a city which seemed French despite being officially Italian, where he could indulge his new passion for climbing on the rocks, sketchbook in hand, keep in touch with his family and feel more intensely alive than ever before. Seducing a girl one evening on the beach firmly exorcized his thoughts of Camille. *Lélio* was in his mind, but he gave priority to an overture on *King Lear* and promptly finished it, following it at once with another on Scott's *Rob Roy*. The month in Nice was a period of recovery and genuine happiness, an unexpected sequel to the feverish months, or rather years, that preceded it, and the remainder of the Italian sojourn was unclouded by nervous or emotional tensions, a period of discovery and youthful adventure.

Much of it was spent at the Villa Medici in Rome, but he preferred to be out in the mountains, swimming (as the sculptor Etex recalled), going for long walks, searching for brigands, playing practical jokes and singing. He read little and composed less. But he does seem to have kept a journal for, although no such thing has survived, his letters take on a more self-consciously literary and descriptive character close to that of the *Memoirs*, both of which are indispensable reading for anyone who seeks the flavour or influence of his stay in Italy and, by extension, the background for *Harold en Italie*. Some passages from letters written on the leisurely return from Nice to Rome turn up unaltered in the spoken text of *Lélio*. He sent back a serialized account of his Italian visit to *L'europe littéraire* in Paris, to be re-used many times later, ultimately in the *Memoirs*. His powers of observation and description were certainly sharpened, so too was his sense of humour and adventure. His mind opened to the Mediterranean landscape essential for the settings of many works: *Benvenuto Cellini, Roméo et Juliette, Les Troyens, Béatrice et Bénédict* and of course *Harold en Italie* with its explicit evocation of scenes of Italian life. So much that left an impression on Berlioz is transmitted to us by his pen: the carnival in Rome (later inserted into his Cellini opera), the trip to Naples, the ruins of Pompeii, his horror of the paltry music in St Peter's, the *pifferari*, his happy memories of Virgil, Chateaubriand's cult of torrents, rocks and mountain streams, his openness to unusual ideas, his 'spleen' and romantic melancholia, his fanciful delight in brigands. No biographer can add much to his own stirring, vibrant account, and at the end of one of the *Memoirs'* more exuberant chapters he sums it up:

> Poignant memories of days of freedom now vanished! Freedom of the heart, of the mind, of the soul, of everything. Freedom to do nothing, not even to think; freedom to forget time, to despise ambition, to laugh at fame, to dismiss love; freedom to go north, south, east or west, to sleep in the open, to live on little, to wander at large, without premeditation to dream, to drowse away whole days immobile in the breath of the *sirocco*. Oh great, strong Italy, wild Italy, heedless of your sister, the Italy of art:
> *The lovely Juliet stretched upon her bier.*

Lélio was completed in Rome and the *Rob Roy* overture on a visit to Subiaco. The little song *La captive*, later to be elaborated and orchestrated, was also written at Subiaco. Otherwise he composed very little in Italy, and submitted various early works to the Académie as fallacious evidence of his activity there. A huge project on *Le dernier jour du monde* included the *Resurrexit* from the 1824 *Mass* but never materialized until the great *Tuba mirum* in the *Requiem* of 1837. Another grandiose project, on a Napoleonic subject, stirred him on his way home in 1832. But it is easy to discern that composition was uncongenial when he was far from Paris and far from musicians with whom he could happily work. He began to be impatient to return, to recapture the acclaim of 1830, to present the revised *Symphonie fantastique*, its sequel *Lélio* and his two new overtures. He was impatient too at missing the great events of Parisian music: the first French performance of the Choral Symphony, the première of Meyerbeer's *Robert le diable* and the sensational appearance of Paganini. (He never did hear Paganini, but he was able to make belated acquaintance with the other two.) He obtained permission to leave Italy but not yet to reappear in Paris. So he left Rome in May 1832 and spent five months at La Côte, still bored, still 'stifling for lack of music', but at least in harmony with his family, and preparing parts for *Lélio*. He finally returned to Paris in November 1832, not quite 29, ready for a prolonged attack on the stronghold of European music.

   The ten years Berlioz now spent in Paris were vigorously productive on all fronts, and they established him as the leading French composer of his generation in the eyes of the more discerning spirits even though official recognition and popular success never came his way. It is the decade in which Meyerbeer, Auber and Halévy established their supremacy at the Opéra and the Opéra-comique and Chopin, Liszt and many scarcely less brilliant virtuosi dominated the salon. The republican hopes of 1830 were soon deflected by French maritime expansion and bourgeois success so that in 1848 yet another revolutionary sputter became necessary. For a while the freshest romantic ideas led the way in the arts; the best work of Hugo, Delacroix and de Musset all belongs to this decade, and the fire of a new movement still burned strongly, with the hated spirit of compromise still kept firmly at arm's length, but the tide of respectable and middle-brow tastes quickly made itself felt with a perceptible decline in the understanding that Berlioz could expect from his audience. Paris was an intensely cosmopolitan city, seething with artists and musicians of every nationality, and the fact that Berlioz shone out as a home-bred Frenchman seems to have escaped everyone including himself in an age when national consciousness counted for nothing. Berlioz was wholly absorbed in his dedication to music: he read widely and mixed freely with men of letters, but although he counted Hugo and Chopin, de Vigny and Sand among his friends, his intimates were few, and the easy camaraderie in which the Romantics are always imagined to have lived and loved is far from the correct picture. He simply had too little time to spend languorous hours reading poetry with his friends. His was a life of commitment, travail and action, with the essential task of marshalling his relentless creative impulse and putting his compositions before the public.

The compositions flowed in a scarcely broken stream. Between 1834 and 1841 five of his major works were composed: *Harold en Italie* (1834), *Benvenuto Cellini* (1836), the *Requiem* (1837), *Roméo et Juliette* (1839) and the *Grande symphonie funèbre et triomphale* (1840). *Le cinq mai* (1835) and *Les nuits d'été* (1840–1), many songs and choruses, and a host of unfinished and unstarted projects also belong here. His concerts provided the outlet denied him elsewhere, for the Société des Concerts, which should have been promoting new music, played only one work by Berlioz in this period, the *Rob Roy* overture's first and only performance before he withdrew it, in 1833 (even later in his lifetime they only ever played extracts from *La damnation de Faust*). His own concerts were a novel feature of Parisian life, unattempted on the same scale by anyone else, and though they scarcely ever made any money despite his eternal optimism and usually cost him dearly, they were the centre of musical attention, feeding the natural French appetite for artistic controversy. Administrative difficulties or resistance often barred him from the Conservatoire hall, which he preferred; singers' commitments to opera or Conservatoire always came first, even at short notice; and a tax, paid to the poor, brutally reduced such takings as he could ever lay his hands on. The recurrent experience provided him with a bottomless well of irony and anecdote when he came to contemplate the follies of singers and administrators with maturer eyes.

It was a truly heroic task. He gave an average of three or four concerts a year, usually in the winter season, having to prepare the material for new works, engage all the musicians and hire a hall. The players even expected him to provide them with mutes and strings. One valuable offshoot was that after Girard bungled a performance of *Harold en Italie* in 1835, he resolved to conduct his concerts himself, leading in turn to his career as one of the first specialist orchestral conductors, in demand all over Europe as an interpreter, as much as for his own music.

From his work as a composer he made virtually no money. Concerts in Paris hardly ever ended with a surplus, and few of his larger works were published at this time, largely because he withheld them until he had had the opportunity to take his own music to foreign cities before false impressions had been allowed to settle. Government commissions, such as for the *Requiem* and the *Grande symphonie funèbre et triomphale* were less generous than they seemed when the fee was expected to pay the cost of performance and when payment had to be milked, in arrears, from the authorities. He was barred from a post at the Conservatoire since his rebellious views about traditional teaching were well known and because he had been on uneasy terms with Cherubini from his earliest days in Paris. Furthermore he eschewed the piano and organ, instruments on which professional musicians were then, as now, expected to be proficient.

Yet for income Berlioz was not at first in any desperate plight. The Prix de Rome was worth 3,000 francs a year, and it continued until the end of 1835 despite the requirement that the holder should spend a period of study in Germany as well as in Italy; to the authorities Berlioz piously asserted his intention of going, but he probably never meant to and they probably never cared. It was not until 1836 that his financial difficulties became serious, exactly when he most needed support during the long labour of composing *Benvenuto Cellini*. His solution was to become a critic. He had written intermittently for the press before he went to Italy and he began again in earnest for the *Rénovateur* in 1833, as their regular critic for two and a half years. The new *Gazette musicale*, soon to merge with the *Revue musicale* and become the leading music journal in France, employed Berlioz as writer and assistant editor all his working life, supporting his efforts staunchly. On 10th October 1833 he contributed an article, *Rubini à Calais*, the first of many, to the *Journal des débats*, an influential daily paper with which he remained associated for thirty years. To his work as a critic we shall later return; here it must suffice to realize how quickly and how deeply he became involved in the critic's world, how he depended on it for a livelihood, how much of his time and effort it absorbed (articles were always of substantial length), how easily in that world he made friends and enemies, and how he eventually came to be thought of as a critic who composed rather than as a composer who eked a living from writing. Despite the brilliance of his prose and the fascination it can have for the reader today, he regarded writing as an accursed drudgery, a millstone which oppressed him body and soul.

The chronicle of this period begins with his swift assault on the Paris public, with two concerts in the Conservatoire on 9th and 30th December 1832 with Habeneck conducting. The *Épisode de la vie d'un artiste*, that is to say the *Symphonie fantastique* followed by the new *Lélio*, was heard for the first time in its full form, with the actor Bocage playing the part of the artist. Hugo and Liszt were in the audience, and so too, by a subterfuge on the part of some friends, was Harriet Smithson, astonished to find herself not only the centre of attention as an actress of celebrity but also the object of the work's obsessed longings (*Lélio* invokes Juliet and Ophelia by name). A few days later Berlioz was introduced to her, and he declared his passion at once, as though the three-year period of suspension had never intervened. To Liszt, who rapidly became a close confidant, Berlioz wrote:

> I shall never leave her. She is my star. She understands me. If I am making a mistake, I must be allowed to make it. She will adorn the evening of my life, which, I trust, will not be prolonged. Such emotion cannot be gainsaid . . .

Yes, I love her, I love her! And she loves me. She said so yesterday,
in front of her sister. Yes she loves me, but I shall tell no one but you,
I want to hide my happiness – if I can.
So . . . keep silence! Nothing now can separate us.[4]

The ensuing year saw Berlioz moving heaven and earth to make his
Juliet his own and to transform his idealized passion of 1827 into
reality. Every kind of opposition was put in his way, including, it
seems, the cautious advice of young Liszt. Her mother and sister
were intransigent; his parents were implacably hostile. Her own
state of affairs was not propitious since her recent theatrical ventures
had failed and the appeal of Shakespeare in English was already
declining. Furthermore she broke her leg in March 1833 as a further
impediment to her theatrical career. She spoke little French and had a
severe accumulation of debt.

The affair soured Berlioz's standing with his family, relatively
calm since his successes of 1830. His father was bitterly opposed to
marriage with an actress of failing gifts, and relations quickly
reached the point where Berlioz had to take legal steps to procure his
freedom to marry. It was a period of intense emotional stress: Berlioz
overwhelmed by the force of his own passion, scarcely able to
communicate with an indecisive actress of delicate nervous sensibility, reduced invariably to tears by the vehemence of his ardour, while
his father and uncle pointed relentlessly to the poor omens of such a
match, of the burdens it would impose on his career. The curious and
inescapable fact is that with the exception of their belief that actres-
ses were disreputable characters, they, his parents, were right and
Berlioz was wrong. His promises to stay by her side to his dying day
proved hollow and the suffering the marriage was to bring on them
both was incalculable. Furthermore, if Berlioz's deficiencies of
character are here most gapingly displayed, there was the additional
element of emotional blackmail when, in August 1833, Berlioz coun-
tered her wavering spirit by threatening to depart and by taking
poison before her eyes, sufficient at least to secure her final consent.
So on 3rd October 1833 they were married in the chapel of the
British Embassy with Liszt acting as witness. After a honeymoon in
Vincennes and a short period in Berlioz's bachelor flat they moved to
the little cottage over the top of the hill of Montmartre, lovingly
painted by Utrillo on many occasions and now demolished, where
their only child, a son, Louis, was born the following August. To
begin with, at least, the stormy courtship settled into a happy young
ménage.

Arranging benefit performances for her and concerts for himself preoccupied his energies. In April 1833 *Rob Roy* was played by the Société des Concerts: Berlioz withdrew it at once and never put it forward again. That winter he brought out the *Roi Lear* overture for the first time, as well as *Le jeune pâtre breton* and the now lost *Romance* from Hugo's *Marie Tudor*. After the concert, at which the *Symphonie fantastique* was also played,

> . . . one member of the audience stayed behind in the empty hall, a man with flowing hair, piercing eyes and a strange, ravaged countenance, a creature haunted by genius, a Titan among giants, whom I had never seen before, the first sight of whom stirred me to the depths. He stopped me in passing and seizing my hand uttered such glowing eulogies that my heart and brain were set on fire. It was Paganini.[5]

Out of this meeting came Paganini's commission of a work in which he could display his Stradivarius viola. In the piece which Berlioz began at once to compose, the viola was prominent as soloist but the orchestra was not restricted, as in a concerto; it was freely expressive. He showed one movement to Paganini who was not impressed by the relatively modest part for the soloist and took no further interest, leaving Berlioz to develop the work into four movements depicting scenes of Italian life through Byronic eyes. *Harold en Italie* turned out to be not a concerto but a symphony in four movements with solo viola, and it was first heard on 23rd November 1834.

In 1835 the main new work was a cantata on the death of Napoleon, *Le cinq mai*, which Berlioz performed often but came not to like. His repertory now consisted of three overtures, two symphonies, *Lélio* (still enjoying the whiff of scandal arising from its reference both to Berlioz's personal life and to the musical atrocities of the senior lexicographer Fétis) and some smaller vocal and choral pieces. He also took to conducting his concerts himself. In 1836 he was absorbed in the composition of *Benvenuto Cellini*, made more difficult by the expiry of his pension, and his necessity to borrow money (from the devoted Legouvé) and work unceasingly for the press. A desire to write an opera was uppermost after his return from Italy, since only there lay a composer's recognized avenue to success and to the ears of the Parisian public. Many ideas for libretti came and went, among them *Hamlet, Much Ado About Nothing* (eventually set as *Béatrice et Bénédict* in 1862), *The Robbers* (Schiller – later set by Verdi as *I Masnadieri*), and a re-working of *Les francs-juges*.

At the Opéra the current successes were *William Tell, Robert le diable* and *Don Giovanni*. Halévy's *La juive* came out in 1835 and Meyerbeer's *Les Huguenots* in February 1836, spurring Berlioz to keener efforts with his own opera. The subject of Benvenuto Cellini's *Life* had been suggested to him, probably by Alfred de Vigny, when he was working on *Harold en Italie* in 1834; he certainly knew the great statue of Perseus in Florence, round which the opera's final scene is built. De Vigny enlisted two friends, Auguste Barbier, a poet, and Léon de Wailly, a translator and novelist, to fashion a libretto out of Cellini's swashbuckling adventures, and though Berlioz wanted a more serious drama to offer the Opéra, probably counting on the idea of the artist working against all odds as a central theme, the librettists came up with an opéra-comique with spoken dialogue, and much colourful and humorous incident. The Opéra-comique turned this down in 1834 so the piece was after all upgraded to an 'opera semi-seria' and in that form accepted by the Opéra late in 1835. Within a year the music was almost finished, but the production had to wait until 1838, after the composition and performance of the *Requiem*, whose history must therefore precede it here.

As well as the symphonic and operatic impulses in Berlioz's psyche, there was another, which we can only term 'monumental' and which may be traced back to his earliest studies with Lesueur and beyond that to the music of the French Revolution itself. The 1824 *Mass*, for all its immaturity, was clearly designed on monumental lines, and his recurrent desire in the following years to write a large-scale work for soloists, chorus and orchestra on some immense, apocalyptic theme persists in his letters and notebooks. Sometimes the plan is biblical and visionary, sometimes purely Napoleonic; for whatever purpose, Berlioz was evidently assembling a body of sketches and drafts which may never have seen the light. On the other hand there is plenty of reason to believe that some of this music found its way into the monumental or 'architectural' works which he later wrote: the *Requiem* (1837), the *Grande symphonie funèbre et triomphale* (1840), the *Te deum* (1849) and *L'impériale* (1854).

He admits that when the chance of composing a *Requiem* came his way he fell on it like a man possessed. 'The text of the *Requiem* was a quarry that I had long coveted.' The opportunity was a philanthropic commission set up by Gasparin, Minister of the Interior, in order to re-establish the prestige of sacred music, and

Berlioz was the first to receive such a commission. It was briskly composed, in a fever of inspiration, in the summer of 1837, but as is the way with bureaucratic patronage, the performance was cancelled for political reasons *after* Berlioz had gone to the expense of copying the parts and engaging performers. Only after urgent appeals and persistent complaints was an excuse found for staging the performance after all: the death of a French general in the war of conquest in Algeria.

So the *Requiem* was first heard in the church of the Invalides (Napoleon's remains had not yet been laid there) on 5th December 1837 in a ceremony of pomp and grandeur which the French do with particular style. It was a stirring public occasion and although it was marred for Berlioz by the conductor Habeneck taking a pinch of snuff at the most dramatic entry of the *Tuba mirum* (the truth of the anecdote is disputed), it signified for him the blessing of official approval and the wider knowledge in Parisian circles of how powerful and novel his music was. No one was left in any doubt of the force and originality of Berlioz's genius, an impression which is made equally strongly by the work in performances today. Although the full score was published soon after, Berlioz gained more prestige than money from the event, and with that he was content enough.

It was auspiciously timed for his first venture at the Opéra, scheduled for 1838. *Benvenuto Cellini* was put into rehearsal in May, but immediately disaster threatened:

> I shall never forget the horror of those three months. The indifference, the distaste manifested by most of the singers (who were already convinced that it would be a flop); Habeneck's ill-humour, and the vague rumours that were constantly going round the theatre; the crass objections raised by that whole crowd of illiterates by certain turns of phrase in a libretto so different in style from the empty mechanical rhyming prose of the Scribe school – all this was eloquent of an atmosphere of general hostility against which I was powerless, but which I had to pretend not to notice.[6]

The libretto was certainly unorthodox in style and the music was even more so. It was also extremely difficult to play and sing, being abrupt, very vivacious and constantly changing in rhythm and direction. The orchestra had nineteen rehearsals yet must still have been perplexed. No technical problem is too great if good will is there, but clearly at the Opéra, from the director Duponchel to the chorus and orchestra, opposition to Berlioz' terrifyingly demanding style was entrenched. Ultimately the production was wrecked by the

Letter to Duponchel, Director of the Opéra, March 1839.

'Sir,

    I have the honour to inform you that I *withdraw my opera Benvenuto*. I am perfectly convinced that you will receive this news with pleasure.

    I have the honour to be, Sir, your devoted servant

H. Berlioz.'

principal tenor Duprez abandoning his part after three performances (all in September 1838), a blow which the management were happy to interpret as the definitive failure of the work.

It is difficult to estimate the setback this represented for Berlioz, for his faith in his public and his faith in himself. He was now forever shut out from any return to the Opéra, whether he knew it or not. So much of his most brilliant genius had gone into the composition of the opera that he must have felt the first insistent scent of the disillusionment that oppressed the last years of his life. In the press debate centred on whether Berlioz's music was or was not melodious, with many critics siding firmly with the composer, ranged in opposition with those who would not tolerate his music at any price. D'Ortigue took Berlioz's side with a whole pamphlet, and Liszt, in a long article, proclaimed Berlioz to be the great sculptor carving his masterpiece from marble. Paganini too was there at the first night, deeply impressed. Salvaging his battered fortunes with a couple of Conservatoire concerts that winter, Berlioz gave two more performances of the now popular *Symphonie fantastique*, some extracts from *Cellini*, and *Harold en Italie*. At this second concert, on 16th December 1838, Paganini heard for the first time the work he had brought into being in 1834 and spurned, and being overwhelmed by his conscience, he at once sent Berlioz a cheque for 20,000 francs. The gift caused a sensation: scarcely anyone believed that the old miser, a diabolical miser at that, could part with such a sum, worth £800 at that time – more than twice a reasonable annual salary. Berlioz knew better, and set about expressing his gratitude in the way Paganini intended. He settled his debts and immediately planned a large new work. It was not to be an opera but another symphony, conceived on the broadest scale with chorus, soloists and orchestra and seven movements, reaching often into operatic territory. He quickly settled on *Romeo and Juliet* as its subject, reverting to the play which had haunted him since 1827 and for which he had already planned some kind of musical setting before and during his stay in Italy. Emile Deschamps, who had already translated the play into French, made a verse libretto to Berlioz's design featuring a narrative chorus, Mercutio, Friar Laurence and a contralto soloist but no sung music for the lovers. Composition began in January 1839:

> Oh, the ardent existence I lived during that time! I struck out boldly across that great ocean of poetry, caressed by the wild, sweet breeze of fancy, under that fiery sun of love that Shakespeare kindled. I felt

within me the strength to reach the enchanted isle where the temple
of pure art stands serene under a clear sky.[7]

He contributed less than usual to the *Revue et gazette musicale* that
year but for the *Journal des débats* he continued much as before, with
feuilletons on the major musical events of the day. By September the
new symphony was finished, and he proceeded at once to arrange
performances. Three were given, in the Conservatoire hall, with the
first on 24th November 1839, and the seating plans (which have
survived) show that all the great figures of French romanticism
gathered to hear this tribute to their presiding genius, Shakespeare.
The old fires of 1827 were not dead, and the ardent acclamations
that Berlioz's music won from his friends and admirers convinced
him that the struggle, though arduous and full of setbacks, was
worth it. He was accused, of course, of misunderstanding Shakespeare, but he knew that the symphony contained some of the best
music he had yet written and that it opened the way to an immense
broadening of his musical horizons. All he needed was time, opportunity and public sympathy to pursue his goals.

One notable member of the audience hearing *Roméo et Juliette*
was the young Wagner, newly arrived in Paris, and though he never
came to admire Berlioz's music without reserve, his response to this
work was whole-hearted and profound. They recognized each other
at once (and for the moment) as kindred spirits. Wagner was also
impressed by Berlioz's next new work, a three-movement symphony
for military band, the *Grande symphonie funèbre et triomphale*.
This was a second government commission and, like the *Requiem*, a
grand formal work for massed forces. The occasion of its commission was the tenth anniversary of the 1830 revolution which had
brought Louis-Philippe to power. The régime was already beginning
to need the prop of public commemoration, so the dead of 1830 were
reburied under a fine new column in the Place de la Bastille (around
which today's mindless traffic rushes) to the accompaniment of
Berlioz's three grand movements: a funeral march, a funeral oration,
and a symbolic triumphal march. On the day itself (28th July 1840)
Berlioz headed his massed bands of 200 players marching down the
boulevards in sweltering heat. The unfavourable acoustics and din of
confusion were such that he gave two indoor performances soon
afterwards, and repeated the work that November in an immense
concert at the Opéra, this time with 450 players.

His next work could scarcely have been more different, being intimate and personal, not grandiose and public, inspired by poetry rather than politics and composed for no immediate purpose, not to a commission. Furthermore no reference to it is found in his *Memoirs* or correspondence at that time. In November 1840 two songs, *Absence* and *Le spectre de la rose*, settings of love poems by Théophile Gautier, were announced for a concert but not, apparently, given. Another song, *Villanelle*, had already been composed in March. By September 1841 six songs for mezzo-soprano or tenor and piano under the title *Les nuits d'été* were ready for publication, although no public performances are recorded; Berlioz was shy to the point of silence about one of his most beautiful works.

Since he thought of the songs evidently more as individual pieces than as a cycle, there was perhaps nothing untoward in the veiled apparition the work made. But the ten-year sequence of compositions and concerts in an unbroken tourney with the forces of Parisian music was coming to a critical point, and his career now faced a cross-roads. The strongest pressure within him was impatience with Paris and an urgent desire to take his music abroad. A wider fame was already beckoning, for although he still withheld publication of his symphonies, the overtures were available to all. *Les francs-juges* had been tried out in London as early as 1834, with performances in Leipzig (four times), Berlin (twice), Weimar (twice), Bremen, Mainz, Cologne, Vienna, St Petersburg, Lille, Dijon, Aix-la-Chapelle and Montpellier in the next few years. *Waverley* was heard in London and Leipzig in 1839, *Roi Lear* in London, Bremen and Marseilles in 1840. The *Requiem* was heard in Lille in 1838 and St Petersburg in 1841. Schumann had acclaimed the *Symphonie fantastique* in the *Neue Zeitschrift für Musik* in 1835 from Liszt's piano transcription.

Plans for a visit to Germany had long been growing in his mind. Without any doubt it was Harriet who prevented his going any earlier, for her sense of isolation was probably already acute with her career prematurely over and her sense of estrangement exacerbated by Berlioz's deep involvement in the everyday whirl of Parisian musical life. We can do little more than guess at the true state of their marriage in these years; Berlioz seems always to have kept his pied-à-terre in Paris as well as the Montmartre cottage, where after 1836 he spent less and less time. But there is no evidence of disturbance until Berlioz's first visit abroad, to Brussels in September 1842. As he discreetly mentions in the *Memoirs* he left for Brussels clandestinely, without telling Harriet, and taking with him a singer,

Marie Recio. This new liaison can be traced back to June 1841, when he inscribed an album-leaf to her, and may account, mysteriously, for the inactivity which uncharacteristically descended on Berlioz's life in 1841 and 1842. These years are lightly glossed over in the *Memoirs*, and fewer letters than usual survive from this period; perhaps he wrote fewer. In 1841 he accepted the Opéra's invitation to compose recitatives for Weber's *Der Freischütz* explaining that he was only doing it for fear of less sympathetic handling by someone else, and in 1841 too he began to work on a Scribe libretto, *La nonne sanglante*, which he never felt much drawn to and which remained inevitably unfinished. Prompted by the appearance of two books on instrumentation by his friend Georges Kastner, the first of their kind, his mind turned from composition to a study of instruments and their combination in the art of orchestration. What began as a review of Kastner's books became a series of articles on this novel aspect of the musician's craft and finally emerged two years later as the *Grand traité d'instrumentation*, a large and definitive text-book which served many generations of student composers.

So it is perhaps not right to speak of inactivity in Berlioz's life, better to observe how the encounters with Harriet Smithson and Camille Moke had ignited compositions of brazenly autobiographical content, while Marie Recio aroused no trace of élan or romantic passion, and thus no music. She was the daughter of a French soldier and a Spanish mother brought together by the Peninsular War, and quite apart from the indiscretion of praising her singing in the press (as he did once), he would have had every reason for keeping silent, fearing both Harriet's now less equable moods and the effect that a scandal would have had on his family. For the public successes of the 1830s had reconciled his father to his career as a musician, and something of a deeper understanding between the two men began to emerge; they had, after all, many attitudes in common. His parents would never meet his wife, and neither of them ever heard a note of his music. His mother died in 1838, and his younger brother Prosper one year later, soon after coming to Paris, like Berlioz seventeen years before, to begin his higher studies. But shortly after that his younger sister Adèle, whom he had not seen for seven years, got married and came with her new husband to Paris; thereafter their affection and understanding became ever stronger.

The visit to Brussels in 1842 opens a new stage in Berlioz's career. The next twenty years were largely taken up with concert tours abroad, and the enthusiasm and support he found seemed to grow exactly in proportion as the support of his compatriots diminished. His attitudes to Parisian music began to divide into that two-edged sword of mockery and bitterness which he wielded relentlessly in his later writings, and though he never abandoned his home in Paris, he spent long periods in London, Prague, Vienna and all the most musical capitals of Europe, enjoying their superior musical priorities, able to profit handsomely from giving concerts, and, to begin with, taking refuge from a deteriorating marriage.

The catalogue of travelling and concerts would be wearisome to narrate in full; many of the early tours are in any case fully recounted in the *Memoirs*, having provided him with good material for articles, which are, too, an invaluable source for the student of musical life in the German empire in the 1840s. As a trial run, Berlioz gave two concerts in Brussels, returned to Paris, *reculant pour mieux sauter*, and then set off on a longer trip taking in Brussels, Mainz, Frankfurt, Stuttgart, Hechingen, Karlsruhe, Mannheim, Weimar, Leipzig, Dresden, Brunswick, Hamburg, Berlin, Hanover and Darmstadt, the whole trip taking up the first five months of 1843. He did not give concerts in all of those cities, but wherever he could he did, and he visited the opera, heard the orchestra and met the musicians in each place. He spoke no German but relied on the goodwill and enthusiasm of supporters and colleagues. His reputation rested on his overtures, with which many German musicians were familiar, and on legend and hearsay seeping out of Paris. Marie Recio was by all accounts more of a hindrance than a help, and she sang in many of his concerts. Ferdinand Hiller, now Kapellmeister at Cologne, was delighted to meet Berlioz again, in Frankfurt, and he later told of an unsuccessful ruse by which Berlioz attempted to give Marie the slip and travel on to Weimar without her. Another old friend was Mendelssohn, who assisted Berlioz in his two Leipzig concerts and swapped memories and batons. A more recent friend was Wagner, now Kapellmeister at Dresden. A new friend was Schumann, '. . . the silent Schumann, who was electrified by the *Offertoire* of my *Requiem*. He opened his mouth the other day, to the great astonishment of all his acquaintances, to tell me, grasping me by the hand: "This *Offertorium* surpasses everything".'[8] Meyerbeer helped promote Berlioz's two concerts in Berlin. Marschner assisted in Hanover. 'I pass through Kassel at seven in the morning; Spohr is asleep and not to be disturbed.'[9]

He encountered some leading performers too: the violinist Ferdinand David in Leipzig, the great harpist Parish-Alvars in Dresden and Frankfurt, the legendary Leonora Mme Schröder-Devrient, whom he had heard before in Paris, and the great baritone Pischek. He heard German interpretations of the French repertory (Gluck, Auber and Meyerbeer) and he heard the classical German repertory (*The Marriage of Figaro, The Magic Flute, Fidelio*) as well as the newer operas (*Der Freischütz*, Marschner's *Der Vampyr, The Flying Dutchman*, half of *Rienzi*). He heard a number of Beethoven's quartets, some probably for the first time. He was compelled to come to terms with eighteenth-century German music, since it was being keenly revived: Graun's *Der Tod Jesu*, Hasse's *Te deum* and Bach's *St Matthew Passion*. The Bach, which he heard in Berlin, he freely acknowledged to be great, although he was unable to disguise his distaste for fugues and for the earnest Protestant tradition well exemplified in the person of Mendelssohn. The *St Matthew Passion* came to influence his own *Te deum* six years later. None of this music from the eighteenth century, in Berlioz's view, approached Gluck for expressive and dramatic power.

Being preoccupied with his treatise on instrumentation, he was anxious to see recent German developments in invention and design, particularly of wind instruments, and his observations thus fill a large share of his travel articles. He heard piston-valve horns, he heard chords played on a single trombone and he heard the new tuba for the first time. He marvelled to find the cor anglais and the harp so little cultivated. The Germans, in turn, were dazzled by his virtuoso command of the orchestra and its instruments.

He saw the Black Forest and he sailed up the Rhine. He met royalty and aristocracy who adored and supported music, something unknown in France. He found critics who took his music seriously, one of whom, Robert Griepenkerl of Brunswick, rushed out a little book about him on the spot, and he found a public who responded at once and ungrudgingly to his music, and stamped and clapped for more. The experience was rewarding in every way and his outlook was immeasurably broadened. His commitment to Paris was accordingly reduced and the lure of *outre-rhin* drew him irresistibly for the next twenty years. He began to write a *nouvelle* entitled *Euphonia*, a portrayal of the ideal musical city wherein everything is committed to the service of art. What he had recently seen pointed the way to a civilization where all his cherished ideals of music-making might come true. The time of this fantasy was accordingly the distant future and its place was, unequivocally, Germany.

The two years that intervened before his travels resumed were filled with almost every musical activity as well as composition. He may have done a little work on *La nonne sanglante*, but certainly not much; a proposed performance of *Hamlet* in 1844 probably produced the mighty *March funèbre pour la dernière scène d'Hamlet* even though the production never took place. Small but characteristic pieces like the song *La belle Isabeau* and the choral *Hymne à la France* date from these years. He also put together *Le carnaval romain* overture out of the opera *Benvenuto Cellini* and composed another overture *La tour de Nice* while on holiday in Nice; later it became the *Corsaire* overture. He was commissioned to write three little pieces for harmonium by the manufacturer Alexandre. He was not inactive as a composer but the pieces came more haphazardly into the world, without the total absorption and commitment that he had given his work in the 1830s.

This was undoubtedly due to the greater struggle he now faced in having to win an increasingly recalcitrant public to his concerts, and the burden of maintaining two households. There was, too, much to publish; his open letters about the German trip appeared in ten instalments in the *Débats* between August 1843 and January 1844, then in book form, with the Italian account, later in 1844, under the title *Voyage musical en Allemagne et en Italie*. The *Traité* appeared in handsome format, dedicated to the King of Prussia, in December 1843. *Euphonia* started serial publication in January 1844. The *Grande symphonie funèbre et triomphale* and *Le cinq mai* were both ready for publication, and the *Symphonie fantastique* also went to the engravers, at last released by the composer for general circulation.

The *Memoirs* say: 'My life in the period which followed [the German tour] offers no musical event worth mentioning. I remained in Paris, occupied almost exclusively with my trade, I will not say of critic, but of feuilletonist – a very different thing.'[10] This passage (Chapter 53) continues as a bitter cry against the misery of writing 'nothing about nothing', of having to write about masterpieces and claptrap side by side, of wracking his brains for even a few words to say about trivial entertainments by minor – or even established – composers. Of the twenty-five articles he wrote in 1844 (to take a one-year sample) eight made up the long fantasy *Euphonia* (later reprinted in *Les soirées de l'orchestre*), two were autobiographical; one discussed new instruments (including the 'orgue-mélodium'), one reviewed new instrumental methods, three covered Paris concerts, including notices of Mendelssohn's *Antigone* and David's *Le désert*. The remaining ten reviewed operas by Adam, Auber, Halévy, Balfe, Boily, Cadaux, Bousquet, Catel (a revival), Kastner and Niedermeyer. Even when these composers' names are familiar today their music is not, and these particular operas were every one consigned to immediate oblivion.

Yet if we read these reviews today the pain of their writing is never obvious. Berlioz's fondness for digressing into anecdote, memory and serious discussion of quite different matters keeps them alive, even for the modern reader with little interest in the works under review. One of the commonest digressions was a tirade against his irksome métier, and the bitterness grew as the years passed. Not only did he hate the writing of reviews for itself: he resented its consumption of time better given to other things. A memorable passage vividly illustrates this:

> Let me only be given scores to compose, orchestras to conduct, rehearsals to direct; be made to stay on my feet eight or ten hours at a stretch, baton in hand, training choirs, until I cough blood and my arm is rigid with cramp; be made to carry desks, double basses, harps, to shift platforms, nail planks, like a porter or a carpenter; and then be forced, as a relaxation, to sit up all night correcting the mistakes of engravers and copyists: I have done it, I do it, I will do it again; it is part of my life as a musician, and I bear it without complaint, without even a thought, as a sportsman endures cold, heat, hunger, thirst, sunshine and downpour, mud, dust and all the countless exertions of the chase.
> But eternally to scratch feuilletons for a living! . . .[11]

Berlioz passes over a few concerts without mention, recalling more vividly the monster concert of 1st August 1844 in which about a thousand performers took part with twenty-four horns, twenty-five harps, and everything else in proportion to the huge building of the Festival de l'Industrie. His description of it gives a convincing picture of the practical problems that concerts of this kind presented, and it rankled that he had to pay 4000 francs alms tax, keeping only 800 francs profit for himself out of total takings of 32,000 francs. He did a further series of four big concerts in 1845, but this time not as his own impresario, and the cartoonists began to depict Berlioz as a purveyor of noise with cannons and mortar in his orchestra, implanting a reputation that has clung to him ever since.

His domestic affairs were now in a wretched state. At the imploring insistence of his wife he refused an attractive invitation to conduct the Philharmonic Society in London. 'Her state of mind is always deteriorating, her alarm and jealousy exceed belief. I need an immense store of patience', he told Adèle.[12] With no further expectation in the theatre, she sold her costumes. In June 1844 Berlioz reported her habitual drinking and described the disorder of their marriage in depressing detail: 'Oh pity me, I don't know how it will all end; yet it must come to an end. Don't say a word about this to our father. My life is wrecked.'[13] The holiday in Nice in 1844 was as much a flight from this desperate state of affairs as recuperation after an exhausting concert: he seems to have set up house with Marie more or less permanently when he came back.

From 1845 to 1848 he was more often away than in Paris. He first gave concerts in Marseilles and Lyons; he paid a visit to his father, but none of the family troubled to hear his concerts in Lyons, to his chagrin. Next to Bonn for the inauguration of the Beethoven monument under the energetic guidance of Liszt who had summoned the leading musicians and many crowned heads of Europe for the occasion. The festivities provided subject-matter for two piquant feuilletons in the *Débats* on his return. He then set off on a second long tour, leaving Paris in October 1845 with Marie and heading directly for Vienna. His mission was the conquest of the farther capitals of Europe where he had not so far been, and he succeeded with even greater satisfaction and rewards than on the first trip. Where audiences had before been enthusiastic, now they were rapturous: where his music had been admired, now it was adored. Vienna itself, where he spent the first two or three months and gave three concerts, was relatively reserved in its ovation, but Prague and Pest, early in 1846, exceeded his wildest expectations, overwhelming him with honours and applause such as he never knew at any point in his whole career. Prague struck him as it had struck Mozart sixty years earlier, as the most musical of cities and the Bohemians as the most musical of peoples.

Once again we have an exhilarating account of the tour from his own pen, first as open letters in the *Revue et gazette musicale*, later published in the *Memoirs*. He was now more drawn to reflecting on the nature of conservatoires, theatres, orchestras and so on, and less on recounting the details of his tour. It is clear, however, that Vienna, for Berlioz, meant Beethoven. To hear of Beethoven having once been scorned there was nearly as galling as to discover that Gluck was no longer played in Vienna at all. The present leader of Vienna's music was Nicolai, and he also met the young Joachim there. For his Vienna concerts he produced two new orchestral songs, *Zaïde* and *Le chasseur danois* for soprano and bass respectively, and for Pest he acceded to the suggestion of arranging their national Rákóczy March for orchestra. Touching on the explosive nationalist mood of the Hungarians, Berlioz's piece roused his audience to a frenzy of enthusiasm. In the ballroom as in the concert hall he found Hungarian behaviour engagingly more exuberant than any he had seen before. Then in Prague he gave altogether six concerts amid enthusiasm and musical understanding he had never before encountered. He gave *Roméo et Juliette* complete both there and in Vienna. He also visited Breslau (present-day Wrocław), capital of Silesia, and went again to Brunswick. In Vienna he was even offered the post of Kapellmeister to the Imperial Chapel, but declined it without much hesitation knowing that 'it would be impossible for me to live anywhere else but Paris'.

He came home in May 1846 with pride in his heart and money in his pocket, and, furthermore, a large new composition almost complete. This was *La damnation de Faust*, which he wrote on his travels whenever the moment was opportune or whenever inspiration struck. Taking up the spurned *Huit scènes de Faust* of 1829 he worked at first with a little-known writer, Gandonnière, as librettist, but finally provided much of the text himself. From now on he always wrote his own librettos. He saw the new work as a 'concert opera', more of an opera than *Roméo et Juliette*, but still designed for the concert hall. The summer months were devoted to its completion, with a break for a visit to Lille where the new railway line from Paris was inaugurated with his *Chant des chemins de fer*, commissioned for the occasion. (Berlioz had good reason to be grateful to the railways for making his travels in the coming years less arduous.) The account of those few days provided a feuilleton of surpassing hilarity two years later. He also conducted a performance of the *Requiem*, not in the Invalides for which it was written, but in the church of St-Eustache. It was given in honour of Gluck's memory.

For the first time in seven years the winter Paris season offered a large new Berlioz work: *La damnation de Faust* was performed twice, in December 1846, but because the gap had been long, more probably because public taste was slipping ever faster towards its Second Empire nadir, the work was a failure. The natural sympathy of his fellow artists which he had been able to count on in the 1830s was scarcely at all in evidence, and while there were critics who admired and respected the work from the first, the public was indifferent. 'Nothing in my career as an artist wounded me more deeply.' Only two years before all Paris had gone mad with delight at the pretty oriental pictures of Félicien David's *Le désert*. The more disquieting world of Berlioz's *Faust*, for all its brilliant colours and dazzling effects, now meant nothing to them.

So he packed his bags again and made haste to resume his travels, this time yet farther afield to Russia. He had been contemplating this venture for some time. He had been commissioned to arrange a group of Orthodox Hymns for the Russian Imperial Chapel and had dedicated the *Symphonie fantastique*, when it was published, to the Tsar. Meeting Glinka in Paris and Wielhorsky in Vienna provided further encouragement and there was also the lure of money, which he needed to recover the expense of his two concerts. Balzac predicted he would make 150,000 francs. In the event this was over-optimistic; none the less he did profit handsomely and captivated many new listeners. The rising generation of Russian composers were Berlioz's ardent supporters.

The fourteen days' journey through winter snows gave him ample time to reflect on the hideous sufferings endured by Napoleon's army in 1812. Even in Moscow, where he gave one concert, remnants of the French artillery were (and are) still to be seen. He stayed mainly in St Petersburg and gave four concerts there, with two complete performances of *Roméo et Juliette* and parts of *La damnation de Faust*. Vladimir Stasov wrote: 'These were the most magnificent, most crowded, most brilliant, most deafening concerts that were presented that year. Everyone flocked to them; how could they do otherwise, when Berlioz has such a colossal reputation throughout all of Europe?'[14] As an honoured foreign artist he was royally entertained; a diamond ring and precious pin were gifts from the Imperial family. The youthful Berlioz was reawakened by his performance of *Roméo et Juliette* on 5th May:

> Heavens, how sad I am! I'm in such a nervous state, thanks to the performance of *Roméo*, the Greek Orthodox mass, and the spring. I was quite overcome by it yesterday during the concert, in the garden

scene. Then in the Reconciliation Oath, at the end, as the chorus break out with my musical fireworks, instead of the joy such a crowning conclusion brings I felt a horrible convulsion of my heart, watching each bar of the score go by and leading simply to silence, and the night. The audience called me back countless times, so I had to appear before the curtain and acknowledge their applause with a smile when all I wanted to do was lie down in the wings and cry my heart out . . . I have to come to Russia to hear my favourite work properly played, it has always been more or less ruined everywhere else. Although, ill as I was, I was well on the way to catching its essence yesterday. How well I conducted, how well I played the orchestra! Only the *composer* can judge how well the *conductor* has served him! It's so difficult, this score. One lapse of attention and all is lost, one dull moment and it falls flat, the nightingale becomes a blackbird, the orange blossom smells of elderberry and Romeo becomes a student . . . Go on, laugh at me! Adieu.[15]

His original plan had been to travel to Russia alone and he may have succeeded in leaving Marie behind. She is mentioned in a letter from Berlin on the return journey and may only have rejoined him there. For the emotional state the May 5th concert reduced him to (also described in the *Memoirs*) spilled over into (or was triggered by) an enchanting flutter of the heart with a girl from the chorus, a seamstress whose fiancé was conveniently away, with whom he wandered along the magical riverside boulevards of the Neva as the sun set. Love and music had not worked so powerfully in conjunction on his soul for many years.

He returned via Riga, where he saw *Hamlet* in German, and then stayed three weeks in Berlin to mount *La damnation de Faust*, complete. Chorus and orchestra were both superb, and the King of Prussia again proved his devotion to Berlioz by inviting him to Sans-Souci and showering him with compliments and honours.

After a short visit to La Côte in September 1847 to visit his father and to introduce the thirteen-year-old Louis to him for the first time – it was also the last time, as Berlioz surely guessed – the next departure was for London, the one musical capital of Europe still unconquered. This was the longest of any of his absences, eight months in all, for the first five of which Marie was still in Paris.[16] This time Berlioz was not just giving concerts, but was engaged as the conductor of the opera season at Drury Lane Theatre by that astonishing impresario, showman and charlatan, Louis Jullien. 'France is sinking more and more into a morass of stupidity as regards music:

the more I see of other countries, the less I love my own, if you will forgive the blasphemy . . . But art in France is dead and one must therefore go where it is still to be found. England has experienced quite a revolution in musical matters over the last ten years, it seems.'[17] Jullien was not the best example of that revolution, although it is true that things were already improving, especially in orchestral and chamber music. In Jullien Berlioz blindly put his faith, agreeing to accept a six-months' engagement for six years. The first season opened with Donizetti's *Lucia di Lammermoor* with some success, and the second production was Balfe's *Maid of Honour*, conducted by the composer: Berlioz took over the podium in the new year of 1848, along with Donizetti's *Linda di Chamounix*, mounted in great haste when it became clear that the season was in financial trouble. *The Marriage of Figaro* was added in February. Berlioz also gave a successful concert of his own music, sold some pieces to London publishers and prepared a 'Musical Shakespeare Night' at Covent Garden – which never took place. By March, with the season over, it was clear that Jullien's capacity to honour his pledges was dwindling and Berlioz became alarmed. In April Jullien was declared bankrupt. But Berlioz stayed on:

> I have still to get from Beale [the publisher] the fee for two pieces which are not yet done, and a concert has been arranged at little expense for 29th June. If I can earn £50 thereby it will be a great help, whereas in Paris I am sure to earn nothing at all and by going there now I would lose what little I can make here. Besides, my expenses in London are very small . . . Once I am at the end of my resources, there will be nothing for me to do but go and sit in the gutter and die of hunger like a stray dog, or blow my brains out . . .[18]

The benefit concert on 29th June 1848 in Hanover Square Rooms was another triumph, with *Le carnaval romain* overture, the *Marche des pèlerins* from *Harold en Italie* and the *Marche hongroise*, all encored.

He returned to Paris in July 1848, having put off for some months returning to a city which since February had been rent in two by the barricades of revolution. This outbreak coincided with the capsize of Berlioz's hopes of security in London, so his despair at the state of things on both sides of the Channel is scarcely to be wondered at. He liked London, its size, its theatres, its parks, its abundance of quick-witted musicians swollen with refugees from all over Europe, and he was already tempted to make his home permanently there. He had no sympathy for revolution or republics, and treated events in Paris simply as a threat to what little musical life still survived there: he felt no glimmer of utopian fervour at the creation of a new order.

Under these painful impressions and fired by reading the *Memoirs from Beyond the Grave* by Chateaubriand, the inspiring father-figure to the French Romantics, Berlioz began to compile his own memoirs, deciding to have his also reserved for publication after his death. He took refuge in the past and pieced together the account of his childhood, his student years in Paris and his first success there. He had recently mentioned Estelle in a letter to a friend in Russia: 'My first love was at the age of twelve, and I still tremble to think of it.'[18] Dwelling in the past was an obsession that remained with him now for the rest of his life. Despite his reputation as a torch-bearer of modernity he was losing interest in contemporary music; he admired Mendelssohn (now dead) and Liszt but never regarded their music as the equal of Gluck's or Beethoven's. Of the little Wagner he yet knew he had no special opinion. *La damnation de Faust*'s failure in 1846 and the chaos of 1848 generated if not despair in France's musical institutions at least disillusionment which deepened during the rest of his career.

3

1848–1869

On 28th July 1848, soon after Berlioz's return from London, his father died. This was yet another break with the past, and it was ironic that he should recently have been writing an account of his father's years of displeasure, for he realized how deep their mutual affection was. The family gathered at La Côte. Berlioz felt closer now to his two sisters (although Nanci had only two years to live) and presided over the settlement of his father's estate. He later had a modest income from the sale of property, though it made little difference to his precarious finances.

His new preoccupation with his childhood impelled him to revisit Meylan and the house on the hill where he had admired the beautiful Estelle. He even found out where she was living and wrote a letter of repressed passion. Berlioz's loss of faith in the future could scarcely be more touchingly illustrated than by this bewildering quest (on which he had many steps further to travel) for his lost ideal love.

As he wrote the account of the thunderclap of Harriet and Shakespeare, she suffered the first of a series of attacks, probably a form of stroke, from which she never recovered even though she had some years yet to live. Remaining in Paris for the next three years, he was able to visit her regularly and take a closer interest in his lamentably neglected son. Louis, now in boarding school in Rouen, was on the verge of choosing a career in the navy.

Berlioz's only permanent employment was the post of assistant librarian at the Conservatoire, a sinecure which had brought in a small stipend since 1839, but this was hardly a post to suit his talents and he neglected it accordingly. In 1850 the head librarian, Bottée de Toulmon, died, leaving Berlioz the succession. But his remote chance of ever securing regular employment in Paris as a conductor had been brought home to him in 1847 by a wretched piece of skulduggery by which Duponchel and Roqueplan, the two opportunist directors of the Opéra, managed both to steer Berlioz away from occupying the post of chorus master as well as to deprive him (with Scribe's connivance) of *La nonne sanglante*, the work which he had been engaged to compose for the Opéra some years before. The account of the affair in the *Memoirs* sounds one-sided, but it is supported by such documents as are relevant, and it was wholly characteristic of the controllers of Parisian artistic life. Their one concern was the promotion of Meyerbeer's much vaunted and long delayed *Le prophète*, declared to be a historic success long before its first appearance on 15th March 1849. Yet he persistently turned down offers of residential employment abroad, and confirmed his attachment to Paris, a kind of unreasoning bond which held him in the city he never ceased to curse and abuse but which was, when all was said and done, his home.

He spoke more and more frequently of distant shores as the only refuge:

> I dream only of the sea, of distant islands, of adventure and exploration. My musical travels in Europe have only enhanced these feelings, always more or less dormant. Not being able to tour South America or New Zealand or the Pacific Islands without the bonds holding me here, I would begin again to explore the terra firma of old Europe.[1]

> Dreams of voyages obsess me more and more. I have a sickness for faraway countries. If I were free, without any question I would disappear for several years and flee this stupid, worn out, violent, bitter hemisphere.[2]

> Oh, if only I were free I could flee to Tenerife or the Ile de Fer or Madeira to find the sun, calm, nature, beautiful landscapes, good-natured people, and forget the feverish agitation of Paris.[3]

Berlioz's work as a composer had been submerged in the 1840s by his wretchedly insecure professional and domestic life. Apart from *La damnation de Faust* there was too little written between 1841 and 1849 to be proud of. He had given a great deal of time to the abortive *La nonne sanglante* and composed too much for commissions which could not possibly have touched his heart. Songs like *La mort d'Ophélie*, *Zaïde* and the newly elaborated version of *La captive*, made for Pauline Viardot in London, kept his muse alive. To be deprived of works unwritten is a tragedy which posterity cannot begin to assess. Berlioz was fully aware of how much he had to *toil* when he wanted instead to *work*, and being at home now for a longer period he sensed the urge to embark on another large work. 1849 was largely devoted to the composition of the *Te deum*, a brother to the *Requiem* (he termed it), but in this case it was not commissioned, nor is it clear what prompted Berlioz to embark on it. Its origins go back to residual ideas from the Napoleonic project of 1832 and it is certainly grandiose enough for such a conception. Perhaps Berlioz planned to have a work at hand to greet the new government, whatever might emerge from the disorders 'of 1848. In this he was disappointed, for no opportunity for performance came up until 1855.

He gave no concerts at all in 1849, but as soon as the *Te deum* was complete he set about founding a new concert society, named the Société Philharmonique de Paris, as if to prove that art in France was not dead after all. Formed partly in imitation of the London Philharmonic Society, it was an obvious rival to the now long-standing Société des Concerts and it was designed to even out the intolerable risks and burdens of concert promotion as he had usually done it hitherto. Instead of bearing the full responsibility for players, hall, music, publicity and finance himself, he now enlisted a commit-tee for this purpose. He was the society's conductor, but his own music did not feature so prominently in the society's programmes and some concerts contained none of his music at all. The first concert was given in the Salle Sainte-Cécile on 19th February 1850. Joachim came specially from London to play Ernst's *Fantasy* on Rossini's *Otello*; works by Gluck, Méhul and Beethoven were played and, of Berlioz himself, the first two parts of *Faust*. There were five concerts in the first season; *Harold en Italie* was heard and, for the last concert, the *Requiem*, occasioned by a disaster in which a detachment of soldiers was lost, having failed to break step across a bridge. Otherwise they were wide and representative programmes in the fashion of the day. But behind the apparent success of this new venture lay dissension and doubt. Berlioz became even more firmly convinced of the need for dictatorial powers in artistic matters when the chorus (under their chorus-master Dietsch) disagreed with the orchestra over what Berlioz's powers should be and how much of his music should be played. Their funds were fully stretched too. Cer-tainly Berlioz had to spend much of the year arguing, persuading, bullying and pleading to keep the organization alive for a second season.

Through the winter of 1850–1 the concerts proceeded, some dozen in all, with barely any profit to share out. Only because certain composers were prepared to pay to have their works performed were the concerts made possible, poor expedient though it was. A wide selection of Berlioz's works was heard, with a new piece on 12th November, *L'adieu des bergers*, a naive little chorus which Berlioz impudently billed as the work of an imaginary seventeenth-century composer, Pierre Ducré. Most of the critics and audience were duped, their familiarity with the seventeenth century, like Berlioz's, being painfully slight. It amused Berlioz to see it innocently praised for its charm. What came into being as a gentle squib eventually took on larger dimensions, with two extra movements, *Le repos de la sainte famille* and an overture making up the whole *Fuite en Égypte* soon after. This in turn formed the kernel of *L'enfance du Christ*, a 'sacred trilogy', first performed in December 1854. Berlioz strongly denied that his style had changed, as many critics were suggesting; he had merely picked on some (for him) unexpected subject-matter and treated it with the expressive veracity it demanded. But it had an undeniably nostalgic flavour, as though he was still the young medical student sitting at the feet of Lesueur. He had not before written music of such calmness and detachment, but none the less deeply felt.

The second visit to London came about in connection with the 1851 Great Exhibition in Hyde Park. Berlioz, being now a recognized authority on instruments, took his place as a member of the jury charged with examining the latest submissions by instrument manufacturers, and he expressed patriotic pride in seeing Erard, Sax and Vuillaume take the honours for France. The Crystal Palace delighted him and he planned (but did not bring off) a concert there which would feature the *Te deum*. In June he went to St Paul's for the annual service which brought together 6000 children from London charity schools. From the organ loft he experienced the overwhelming effect of all those raw voices intoning 'All People that on Earth Do Dwell', massed on raised benches underneath the dome, and the complete congruity of the place with the musical means fulfilled every musical ideal: 'It is useless to try to give any idea of such a musical effect.' But try he did, for he immediately added a ripieno part for 600 children's voices to his still unperformed *Te deum*.

London delighted him even more on this second visit, bustling with visitors from all over the globe and decked in flags. He gazed at the Chinese, the Indians and the Scots in their curious kilts. He heard Purcell in Westminster Abbey but thought little of it. He gave no concert, but he went to the opera, including three Mozart operas,

EXETER HALL.

New Philharmonic Society.

THE FIRST CONCERT

WILL TAKE PLACE ON

WEDNESDAY EVENING, MARCH 24th, 1852,

To commence at Eight o'Clock.

PROGRAMME.

Part I.

Symphony in C — — — — *(Jupiter)* — — — —	**Mozart.**

Allegro Vivace, Andante Cantabile, Minuetto Trio,
Finale—Allegro Molto.

Selection from **IPHIGENIA IN TAURIDE** — — —	**Gluck.**

Song, Chorus, Ballet, and Chorus.

Triple Concerto in C, Pianoforte, Violin, and Violoncello — —	**Beethoven.**

Allegro, Largo, Rondo alla Polacca.

M. SILAS, Signor SIVORI, and Signor PIATTI.

Overture — — — — *(Oberon)* — — — —	**Weber.**

Adagio, Allegro con Fuoco.

Part II.

THE FIRST PART OF

ROMEO AND JULIET,

A DRAMATIC SYMPHONY WITH SOLOS AND CHORUS.

BY HECTOR BERLIOZ.

No. 1.

Combats—a Tumult—INSTRUMENTAL INTRODUCTION.

PROLOGUE—*in Choral Recitative.* SEMI-CHORUS—*Strofa*, Contralto Solo.

VOCAL SCHERZETTO—*Tenor Solo, with* SEMI-CHORUS RECITATIVE.

No. 2. (Instrumental.)

ROMEO alone. *Distant Sound of Festive Music. Grand Fête at the Mansion of*
CAPULET.

No. 3. (Instrumental and Vocal.)

The Garden of the CAPULETS, *silent and deserted.* JULIET *on the balcony*—ROMEO
in the shade. Love Scene—ADAGIO, CHORUS AND ORCHESTRA.

CHORUS *of Capulet Youths quitting the Feast.*

No. 4.

Queen Mab, or the Fairy of Dreams—SCHERZO ISTRUMENTALE.

Overture — — — — *(Guillaume Tell)* — — —	**Rossini.**

Andante, Allegro, Andante, Allegro Vivace.

THE ORCHESTRA will embrace the highest Talent in Europe.

THE CHORUS will be select.

LEADER - Signor SIVORI.

CONDUCTOR - M. HECTOR BERLIOZ.

Subscription to a Series of Six Concerts, Two Guineas; Single Tickets, 10s. 6d. each;
Gallery, 5s. each; West End of Hall, 2s. 6d. each;
To be had of CRAMER, BEALE, & Co. 201, Regent Street; and the principal Musicsellers.

J. MALLETT, PRINTER, WARDOUR STREET.

Handbill for Berlioz's concert in Exeter Hall, London, on 24th March 1852.

with Mme Sontag stealing all hearts. London seemed a more encouraging place than when he had last been there, so when he was asked back in 1852 to conduct the New Philharmonic Society as a rival to the old, he accepted gladly. He was engaged for six concerts between March and June 1852 in Exeter Hall, Strand, which turned out to be some of the most successful in all his career as a conductor. It was very much as a conductor that he was now presented, even though four parts of *Roméo et Juliette* and various other compositions of his own were done. He conducted some Handel, for example, and gave his interpretations of classics such as the 'Jupiter' Symphony, Beethoven's Fifth Symphony and Mendelssohn's Italian Symphony and Violin Concerto. The climax was undoubtedly two performances of Beethoven's Choral Symphony which were remembered long after. A New York impresario heard the concerts and instantly offered him 25,000 francs to conduct a similar season in New York, but he refused.

Having compiled his *Memoirs* for posthumous publication his mind turned to assembling a group of his longer feuilletons for immediate publication as a book. Thus came about *Les soirées de l'orchestre*, published in 1852 and instantly successful. Presented as a dialogue between orchestral players in a provincial opera house who swap endless tales whenever boring music is being played, leaving the bass drum to carry on on their behalf, but who concentrate with every nerve and fibre whenever a masterpiece is performed, *Les soirées* contains the purest and best of Berlioz's idealistic writing. We are never in any doubt of his views of music and musicians, but he never worries us with preaching or politics: it is laced with romantic fantasy, not unlike E.T.A. Hoffmann, and sparkling with wit. Every side of his writing and every musical obsession is represented.

Committed to London concerts in March 1852 Berlioz was unable to go to Weimar to hear Liszt's revival of *Benvenuto Cellini*. Liszt had been struck by its great qualities in Paris in 1838, and as part of his plan to put Weimar's court music at the head of the German league and at the same time promote the music he felt most deserved performance (this included operas by Schubert, Cornelius, and Wagner), Liszt mounted a new production with the aid of his son-in-law-to-be, Hans von Bülow. Berlioz was deeply touched, and happily agreed to some major revision of the opera for further performances in November when something nearer the final

'Weimar' version was devised. This time Berlioz was there, to hear *Benvenuto Cellini, Roméo et Juliette* and half of *La damnation de Faust* played within a week. Soon after, *Cellini* was accepted at Covent Garden and Berlioz was engaged to conduct the old Philharmonic Society in London. His star which had shone so feebly only four years before was at last giving off its proper brilliance.

All this public fame checked his work as a composer. After *La fuite en Égypte* in 1850 he wrote no music for three years. It was not simply that he was too busy; we know that he was deeply discouraged. It was at this time that a dream of a symphony in A minor came to him, as the *Memoirs* recount. Fearful of the expense and humiliation of completing and performing it and knowing it would deprive his wife and son of care, he drove it from his thoughts and it was never written. In 1852 he toyed for the second time with an opera on *Much Ado About Nothing*, but dropped the idea; and deep in the back of his mind lay the first stirrings of a Virgilian opera, still so daunting that he barely dared mention it, and he felt impelled to resist the urge.

The year of success, 1852, was not to be crowned with another. *Benvenuto Cellini*, when it was played at Covent Garden in June 1853, in the presence of the Queen and Prince Albert, was a pitiful failure, shouted down by the faction that liked only Italian opera, unimpressed by the fact that it was sung in Italian. But then *Rigoletto* had been a failure only a few weeks earlier, so there was little hope for London opera audiences, and *Cellini* was withdrawn. The Covent Garden orchestra offered to give a benefit concert in Exeter Hall to compensate, but it could not be arranged and Berlioz left, still holding English musicians in high regard (even though he found their compulsive preference for sight-reading rather alarming). They subscribed £200 as a present for Berlioz but 'such a gift was too foreign to our French notions for me to feel that I could accept it'.[4]

He went almost directly to Baden-Baden to give a concert during the fashionable summer season, not guessing that this would become his favourite venue in the coming years. Nearly every August in the ensuing ten years he gave concerts there at the invitation of Bénazet, the enlightened manager of the casino, who afforded Berlioz all the freedom of choice and manoeuvre in his concerts that he had always longed for. All fashionable Europe went there, especially the aristocracy of Russia and Germany, and with Turgenev and Pauline Viardot and others generally resident also, artistic circles were not undistinguished. With the wealth that poured into the spa Bénazet was later able to commission an opera from Berlioz, *Béatrice et Bénédict*, first performed in 1862.

Next after Baden came two concerts in Frankfurt and then shortly afterwards a tour that filled the autumn of 1853: Brunswick, Hanover, Bremen and Leipzig. For repertory he relied on fragments from *Harold, Roméo* and *Faust*, with *Roi Lear* and *Le carnaval romain* overtures. The *Symphonie fantastique* was being rested, and the new work, *La fuite en Égypte* was fragmentarily heard in most cities with the first complete performance in Leipzig. The blind King of Hanover (who had shared Queen Victoria's box at *Cellini*) declared himself one of Berlioz's most ardent admirers. In Leipzig Berlioz met a rising star of German music: 'Brams [sic] is enjoying great success here. I was very impressed the other day at Brendel's with his Scherzo and his Adagio. Thank you for introducing me to this bold but shy young man who has taken it into his head to write new music. He will have much to suffer . . .'[5] For his part Brahms reported that Berlioz's praise was so exceedingly warm and hearty that the rest meekly followed suit. 'Yesterday evening at Moscheles's he was just as friendly; I have much to thank him for.'[6] Brahms liked *La fuite en Égypte* and, eventually, *L'enfance du Christ*, which he deemed the best of his works. He later conducted *Harold en Italie* in Vienna and owned the autograph of *La mort d'Ophélie*. This brief friendship is all the more touching for being between composers whose works have so little in common.

Another equally successful tour followed in April 1854, to Hanover, Brunswick and Dresden. In Dresden he gave four concerts in eight days including two complete *Fausts* and two complete *Roméos*, unimaginable in Paris;

> The Dresden musicians came in a body to see me off at the station . . . There are idiots in Germany just like anywhere else, but I must admit they have more warmth and a deeper feeling for art than anywhere in Europe. They showered me with every token of sympathy, respect even, and affection that touched me deeply. I made money there too. This contrast with the indifference of Paris is stirring up a sensation here in Paris itself which can only have good results.[7]

In fact, as he must surely have anticipated, his successes in Germany made no difference to his standing in Paris whatsoever. If he expected to succeed to Halévy's chair at the Institut, Halévy having been elevated to Permanent Secretary, he was sadly mistaken, for not one person voted for him (a nonentity, Clapisson, was elected). It had been the same in 1842 when Cherubini's death left a vacant chair (Onslow was elected) and in 1851 for Spontini's chair (Thomas was elected), Berlioz receiving no votes in either election. Meanwhile the intendant at Dresden was talking of mounting *Benvenuto Cellini* and of offering Berlioz the post of Kapellmeister once held by Wagner until his flight in 1848. Neither project materialized.

On 3rd March 1854 Harriet died after many years of painful suffering. She had been paralysed for four years. Recollections of her moments of glory and remorse at how their lives had turned out crowded in on Berlioz and sharpened his grief. Resignation now dominated his thoughts. Six months later he closed the final chapter of his *Memoirs* with some bitter reflections on his career as though it were now over, summing up his gloomy view of the state of music in France. Despair was not far away, and he admitted his deliberate decision not to write the symphony two years earlier. So now, acknowledging that the notion of composing a full-length opera had been with him for some time, the futility of giving himself wholly to the urgency of inspiration was uppermost in his mind.

Fortunately Louis had been on leave from his ship just before his mother died. More and more of his father's demanding love was devoted to him, especially when he took part in the capture of Bomarsund in the Baltic that August, his first whiff of naval action and a reminder to his father of the reality of his paternal affection. Louis, emerging from a difficult adolescence, gave his father infinite grief with his apparently spendthrift ways and rebellious attitudes. But Berlioz's possessive love merely redoubled until Louis became the very focus of his emotional life.

After a decent interval Berlioz married Marie Recio, who had been his companion for twelve years or more. 'I had to', he wrote. She was not aware of the existence of the *Memoirs*, whose last page was closed the day before their marriage, and is not mentioned in them, except once by allusion. Of their relationship Berlioz had virtually nothing to say; doubtless he was aware of her spiteful tongue and lack of tact, to which many witnesses testify, but he appreciated her good domestic management even if that was properly to the credit of her Spanish mother, living with them.

That summer (1854) he completed *L'enfance du Christ* and

L'impériale, and shortly after wrote to his sister Adèle a letter of passionate honesty:

> I am beginning to look only into the past, and as if to redouble my misfortune, my feelings and imagination and convulsions of the heart and soul simply increase all the time.
>
> My passion for music, or rather for art, breaks all bounds. I feel I have greater powers than ever before, shackled by material obstacles. At this very moment I am sick with the frustration of my love of art. But what can one do? In France! Nothing, absolutely nothing. Indifference and idiocy, gross materialism, bestial government, ignorance, the philistinism of the rich, the vulgar preoccupations of everyone . . . Snakes, hedgehogs, toads, geese, guinea-fowl, crows, lice, vermin . . . that's the charming population of that earthly paradise Paris.
>
> Then my accursed journalism forcing me to ponder so much wretched nonsense and often speak of it with a kind of deference . . .
>
> Oh, how balmy was the air the other day on the high cliffs of Saint-Valéry [in Normandy] with the sea quietly lapping three hundred feet below my grassy bed! What marvellous sunsets! What peace up there! What pure sky! Only this kind of passionate intimacy with nature can make me forget for an instant the pain I suffer from my unrequited love of art. But it reawakens the pain just as quickly, that's the way it is.
>
> I am obsessed by plans for enormous audacious works which I know I can bring off. As soon as I am about to begin, I break off. 'Why undertake such a work' I say to myself and get passionately involved with it? Just to bring smarting agonies on myself when it's done, if I find it beautiful? Just to see it fall into the hands of children, or brutes, or buried alive? . . .[8]

Throughout 1855 the cycle continued: concerts in Weimar, Brussels and London, and on 30th April, the first performance of the *Te deum* in St-Eustache church timed to coincide with the opening of the Paris Exhibition for which Berlioz was engaged, once again, on the jury to assess musical instruments and as conductor of the closing concerts. The somewhat hollow cantata, *L'impériale*, with its gross flattery of the Emperor, proved exactly right in this context. In London he coincided with Wagner, engaged as conductor of the old Philharmonic Society while Berlioz conducted the New. Under the bombardment of critical attack Wagner seemed more hunted and oppressed than Berlioz, so for the duration of a long evening smoking cigars they shared their common woes and felt closer in spirit and friendship than ever before or since. Wagner was at work on *Die*

Walküre: Berlioz was turning over in his mind his plan for an opera on the *Aeneid*, a plan that he had felt drawn to for some years but had felt compelled to resist. That year in Weimar, however, Princess Sayn-Wittgenstein, Liszt's mistress, and a woman of dogged intellectual strength, urged him to yield. He still refused. Yet lines from Virgil appeared more frequently in his feuilletons, often quite irrelevantly, and so too, in one article, did a quotation from *The Merchant of Venice*: 'In such a night as this, when the sweet wind did gently kiss the trees . . .' At this moment, we may guess, the idea for his great love-duet in Act IV of *Les Troyens* was implanted.

A further visit to Weimar in February 1856 was crucial. The Princess renewed her persuasion and Berlioz yielded. The young Peter Cornelius wrote in his diary: 'This summer Berlioz is going to begin a new opera, which I shall translate.'[9] So against all his best judgment, Berlioz reshaped his life to allow the time and leisure to compose what turned out to be the largest and greatest of his works, *Les Troyens*. Discouragement had taken such deep root in him that the effort required to face the task of composition was far greater than we can easily guess, even though the force of a lifelong love of Virgil and dedication to expressive music fuelled his creative instincts.

He first completed the orchestration of *Les nuits d'été* for the Swiss publisher Rieter-Biedermann, whose edition of these orchestral songs is a glorious example of the engraver's art, in particular contrast to the cramped and messy scores Richault and Brandus were producing for Berlioz in Paris. Having completed that, and refusing all concert plans except the annual trip to Baden-Baden, and writing as little for the *Débats* as he could, he set to work on his opera. We know a great deal about the progress of the work, for abundant letters have survived, including the invaluable series to the Princess in Weimar, discussing and reflecting on his progress. They were two ardent years, fulfilling, as he saw it, his lifelong debt to Virgil, and 'living in his score like Lafontaine's rat in his cheese'.[10] The libretto took two months to write, interrupted when he could not resist composing the love duet in Act IV: 'the music settled on this scene like a bird on ripe fruit',[11] coaxed into being (many sketches survive) by the borrowing from the last act of *The Merchant of Venice*. Likewise, although he composed Act I first, he could not then resist jumping ahead to Act IV, the act 'of love, tenderness, festivities, hunting and the starry African nights'. Bit by bit his huge score came into being, with the last page dated 12th April 1858. The last few pages had so absorbed him that 'even if I had been due somewhere to be guillotined I would probably have failed to turn up and kept the poor man waiting in vain', as he wrote to Théophile Gautier.[12]

The satisfaction he drew from this great burst of creative fervour at a time when he felt so discouraged was profound, and the music itself moved him deeply. He wanted his friends to admire it – he would have liked Virgil and Shakespeare and Gluck to admire it – for he knew that its chances of success in Paris were slim. He was right, for the following years saw a series of manoeuvres and campaigns to have the opera mounted in Paris. He made a piano reduction and had it engraved at his own expense; he gave readings of the poem on many occasions to as many influential people as he could; and he exerted his new-found influence as a member of the prestigious Institut, where he succeeded to Adolphe Adam's chair in 1856. This at least assured him regular access to the Emperor, who alas proved to have the most commonplace taste in music. Berlioz once went to an audience with the Emperor thinking it was to be private and found forty-two people present. When high-level authority did back a new operatic venture it was Wagner's *Tannhäuser* that was selected. It was mounted at the Opéra in March 1861 with colossal expense and hullaballoo but failed noisily. Berlioz felt bitterly torn between regarding Wagner as a rival and as a colleague and could scarcely rejoice. At the time he had a tentative undertaking from the independent Théâtre-lyrique to put on *Les Troyens*, but since that theatre was not yet built and its management dragging its feet, he seized the advantage of an offer from the discomfited Opéra and would have seen his work played there if the management had not changed hands late in 1862, leaving the new director no obligation to honour his predecessor's commitments. So Berlioz was forced back to the Théâtre-lyrique, eventually complete, and now in the hands of an entrepreneur of energy and character, Léon Carvalho; Carvalho was one of the most enterprising figures of his time, destined to play a major part in the fortunes of French opera. Although Berlioz abused him roundly in the *Memoirs* for savaging *Les Troyens*, it would be fairer to remember that he alone in Paris had the courage to put it on at all.

The five years between completion (1858) and performance (1863) were a protracted agony for Berlioz, involving him in the kind of begging and bullying he most hated, exposing him to the ceaseless ridicule of the press (who assumed it was ten hours long), and exacerbating his spiritual despair. Furthermore he began to suffer, about 1856, from a severe nervous disorder which was diagnosed as 'intestinal neuralgia', a complaint not generally recognized today though it was real enough to him. By 1859 the pain was so acute that he tried electrical treatment, but it gave little relief. The singer, Pauline Viardot, was a particularly close friend at the time; his admiration for her great artistry and their collaboration on a revival of Gluck's *Orphée* induced an adoring passion which sustained him through a critical period. 'The sight of this man', she wrote, 'suffering so much moral and physical pain, so much intestinal illness, a prey to horrible emotional torments, the violence of his efforts to hide them, this burning soul that bursts its casing, this life which hangs by a thread, the great overflowing tenderness of his gaze and of his slightest utterance – all this has shattered me.'[13]

He continued to write regularly for the *Débats* and his wit seemed sharper the more bitter his real feelings and sufferings became. There can be few books about music more humorous than *Les grotesques de la musique*, which came out in 1859, a second compendium of articles, where the raillery is so mordant it hurts. A third book, *A travers chants*, of 1862, is a more serious collection, containing studies of Beethoven, Gluck, Weber and even his recent articles on Wagner. With these successful publications he became less dependent on writing new articles; he now had a stipend from the Institut and his salary as librarian of the Conservatoire as well as a certain income from his father's estate. Yet he remained as careful as ever and kept scrupulous monthly records of his expenses, which have survived.

There were two consolations in this difficult period. One was the commission of an opera by Bénazet for his new theatre in Baden-Baden. Berlioz was well treated there and always happy conducting his annual concerts. The libretto originally suggested by Bénazet – an episode from the Thirty Years' War – did not appeal to him, but eventually he chose a subject he had pondered in 1833 and worked out in draft in 1852: Shakespeare's *Much Ado About Nothing*, which he turned into a one-act comic opera in 1860–2, expanding it bit by bit into the two-act opera we now have. It was a labour of love, Berlioz delighting in comedy after the epic preoccupations of *Les Troyens*, like Verdi composing *Falstaff* after a career of serious drama. Furthermore it was staged at once, in 1862 in

Account sheet showing Berlioz's personal expenditure for the month of September 1850. The sheet shows separate expenditure for Berlioz's two households: his own, with Marie Recio, in Paris, and Harriet's, with Louis, in Montmartre. It shows payments for household expenses, servants' wages, carriages, postage (some on behalf of the Société Philharmonique), and books, an inkwell and a knife for Louis. Setting up Louis for five months' navigation course (shown on a separate sheet) cost Berlioz 815 francs, of which he had to borrow 500. Other sheets show the purchase of hats and clothing and even record small gambling losses.

Baden-Baden, with none of the tribulation and humiliation he still had to face in Paris. It was a success, with a revival the following year and a production in Weimar in 1863 which he also conducted. It was his last composition.

A further consolation was the slow but definite establishment of a vital understanding with his son, Louis. Both father and son had been at fault, Berlioz expecting too much, Louis underestimating his father's response, but by the time Louis' naval career was under way their relationship was closer than ever, sealed when Louis came to discover and admire his father's music. Berlioz's emotional dependence on him was greatly increased by the death of his beloved sister Adèle in 1860 and then in 1862 by the death of Marie, both still in their forties. Few of Berlioz's friends had much to say in Marie's favour, but it would be rash to underestimate his feelings for her after twenty years shared. He now had her mother to care for him but no companionship.

The 1863 production of *Les Troyens* at the Théâtre-lyrique in Paris precipitated the end of his career. Yet it was not a failure, as *Benvenuto Cellini* and *Tannhäuser* had been at the Opéra. It had twenty-one consecutive performances, it had the finest singer of the day, Mme Charton-Demeur, singing Dido, and royalties from the production and the sale of the vocal score enabled him to resign instantly his post as critic of the *Débats*. Many critics were profuse in their praise, Meyerbeer attended many times. All this gave Berlioz cause for pride, and Louis eagerly assembled the favourable notices.

But as we can tell all too clearly from the *Memoirs*, it broke his heart to see anything less than his real and whole conception worthily presented to an admiring audience. Instead he found that Carvalho, despite his promises, could afford to mount only half of it, so he lopped off the first two acts under the title of *La prise de Troie* (he never heard those acts) and composed a brief prelude to introduce the rest, now entitled *Les Troyens à Carthage*. Even then, many numbers were cut in successive performances. Carvalho plagued him with alterations and cuts; the conductor, Deloffre, seems to have had no commitment to his task; many critics to whom Virgil's name was probably unknown still railed at his 'lack of melody' and the like; and the vocal score was cut down piecemeal to match the performances and was offered for sale 'like the carcass of a calf on a butcher's stall'.

Berlioz was proud at first, then embittered, finally enraged by what happened. He discouraged revivals and none took place for nearly thirty years. He allowed his spirit to be overcome by a despair and disillusionment of appalling intensity. In 1864 he resumed his *Memoirs*, writing:

> I am in my sixty-first year; past hopes, past illusion, past high thoughts and lofty conceptions. My son is almost always far away from me. I am alone. My contempt for the folly and baseness of mankind, my hatred of its atrocious cruelty, have never been so intense. And I say hourly to Death: 'When you will.' What is he waiting for?[14]

Yet he had five years to live, in constant physical discomfort amid a diminishing circle of friends: Stephen Heller, the Damckes, the Massarts and Edouard Alexandre, all musicians of some standing who remained devotedly loyal. When Louis was home on leave from Mexico they went for a walk with Heller along the Seine 'discussing Shakespeare and Beethoven . . . we got into a state of great excitement which my son shared only as far as Shakespeare was concerned, being still unacquainted with Beethoven.'[15] On his own he devoted his days to 'keeping in touch (why?) with the goings-on of the miserable insects that people this earth'.[16] He read travel books again and dreamed once more of going to Tahiti, though his 'full orchestral tutti of boredom' included the pleasures of walking past theatres and not going in, not writing notices afterwards and not correcting proofs. He made an exception for *Don Giovanni* (he went to eight consecutive performances in 1866), for Joachim playing Beethoven, and for Pasdeloup's concert performances of the Septet from *Les Troyens*. Berlioz, uninvited, bought a ticket in the gallery but was spotted and enthusiastically applauded. At his friends' bidding he gave several readings of Shakespeare, sometimes a whole play at a time. He also acted as adviser when the Opéra revived Gluck's *Alceste* in 1866.

The final pages of the *Memoirs*, completed and printed in 1865 and stored in his office at the Conservatoire to await posthumous publication, reveal the single ray of light to penetrate the general gloom of these years. In 1864 he felt again the magnetism of his childhood and the lure of Meylan where his adored Estelle had lived. She was now a widow of 67, he was 60, yet the memory of his infatuation was still strong. He discovered that she was living in Lyons, so he wrote to her as he had in 1848, and this time he received her permission to visit her. 'My soul leapt out towards its idol the moment I saw her, as if she were still in the splendour of her beauty.'[17] He was enraptured to be in her presence, to kiss her hand and, next day, to receive even a brief and formal letter from her. Thereafter he wrote every month for the rest of his life, and paid her a visit every year for three years while he was still well enough to travel. She accepted his attentions with calmness and incomprehension turning gradually to understanding and sympathy. She also preserved his letters, each one bearing a message of autumnal love. On his second visit he seems even to have suggested marriage. Having by then read the *Memoirs* (she was favoured with an advance copy) she should perhaps not have been too surprised. But she rejected him with evident tact and sensitivity, and this strange nostalgic passion continued its narrow, proper course. We cannot easily measure the full depth of his feelings for her nor his dependence on his renewed glimpse of childhood; not for the first time he had fallen in love with an idealized vision, reality transfigured by imagination.

In December 1866 he accepted an invitation to conduct *La damnation de Faust*, which he had not heard for many years, in Vienna. The visit, very fully documented, was a great success despite his failing strength and his ignorance of German, and he relived some of his triumphs of 1845. He was lionized by Cornelius and Herbeck, but given short shrift by the all-powerful Hanslick. Shortly afterwards he conducted *Harold en Italie* and parts of *Béatrice et Bénédict* in Cologne as the guest of his old friend Hiller.

The previous summer, 1866, when Louis was on leave once more from Mexico (where the Emperor was getting French forces messily embroiled), Berlioz took pride that Louis was now in command of his ship and consequently much richer than his father. When Berlioz said goodbye just before his son's thirty-second birthday for what he supposed would be a year's absence, the unspoken thought must have been in both minds, as it might have been on earlier occasions, that Berlioz himself might not survive the interval, wracked as he was by almost continuous pain and debility. But fate had a crueller version: it was Louis who died, in Havana in June 1867 of yellow fever, and his father, on hearing the news, collapsed. Scarcely two years earlier he had written:

> Ah, my poor Louis, supposing I did not have you . . . Let me tell you that I loved you even when you were tiny, and I find it so hard to love small children! Something about you drew me. Later that feeling

declined at the difficult age when you had no common sense; since then it has come back and grown, and I love you as you know; it will only go on growing.[18]

A week later he burned many of his personal papers – letters, honours, notices – and yielded to even deeper resignation. That September he attended his niece's wedding near Lyons and seized the opportunity to visit Estelle. She received him graciously, and her son and daughter-in-law tactfully left them alone several times. But that was to be their last meeting. As if to distract himself Berlioz accepted an invitation to visit Russia again, happy perhaps to occupy his mind and demonstrate that the musician in him was not dead. He left Paris in November, reached St Petersburg at the onset of the Russian winter and conducted six concerts there to the fascinated ears of the new generation of Russian composers. Court and press were boundlessly enthusiastic, and though most of the programmes consisted of Beethoven, Mozart, Gluck and others, he played the *Symphonie fantastique* for the first time since 1855, *Harold en Italie* once more, and, in two Moscow concerts, *Roméo et Juliette* and parts of the *Requiem*.

Overcome by exhaustion and the climate he returned to Paris in February 1868 with little strength left. With memories of 1831 and 1844 in his mind he felt the urge to revisit Nice, to find the sun and the sea. But walking on the rocks he fell, twice, and returned to Paris weaker than ever. The remaining year of his life was spent in steady decline, interrupted by occasional outings in Paris, once even to Grenoble, and darkened by the death in wretched circumstances of his lifelong friend Ferrand. He was cared for by his mother-in-law and sustained by his loyal friends the Damckes and Massarts and by two younger composers who were as much sons to him as pupils: Saint-Saëns and Reyer. When he died, in his Rue de Calais apartment on 8th March 1869, Madame Charton-Demeur, his Dido and Beatrice, was present. He was buried in the Montmartre Cemetery, not far from his home, where he had spent many morbid hours brooding not on the mysteries of death but on the ironies of life, playing Shakespeare's 'walking shadow', and wondering how soon he would 'bring my own share of corruption to the same charnel-house'.

4

Berlioz's character

It is hard to explain the misunderstanding that Berlioz faced in his lifetime and has suffered widely since, when he was so articulate and honest about his attitude to life and art. Few composers have expounded their views with such insistence and such clarity. Any reader of his feuilletons, his *Memoirs* or his letters is instantly introduced to the forceful enthusiasm of his personality, and while it is easy to see how this provoked hostility, even his enemies should have known clearly what they were up against.

Enthusiasm, or as he called it, passion, informed his daily life; the supremacy of feeling dictated his response to persons, music and daily obligations of all kinds. His passionately youthful defence of Gluck and Beethoven against the inroads of 'dilettantes', 'Rossinistes' and against the trivializing of the opéra-comique and the ballroom complement his overflowing adoration of Harriet Smithson; his lifelong faith in expressive music balances his eternal devotion to the distant *stella montis*, Estelle. There is sincerity and conviction in these passions which annihilate any suspicion that he was a *poseur*, for falsity and contrivance were remote from the Romantics' world just as the sincerity of belief mattered more than the cause in which one believed. To burn for a cause, even to die for it, was of supreme value, no matter what that cause was. Berlioz's dedication to expressive music, born of the marriage of Gluck and Beethoven, was not to be deflected, once it had been defined, by any modern distraction of any kind.

He thus strove for an ideal world in which the greatest music was permanently accessible to a discriminating public, and from which 'cretins and toads' and the riff-raff of popular music were excluded. *Euphonia* (1844) describes this world, set far in the future, and pages of the *Traité d'instrumentation* and the *Memoirs* echo the dream of a perfectly musical city in which true art is nobly upheld. As his career proceeded the vision receded. In *Lélio* in 1832 he spoke of the New World discovered by Columbus/Beethoven that now needed a

Pizarro or a Cortez to explore it: he, Berlioz, would be that explorer. The passage was cut from the work in 1855 (when it was re-named), for the boyish spirit of adventure had faded and the utopia seemed further away than ever.

Similarly, by 1854, it was not Euphonia that Berlioz longed for so much as the high cliffs of St-Valéry-en-Caux, in Normandy, where he spent a quiet few days, gazing at the sun and the sky and the sea (see p. 59). This was the nearest approach to heaven on earth simply because there was no music there, no music critics, no newspapers, no composers, no pianists, no singers.

He wrote far-sighted fantasies about the telephone and the aero-plane, predicting that these devices would change the world. 'Fetch me a soprano from Bombay', he would be able to say, 'for my concert tonight.' He came back time and again to his dream of Tahiti and the South Seas. This was pure utopianism, real and fiery in his youth, badly bruised in his later years. By then he had come to realize that the modern world, the world in which he had to fight for a living as a composer, was not approaching his ideals but receding from them at an accelerating pace. This was the cause of his later despair, held in check only by his wit and his deeply-rooted creative convictions. He had failed in his self-appointed mission to build Euphonia.

That is why his response to the real modern world was cautious and unsympathetic, especially in music. Although he could applaud Flaubert (*Salammbô* moved him deeply in 1862), he was not interested in the innovations of Liszt and Wagner: he distrusted them profoundly as undermining the values of Gluck and Beethoven, which they indeed did. He hated the success of Strauss, Offenbach and lesser figures and never appreciated the dramatic genius of Verdi. He clung to a picture of musical progress which he could promulgate in his own works if only the public could hear them (which in the case of many, such as the first two acts of *Les Troyens*, they could not) and which he was of course powerless to promulgate after his own death.

Idealism as strong as this burned vehemently in his youth and never really disappeared however strongly his surroundings cast it in doubt. It meant a refusal to compromise or to play politics for self-advancement. Berlioz was rarely cynical, although a note of resignation crept into his letters when he found himself having to admire works by Meyerbeer or Halévy over which he found it hard to be enthusiastic. The Bertins, who owned the *Journal des débats*, were committed politicians and Berlioz's gratitude to them often had to be expressed in a column of insincerity. But his early confrontations with Cherubini and Fétis were conducted with imprudent folly, for his vocal criticism of their doings lost him influential friends in Paris with incalculable consequences for his career. Both men offered qualities that Berlioz could and did admire; Cherubini's operas and choral works, admired also by Beethoven, were fully within the orbit of Gluck and Spontini in expressive force, and Fétis's energy and enthusiasm marked him out from his contemporaries. Yet Berlioz could suppress his contempt neither for Cherubini's counterpoint and his administration of the Conservatoire nor for Fétis's attempts to 'correct' Beethoven and Mozart. Berlioz's relationship with Habeneck seems to have been equally delicate when a more cunning operator might have secured performances and favour by cultivating his influence. There is a certain defiance, likewise, in his relationship with his father which seems sometimes wilfully unproductive however right he felt himself to be. And there is the sheer obstinacy of his pursuit of Harriet Smithson, impelled by artistic and creative forces stronger than mere common sense or any knowledge of her as a person.

Berlioz's life illustrates well the immense productive energy of so many great men of his century. His output is not as vast in bulk as that of Balzac or Scott, nor was it as rapid and meteoric as those of Schubert or Mrs Beeton, nor does it have the slow unfolding vision of Wagner; but in his manifold activities as composer, critic and conductor Berlioz gave himself unremittingly, only in his later years baulking at the organization of a big concert or the planning of a complicated tour. He would not rescore his works to save himself the trouble of engaging players; he was prepared to write endless notes to musicians and critics and travel from end to end of Paris if the presentation of his music required it. His correspondence was always abundant and informative, no matter how pressed he was by other business; his creative impulses demanded satisfaction whenever circumstances would allow.

This many-layered activity marked off the leading figures of his generation from the feebler spirits seduced by romantic fantasy and poetic make-believe into a life of inert *mal de siècle* or self-destructive frustration. The 'spleen' did attack Berlioz in Italy and he became sufficiently alienated from music during that period to lose his capacity for productive work, but in Paris this was never the case, and only illness and disillusion clipped his wings in his last years. Until then he was both dreamer and man of action, a utopian in his inner thoughts and a realist in the concert hall.

Berlioz made varying impressions on his contemporaries. Like all Frenchmen he was an ardent conversationalist and spent many a late evening locked in discourse. He enjoyed smoking 'un bon cigare' at the Café Cardinal with Balfe, or whoever was in Paris. He loved talking about Shakespeare and Virgil to his closest friends. They can have had no difficulty discerning his feelings. His sister Nanci wrote in her journal in 1824: 'With him everything is open and spontaneous, he always gives himself away – never the slightest effort to conceal the vagaries of his mood.'[1] At the same time there was a certain *hauteur* emphasized by his aquiline profile, spare features, and piercing eyes. In his last years he was a melancholy, dignified figure where before enthusiasm and mockery had jostled side by side, when he would slip from passionate defence of his favourites to humiliating scorn of triviality and baseness. He would weep freely at great music and poetry, the response of feeling always uppermost.

His persistent mockery was sardonic and often bitter, whenever it was directed at the things he hated most: inexpressive music, parasites of the musical world, ornamented singing, overpaid singers, commercially-minded theatre-managers and tune-mongers who made easy fortunes. But his wit is also one of his most endearing qualities, and it saved him from morbid self-pity and despair. His writings and conversation were laced with puns. His sense of the ludicrous in innumerable stories in *Les soirées de l'orchestre* and *Les grotesques de la musique* is self-evident. The latter is an exceptionally funny book, bearing a serious message amid its raillery. Humour and seriousness are in perfect equilibrium, each reinforcing the other, the grotesque magnifying the sublime as Romantic orthodoxy proclaimed it should.

In this respect Berlioz showed himself a true disciple of Shakespeare and Hugo, but was he a typical Romantic? The musical aspects of this question will concern us in Chapter 9; here we should observe that Berlioz most certainly reached maturity on the wave of artistic fervour of the 1820s and 1830s which we call French Romanticism. He read the new poetry of Barbier, de Musset and de Vigny; he read Scott, Byron and Cooper and based compositions on them. He believed in the fertilization of poetry and music, in the diversity of things, in the supremacy of inspiration, in the divine power of love.

He dreamed of distant shores and mountainous landscapes, though he hardly ever visited them. He rebelled against the classicism of Voltaire and the stale teaching of the Conservatoire. He loved listening to Liszt's performance of the 'Moonlight' Sonata in a darkened room, sobbing.

These predilections mark off the Romantic. But in other respects he stood outside the movement. For example, the Middle Ages and things gothic did not interest him; his attempt to write a gothic opera (*La nonne sanglante*) failed. He showed no interest in folksong, even though snatches appear for picturesque reasons in *Benvenuto Cellini* and *La damnation de Faust*; it was too unsophisticated to serve as modern expressive music. French composers were still far from the nationalist self-consciousness that overcame them after the humiliations of 1870; while Germans were imbibing folk poetry from Wunderhorns, and Russians were building a whole tradition on folk-culture, Berlioz remained the perfect cosmopolitan, like most Parisians of his day, proud of his country's Napoleonic past but at home with friends and musicians of many nations. Despite his Irish wife his English was never very fluent; he probably spoke more Italian than English. And despite his many visits to Germany he was never able to say more than a few words in the language. He had little feeling for painting or architecture, and admitted it. He was not attracted by mystical religious feeling nor by progressive politics. In fact his contempt for politics of any kind, especially republicanism, is a recurrent *cri de coeur*. Perhaps in 1830 he was content to see the philistine monarchy swept away and to sympathize with new movements for social improvement, but he quickly came to despise all that and was bitterly scornful of the 1848 revolutionaries for their destructive savagery. His political views were later expressed in his ultimate acceptance of Napoleon III's *coup d'état* even though as Emperor his influence on the arts was wholly unproductive. Such political attitudes as Berlioz can be said to have held were derived by extension from his conviction that artistic matters could not be entrusted to the masses, and that fine music was only intelligible by fine minds. The ignorant and unmusical could not· possibly be expected to appreciate the superior manifestations of the art. A footnote in *Roméo et Juliette* offers a warning that very few will understand the more recherché parts of the symphony and so in most circumstances these parts should not be played. An artistic system based on commerce was doomed to failure since vulgar taste would outweigh refined cultivated taste, a process he saw happening year by year in Paris, reaching its nadir in Offenbach's triumphant success at the Bouffes-Parisiens. In contrast the old-fashioned courts of Germany and Russia provided examples of enlightened court patronage. Berlioz felt happiest in Loewenberg in Silesia or St Petersburg or Hanover where a court orchestra was made available with unlimited rehearsal time and strict orchestral discipline to serve the composer's every wish. As the mutilated production of *Les Troyens* limped on in 1863, Berlioz expressed his profound frustration by declaring that he could never achieve anything in the theatre unless he had despotic powers over all the singers and orchestra as well as over the 'machinists, wardrobe-mistresses and under-candlesnuffers' who insist on their own ideas and bully or blackmail the director into accepting them. Verdi may have called the Paris Opéra a 'grande boutique', but Berlioz's words for theatres in general were less generous: theatres are to music, he said, *sicut amori lupanar* – as brothels are to love.

He was similarly contemptuous of traditional religion. He can fairly be said to have made a religion of his art since it offered a doorway to a heavenly world of perfection and ecstasy, a view shared by many Romantics. It was in church, at his First Communion, that Berlioz first felt stirred by music, mingling in adolescent religious wonder. But he abandoned Catholic orthodoxy, possibly alienated by his mother's strong attachment to it and drawn to his father's more enlightened liberal outlook. He gently mocked his friend d'Ortigue for his faith in plainchant as the basis of all sacred music since Berlioz himself could not see why the ideal of expressive beauty should not apply equally to sacred music as to secular. So it is easy to see that the sacred texts that Berlioz did set, the *Mass*, the *Requiem*, the *Te deum*, and *L'enfance du Christ* derived from loyalty to Lesueur, from the numinous and expressive potential of sacred texts or from the physical experience of church buildings as their setting, not from faith.

Being pragmatic in outlook, Berlioz needed no alternative philosophy by which to conduct his life. He relished the conventional wisdom of La Fontaine, and found that his daily problems needed solutions in action, not in contemplation or prayer. In a letter to Marie d'Agoult, earlier Liszt's mistress, Berlioz wrote in 1866: 'I have never been able to endure the works of La Rochefoucauld, nor those of La Bruyère nor of Vauvenargues nor of Epictetus, nor any other multiplier of maxims.'² Philosophy was uncongenial, political philosophy especially so, and the only contemplative vision he could allow was that of poetry or music, the human universality of Shakespeare, of which he never tired, and the aspiration of Goethe's *Faust*, whose essence he captured so perfectly in 'Nature immense', Faust's 'Invocation to Nature'.

In one important aspect Berlioz's unique character as man and artist is well displayed: he refused to acknowledge rigid demarcations between traditional categories devised by neo-classical man: between opera and symphony, between art and life, or between the seen and the unseen, the real and the imaginary. In Berlioz's mind reality and imagination were indistinguishable. At one end of the scale we can perceive this in his love of off-stage effects in his operas. The wooden horse in Act I of *Les Troyens* is not actually seen; a whole comic scene at the beginning of Act II of *Béatrice et Bénédict* is audible but not visible; there is an important off-stage number at the beginning of *Benvenuto Cellini*. This derives partly from his love of spatial separation and direction, but it also reflects the intense vividness of his imaginative faculty. He clearly *saw* the *Symphonie fantastique* as a drama; the love scene in *Roméo et Juliette* abounds in speech and song but no voices are heard; and both *La damnation de Faust* and *L'enfance du Christ* rest on vivid dramatic imagery and actual stage directions even though they are intended for the concert hall, not for the stage. Modern audiences may be troubled by this apparent confusion, but Berlioz was not. These works lived in his mind as intensely as if in real life, and he needed no stage to supplement the theatre of his imagination.

At the opposite pole we may observe how his relationships with women were dictated more by what he imagined each lady to be than what she actually was. This was acutely so in the cases of Harriet Smithson and Estelle Dubœuf, both of whom had a complex fabric of imaginary symbols and virtues thrust on them unawares. Poor Harriet was expected to embody Juliet and Ophelia and Desdemona rather than be herself, and dear Estelle, in elderly widowhood, was cast as a perennial vision in little pink boots entrancing a twelve-year-old boy just awakening to the power of love and beauty. He even told her, many years after the event, that she had inspired certain pages of the *Symphonie fantastique*, 'illuminating the morning of my life'. No wonder he had nothing to say about Marie Recio, who alone succeeded in simply being herself.

Since imagination and reality merge thus imperceptibly one into the other, there was no distinction between art and life either. He thought of his life as a work of art, not as Oscar Wilde did, but as a 'romance which interests me greatly'. No composer wove his own experience so densely into the fabric of his music; neither is intelligible without reference to the other. None of his music is 'pure' or self-explanatory or abstract. He frequently observed how the creative process was part of living, not something which he would water in a rose-garden or lock up in an ivory tower. We have seen how the *Symphonie fantastique* and *Lélio* grew out of two, perhaps three, love affairs. *Harold en Italie* might well be *Hector in Italy*; Berlioz felt the soul-searching and frustrations of Faust as his own personal experiences, he identified wholly with Benvenuto Cellini in his efforts to cast the great statue of Perseus; he wrote that he had known Dido and Aeneas all his life, as familiar figures with whom one might converse.

There are similarly no clear formal categories into which his music falls. There are no pure symphonies or pure concertos, no oratorios of conventional type. Throughout the choral works and operas we find elements belonging to different spheres of composition. Heterogeneous collections are numerous, with song and symphony, reflection and drama, and any combination of opposites found side by side. Each work required its own genre and its own form. One cannot treat Berlioz 'as a songwriter' or 'as a symphonist', one cannot easily separate sacred from secular nor even vocal from instrumental.

In the ensuing chapters, therefore, our discussion of the music will be by chronology rather than by category. To have separated this from the pages of biography is arguably a misrepresentation of the intimate connection between life and music that is evident in everything he wrote, but I hope that the division will be justified by ease of reference and that any essential repetition will be borne with patience.

5

The music 1818–1830

Berlioz never wavered in his assumption that composing music was his prime vocation. Circumstances and necessity steered him, like so many other composers, along many other paths, but to be composing was for him the highest source of fulfilment. He was not prolific and composed always with great care, as he explained during work on *Les Troyens*, drafting, polishing, revising, orchestrating. He rarely dashed off a short work in a moment of inspiration, preferring to let great subjects gestate in his mind before the hard work of composition began. The idea of the *Symphonie fantastique* was implanted two years before composition, that of *Roméo et Juliette* probably twelve years before, *Faust* seventeen years before, *Béatrice et Bénédict* twenty-seven years before and *Les Troyens* forty years before. Only in the vaguest sense can he have been composing in these periods of incubation (and *Faust* provides an interesting exception in that Berlioz did some of the composing too soon), but they were, none the less, important to him. Into his largest works he put his greatest effort, not just because they took longer to write but because they drew on the deepest resources of his art.

One self-imposed difficulty was that Berlioz never assumed that a form devised for one work could serve later for another. For each work there had to be found a new tailor-made form apposite to its subject. There are no standard forms in Berlioz's oeuvre (except a few strophic songs); each work calls on voices, instruments, stage or concert hall, themes, forms and movements suggested by its subject, and in the combining of these elements resides the unique quality of each. Musical inspiration did not require a subject, of course, in order to happen: but the musical ideas were often homeless until they found their place in a finished work. This should help us to understand the regular occurrence of self-borrowing, of which many cases will be noted, a habit which reflects partly the thrifty composer's reluctance to waste good ideas in less good (and so less often heard) pieces but also reveals a more profound mental process whereby the composer's natural spring of music operates independently of the more intellectual shaping of finished works. If Berlioz's works had come quickly and effortlessly into existence, no self-borrowing would ever have been necessary or possible.

Responding to a commission was only possible when it offered an outlet for ideas which had already had time to gestate. We may observe how the *Requiem* and the *Grande symphonie funèbre et triomphale* both drew on long-nourished projects for which music had been partially sketched or finished and were both quickly completed. On the other hand he declined, in 1834, a request to set some verses for publication in the *Journal des jeunes personnes* on the grounds that he could not find inspiration in them: 'I have sought in vain for some acceptable ideas for M. Guérin's pretty romance. All I can think of is trivial and incomplete.'[1] His collaboration with Scribe on *La nonne sanglante* was doomed to failure because he could find nothing to identify with in the subject and because the form was imposed by someone else.

The slow process of maturation helps to explain Berlioz's gradual growth as an artist during his career and the supreme quality of his late works. It also explains why new directions in music, for example that of Liszt, are rarely, if at all, reflected in his own. He could not assimilate new styles since he was waiting for the old ones to reach maturity. On this subject more will be said in the last chapter: here we must simply note that despite his reputation as a wild outlaw of music, very little of his music is experimental or exploratory. The *Symphonie fantastique* is clearly a pathbreaker in new concepts and new sounds, *Harold en Italie* and *Benvenuto Cellini* in new rhythms. Thereafter Berlioz clung tenaciously to technical resources which he had mastered, refining from within but never seeking ideas from outside.

His earliest music shows, as one would expect, the child's imitation of received models, but since so many of his first works are lost it is hard to form a sustained judgment until the late 1820s; tracing the acquisition of individual characteristics must remain largely a matter of guesswork. In his *Memoirs* he dismissed much of his own early music and never regretted destroying any of it: some ideas almost certainly lie buried in later works, transformed probably from their first identity. Thus the earliest bars to survive are the A flat theme later inserted in the *Francs-juges* overture (see Ex. 1 on p. 3), composed probably at the age of fourteen for a sextet (himself on the flute, Imbert *fils* on the horn and a local string quartet). The theme is symmetrical and regular, but already distinctive in its leaping, disjunct arpeggio, also found in the *idée fixe* of the *Symphonie fantastique* (see Ex. 5). Pleyel's music was apparently then the only accessible model, Rameau's and Catel's treatises on harmony the only textbooks. Before he went to Paris his experience of music remained very narrow, confined to tunes from *opéras-comiques* and romances by minor figures of the day, and the earliest pieces that survive intact reflect this slight, charming style. Seven songs, for one, two and three voices, were published in Paris before he was twenty. *Le dépit de la bergère* is the first, and despite minor solecisms there is some touching variation in the fourth strophe and a nostalgic coda which suggest an older composer or perhaps simply an instinct for poetic feeling. The melody came back to Berlioz (in the minor) for the *Sicilienne* in *Béatrice et Bénédict* over forty years later. The codas often show a hidden spark: this is true of *Le montagnard exilé*, otherwise rather long, and of the *Canon libre à la quinte*, the canon producing a typically Berliozian wail at the end:

Ex. 3

Two songs have sudden eruptions of drama: in *Le maure jaloux*, twice, when jealousy breaks out, and in the second strophe of *Le montagnard exilé*, both identical in rhythm, both responding to the word 'fureur' in the text. Such things serve as Berlioz's signature already legible in the music, along with awkward harmonic movements which he later learned to handle more carefully and which must have led Lesueur to discourage him from publishing any more. In any case he was impatient to try larger works, dazzled by the resources he encountered in Paris. *Estelle et Némorin*, of 1823, now lost, was an opera probably made up of youthful songs; *Le passage de la mer rouge*, an oratorio with Latin text was obviously modelled on Lesueur's Latin oratorios *Noémi, Ruth* and *Déborah*, regularly sung in the Chapel Royal at that time. *Beverley, ou le Joueur*, from the winter of 1823–4, likewise destroyed, was probably the first work to give a hint of Berlioz's more modern manner, being a setting for bass voice and orchestra of a highly dramatic, in fact romantic, adaptation of a scene from Edward Moore's play, *The Gamester*, of 1753, although he still knew neither Weber nor Beethoven. The following extract from the profligate gambler's words gives an idea of what the composition might have attempted:

> Why, there's an end then; I have judged deliberately, and the result is death! How the self-murderer's account may stand, I know not. But this I know — the load of hateful life oppresses me too much —. The horrors of my soul are more than I can bear —. Father of mercy! I cannot pray —. Despair has laid his iron hand upon me, and sealed me for perdition. Conscience! Conscience! Thy clamours are too loud.

Having abandoned romances as unworthy trivia, Berlioz's canvas was taking larger dimensions with every work, and in 1824 he composed a full-scale *Mass*, again modelled on Lesueur, a 'clumsy imitation' Berlioz called it. Of its nine movements one alone, the *Et Resurrexit*, has survived, passages of which found their way into later works, *Benvenuto Cellini*, the *Requiem* and the *Te deum*. The mere fact that it prefigures the great brass fanfares of the *Requiem* is sufficient to indicate the power of Berlioz's imagination, with many years of growth still to come. Eschewing conventional churchy counterpoint, Berlioz depicts the Resurrection with raw choral blocks, often unisons. It is already the dramatic potential of the sacred text that attracts him here. In the *Traité* Berlioz printed a fragment of an *Agnus dei* to illustrate the 'pious, angelic expression' of soprano vocalizing above the men's voices, and if this does not come from the *Mass* of 1824 we may be sure its music was very similar:

Ex. 4

There followed the *Scène héroïque*, also called *La révolution grecque*, on a text by Ferrand, influenced strongly, as Berlioz acknowledged, by Spontini. It approaches more nearly than any other of his works the popular style of the 1790s, with a deliberately plain, not to say crude, harmonic interest, solid rhythms and rousing choral cries of 'victoire', 'triomphe' and so on, patriotism on behalf of the Greeks being equivalent to patriotism on behalf of the French. Most of it is disappointing, hardly even characteristic, though two passages stand out: one is the close of the central *Prière* for the women's voices, to the words 'sans crainte bénissent la loi', with all voices weaving in turn around the others. Also, amid the blustering heroics of the last section we find a passage of relentless galloping momentum which summons the heroes to action with something of the urgency with which Aeneas drove his people on to Italy in Act V of *Les Troyens*.

Still collaborating with Ferrand, Berlioz next embarked on *Les francs-juges*, anxious as every aspiring composer was, to offer the public an opera. He had been pondering a libretto on *The Talisman*, by Scott, then on a wave of Parisian fashion, to be made into an *opéra-comique* under the title *Richard en Palestine*, but no music seems to have been written. Of *Les francs-juges*, however, the music was quickly written and completed, in the summer and autumn of 1826. After many attempts to revise it Berlioz eventually abandoned all but the overture and pillaged his score for usable material in later works, the most famous being the *Marche au supplice* in the *Symphonie fantastique*. Yet enough survives (five movements and some fragments, as well as the overture) to give a good idea of the whole.

Set in dark medieval forests, it tells of tyranny, heroism and rescue, after the model of Cherubini's *Lodoïska*, flavoured with Weber in orchestral colour. Some scenes are grim and sinister, like the *Hymne des francs-juges*; some are pastoral, like the *Chœur de bergers*, with its double echoes already declaiming Berlioz's feeling for space. Every scene can be related to Revolutionary opera, with Méhul, Spontini and Cherubini his clearest models in musical style. The overture, which Berlioz rightly prized, is one of his most powerful compositions, with broad statements in the brass, a taut, forceful allegro, and an urgent close which brings out the demonic in Berlioz long before *La damnation de Faust* as well as combining the tempi of both slow and fast sections in a grand restatement of the D flat brass theme. Berlioz would have been entirely unaware of Schubert doing the same thing at the close of the first movement of his Great C Major symphony only a year before. With a contrabassoon, a third trumpet and two ophicleides he seems wholly in command of a large, complex orchestra. When it was first heard in Paris – Beethoven had been dead for scarcely more than a year – few could have realized how uncompromisingly modern the music was, the first hint of a new orchestral style.

He followed it up with another overture, based on Scott's *Waverley*. We may compare it to Beethoven's or Mendelssohn's concert overtures with no opera or play to precede, but Berlioz certainly hit on the idea independently. The overture is simply headed with the lines:

> Dreams of love and ladies' charms
> Give place to honour and to arms.

providing a neat balance of slow, tender introduction in triple time followed by a sprightly (though not military) allegro. *Waverley* does not match the *Les francs-juges* overture in sheer power and it lapses at times into commonplaces of rhythm and phrasing, but it does use the orchestra interestingly, notably in the canonic treatment of the cello's theme in the introduction, and in the eerie passage of the coda where the wind hold shifting chromatic chords while the strings (tirelessly energetic in this overture) sputter little fragments of the allegro theme. The sonata form is transparent, with a second subject smacking of *opéra-comique*, as if Boieldieu's *Dame blanche* (1825) provided a short cut to the Scottish highlands. It even concludes with the second subject treated simultaneously to diminution and a Rossini crescendo. Was Berlioz ironically mocking a style he hated?

By 1827 it was apparent that Berlioz was using the orchestra with a resourcefulness that exceeded even that of his teacher Lesueur. He was eager to exploit the technical and expressive potential of every instrument, by listening attentively to what they could do and by combining timbres and groups so that nothing was needlessly duplicated and nothing was wasted. He discovered that the players themselves did not know the potential of their instruments, so it was hardly surprising that composers too, whether teachers or students, were often ignorant of what he regarded as the *science* of instrumentation. But more than that, his imagination conceived colour as an integral part of his music so that rather than filling out the instrumentation like adding colour to a finished painting, his task was to realize in score a sound which he perceived in his mind. Time and again in his early music, and even as late as *La damnation de*

Faust, we find strikingly original combinations and colours that seem to have been spirited into existence by the poetic idea of the piece.

This is true of *La mort d'Orphée*, the cantata submitted for the first Prix de Rome for which he qualified to enter, in 1827. Much of it has a haunting quality new to Berlioz's music. After some evocative forest murmurs a solo viola and two flutes give out a long placid theme (later to be *Le chant de bonheur* in *Lélio*); this symbolizes the enchantment of Orpheus's lyre. Orpheus himself enters to some forceful recitative and sings rapturously of his love and his art. In the *Bacchanale*, which follows, an aggressive motive, endlessly repeated, urges the chorus of Bacchantes in their onslaught and Orpheus dies under a thunderous climax with Euridice's name on his lips. Not only do the woodwind echo his cry; we then hear, in a *Tableau musical* of magical enchantment, the strings of his broken lyre caressed by the breeze while a Thracian flute (actually a clarinet) recalls the opening theme of the cantata and subsides into 'calm . . . silence . . . solitude . . .'. It is a page of the highest poetry, far beyond the comprehension of the Prix de Rome judges who dismissed it as unplayable, and more subtle than any music he had yet written.

By the time he next entered the competition, he had suffered the impacts of Harriet Smithson, Shakespeare and Beethoven. Instead of inspiring immediate composition, these thunderblows seem to have checked his muse as if to allow it time to absorb them, otherwise he would certainly have conceived new grander plans for which his style and resources were still inadequate. In the 1828 prize cantata *Herminie* there appears, at the very opening, a melody destined to represent his beloved in all five movements of the *Symphonie fantastique*, and even in the earlier work it probably stood for his helpless insatiable passion:

Ex. 5

(a)

(1828) Moderato

(b)

(1830)(Allegro agitato e appassionato assai)

It serves well enough for Herminia's helpless passion, with its impulsive neurotic bulges, and in a manner that had already been effectively used in the wild scene of *La mort d'Orphée*, it is a mainly instrumental motive, confined principally to the orchestra. *Herminie* has touches of eighteenth-century propriety as well as modern Spontinian recitative, three airs of different character and a *Prière* of broad solemnity which Berlioz took great pride in and re-used the following year as the *Chant sacré* in the *Neuf mélodies irlandaises*. In his account of the cantata in his *Memoirs* he should also have mentioned the close, not as striking as that of *La mort d'Orphée*, but dramatically imaginative in its evocation of Herminia as she disguises herself in Clorinda's armour and invoking the Christians' God sets off in quest of Tancred. The *Prière* returns in long notes against the rapid pace of the music (the device he had so successfully worked in the overture to *Les francs-juges*) and the galloping recedes graphically into the distance. The cantata won second prize.

Berlioz might then have embarked on a *Roméo et Juliette* of some kind if he had not discovered Goethe's *Faust*, a work which produced immediate creative response, unlike those of Shakespeare and Beethoven. The writing down of the ballad *Le roi de Thulé* in September 1828 was an instantaneous discharge of inspiration which may account for its strongly individual character, conveniently labelled 'caractère simple et ingenu' by Berlioz himself. From Gérard de Nerval's translation he took eight picturesque verse texts and set them for widely differing combinations of voices and instruments, an early illustration of how he preferred to find the right setting for each piece than to construct a unified work making balanced use of specified forces. Unity is supplied by Goethe's *Faust*, while Berlioz draws on Shakespeare to provide quotations for each piece and Thomas Moore for a superscription to the whole work, poetic intrusions coming from any source that supplied something apposite. The eight scenes, all later adapted for incorporation in *La damnation de Faust*, open with the *Chants de la fête de pâques*, the Easter Hymn, and even allowing for the considerable improvements he made to it in the later adaptation, this first version is one of the boldest samples of harmonic thinking he had then ventured upon, freely colliding the moving parts and striding across the flat keys at will. The reprise of the main melody is adorned by a long pedal (not as long as in the later version) and by a choir of angels, later removed, decorating the disciples' line. He also changed the fading ending which we are beginning to recognize as one of his private signatures. The harps play a prominent role in this version.

No. 2, *Paysans sous les tilleuls* is the later *Ronde de paysans*, with provocative rhythms and the strident sound of two piccolos. It simply has four verses of the 6/8 song, with a little coda. Even without its teasing accompaniment the vocal line, lurching like an idiot, is graphic enough:

Ex. 6

Dan - sant, sau-tant, dan - sant, sau-tant, sau - tant com - me des fous. Ha! ha! ha! ____

The *Concert de sylphes*, no. 3, was to be more changed than any other movement, and is the most substantial part of the *Huit scènes*. There is an intricacy in the string parts which Berlioz had not attempted before, with tremolos of both left and right hands, alternating bowed and pizzicato notes, divisi passages with even the double basses dividing into three parts, and the wispy muted runs which are familiar from the later version. He scores also for a glass harmonica and virtuoso harp and the vocal setting is for six solo voices. Even in its forces, then, it is a boldly progressive piece, and what sets out as a broad but simple melodic refrain in D major gets progressively elaborated, first by intricate vocal decoration, and then, after an extraordinary passage showing the birds in timid flight, by combining the broad melody now in F, with a brisk and noisy dance in 6/8, producing different layers of tempo, colour and rhythm all at once. His passion for 'combinations', already tasted in *Les francs-juges*, bursts out, and though he modified the passage considerably in 1846, it served as a starting point for many other proud and characteristic attempts to do the same again. There is, even after that passage, a long, fading coda of very poetic effect, with four solo cellos sustaining a high chord on harmonics.

The three verses of *Ecot de joyeux compagnons*, no. 4, Brander's song, are strophic, the boozy hiccuping carouser finding his embodiment in four bassoons and a phrase-structure which feels lopsided when it is not. Its companion piece is the *Chanson de Méphistophélès*, no. 5, the song of the flea, also strophic, except that here only the vocal line is repeated: the accompaniment is different for each verse, depicting the velvet-clad flea in unctuous counterpoint in verse two and the courtiers all scratching themselves in verse three; the humour, conveyed both in the scoring and in subtle harmonic variations, fixes this brilliant little song leagues away from the bland romances he had been composing only a few years earlier. Neither song needed any touching up in 1846.

Le roi de Thulé, no. 6, is a 'gothic' song by reason of its melancholy viola solo and the sharpened fourth in the melody, close to a flattened sixth, creating a mode of imagined antiquity. Rarely does Berlioz depend so on the beauty of his melodic line, since the low-pitched accompaniment (cellos and double basses in three separate parts) throws the singer into relief. The haunting, unusual shape of the melody vindicates his trust. At the end Berlioz fragments the line, learning already from the *Eroica*'s funeral march and *Coriolan* overture, and Marguerite sinks into silence on a 'profound sigh'. She then sings the *Romance*, no. 7, in which a cor anglais vies with her for expressive richness. Between each refrain the music moves off into agitated regions (the bass line of the refrain was already agitated) as her regrets crowd in on her. The passage where her heart beats in feverish expectation dissolves in tremolos and a long heartfelt cadence before the cor anglais has the last refrain. Then at the end, intruding on her last longings and intensifying their effect, we hear the trumpets and drums of a detachment of soldiers in the street below, approaching from so far that we miss the beginning of their tune. To an incessant bugle call (a well-known retreat of the day) they approach, pass, and march off into the distance, and yet another disappearing end closes this intensely felt and dramatic scene, a vivid recreation of Goethe's scene in the mind's eye.

Finally Mephistopheles takes his guitar and sings her two verses of his 'chanson morale'. In admiring the orchestral wizardry of the later version we forget the sardonic character of the vocal line, whereas here in the *Huit scènes*, with a single guitar for support, its mocking tone is strikingly clear, and we almost wish that Mephistopheles had remained a tenor in the later work.

The *Huit scènes de Faust* were quickly finished and quickly engraved, at Berlioz's expense, as his op. 1. Within six months of publication, and soon after a performance of no. 3, the *Concert de sylphes*, he took a dislike to the work and withdrew it, thinking it 'crude and badly written', harsh words for his most inventive and far-sighted work yet. But with hindsight it is evident that he had not allowed himself to digest Goethe properly. The work needed to grow in his inner consciousness, and he later learned to withhold a work's publication until he was satisfied with it. The fact that both these principles had been denied explains his swift dissatisfaction more readily than the intrinsic quality of the music.

At much the same time he composed *Le ballet des ombres*, published it as op. 2, and withdrew it also. Based on a poem by Herder, it echoes the satanical mood of *Faust* and *Hamlet* as the Shades intone their ghostly song. Chromatics and dissonance make a striking appearance and the end, yet another graphic picture of disappearance, leaves the voices hanging on a D flat chord as the piano clings to C minor, and fades away to nothing. To the three men's voices Berlioz adds sopranos singing in octaves with the first tenors, a sonority of haunting strangeness.

This piece has survived by a miracle, but other compositions of the period are lost: the guitar variations on Mozart's *Là ci darem*, for example, probably the fruit of living off guitar lessons at that time, also a *Salutaris* for solo voices and organ. A setting of Victor Hugo's swashbuckling *Chanson des pirates* is also lost, though it is probably the same work as the *Scène de brigands* in *Lélio*. Berlioz described it in 1829 as the 'music of corsairs, brigands, buccaneers, freebooters, with wild raucous voices', an apt description of the music we find only slightly disguised in *Lélio*. This ultra-fashionable subject produced crude and blatant music, full of abrupt harmonic juxtaposition. But he did also apply the discovery of Mephistopheles' song of the flea by varying the accompaniment of each verse to match the different words.

Fortunately the third Prix de Rome Cantata survives, for it is the finest of the three and has been deservedly revived in recent years. Into *Cléopatre* (1829) Berlioz poured his most passionate feeling, the overspill of enthusiasm for Shakespeare and Beethoven, and despite confidently expecting to win, he found himself rejected for overstepping the academic mark. We should not be surprised at the judges' incomprehension, for the music is nothing if not bold. Within two bars the wind pause dramatically on the chord:

Ex. 7

1   Portrait of Berlioz by Emile Signol, 1831.

2   Pencil drawing of Berlioz by Alphonse Legros.

3   Photograph of Berlioz by Pierre Petit, *c*.1863.

4   Portrait of Harriet Smithson by an unknown artist.

'Aeneas Recounting to Dido the Misfortunes of Troy' by
ierre-Narcisse Guérin.

Paris 4 avril 1860
4 rue de Calais

Mon cher Hallé

Je vous félicite du succès éclatant
de votre ~~tentative~~ pour révéler Gluck
aux anglais. Il est donc vrai que
tôt ou tard, la flamme finit par
briller, si épaisse que soit la couche
d'immondices sous laquelle on la
croyait étouffée. Ce succès est prodigieux
si l'on songe combien peu
l'Iphigénie est appréciable au concert,
et combien l'œuvre de Gluck en général
est inhérente à la scène. Tous les

6   Letter to Charles Hallé, 4th April 1860, first and last pages. Berlioz congratulates Hallé for performing Gluck's *Iphigénie en Tauride* in Manchester. A melody from Act II of the opera is quoted.

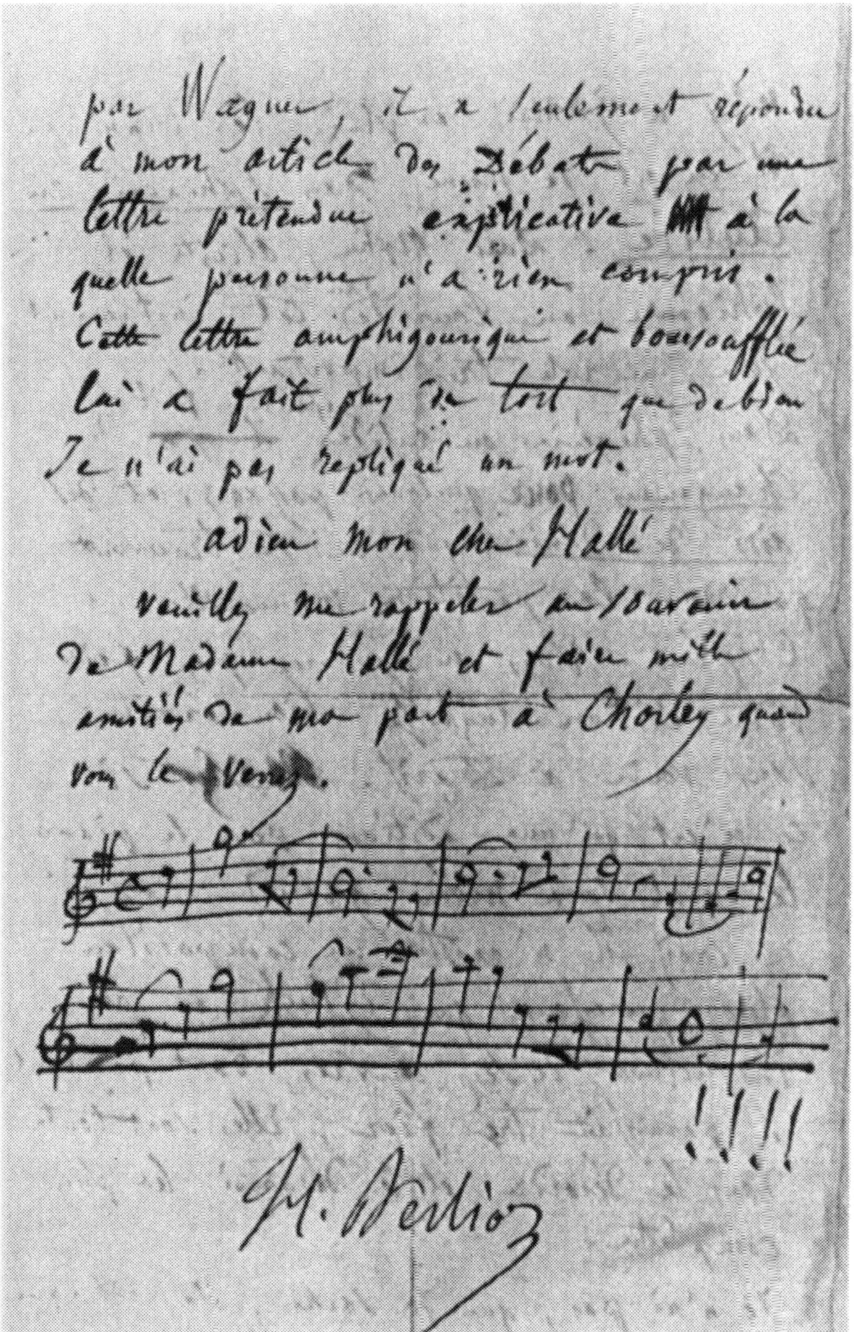

par Wagner, il a seulement répondu
à mon article des Débats par une
lettre prétendue explicative à la
quelle personne n'a rien compris.
Cette lettre amphigourique et boursoufflée
lui a fait plus de tort que de bien.
Je n'ai pas répliqué un mot.

adieu mon cher Hallé
veuillez me rappeler au souvenir
de Madame Hallé et faire mes
amitiés de ma part à Chorley quand
vous le verrez.

!!!!

H. Berlioz

7 Autograph albumleaf dated London, 12th November 1847. The words are a parody of Dante's

'Nessun maggior dolor
Che ricordarsi del tempo felice
Nella miseria.'

and audacious ideas persist throughout. Low divided strings, violent recitatives, wide leaps and complex rhythms abound, not out of a spirit of adventure but because Cleopatra's dying hysteria called for music of equally strong expression. It is a great vehicle for a dramatic soprano, and it gives much more palpable hints than *Herminie* of the two great heroines of *Les Troyens*, Cassandra and Dido, both of whom die at their own hand in scenes of intense passion. So too does Juliet, whose delirious death scene is strongly adumbrated in Cleopatra's closing moments with tonality, rhythm and timbre all stretched to their known limits. Berlioz has lost sight of any Gluckian sense of classical poise in this cantata; even Lesueur must have recognized it as bizarrely adventurous, but Berlioz never performed or published it. Instead he preserved the best ideas in various later works, in *Benvenuto Cellini*, in the *Tempest* fantasy and in the *Chœur d'ombres* in *Lélio*, a simple choral arrangement of Cleopatra's *Méditation*, her invocation to the Pharaohs. In *Lélio* Berlioz is his own commentator, describing the music as 'dark-sounding instruments . . . broad, sinister harmony . . . a gloomy melody . . .' He could have mentioned the relentless rhythm, the slowly unfolding cumulative force of the harmony and the violent dynamic changes. In a letter Berlioz related this movement to the tomb scene in *Roméo et Juliette* reinforcing our suspicion that he was already working on a setting of the play and had some ready material when he went into the Institut to sit for the Prix de Rome.

The later part of 1829 produced a lighter group of works, growing out of neither Shakespeare nor Beethoven nor Goethe, but inspired by Thomas Moore's very popular *Irish Melodies*. For the *Neuf mélodies irlandaises* he selected nine poems and set them for a variety of different voices. Five are for solo voice, one for duet, and three for chorus, all with piano accompaniment. Like the *Huit scènes de Faust* they are a miscellany, not a cycle, and with the exception of the last song, *Elégie*, they strike a less intensely emotional note than we would have expected from him at this period, his enthusiasm for Moore notwithstanding. Two of the songs bear superscriptions from *Faust*, and three are headed with anonymous epigraphs.

Strophic form is still predominant, within the tradition of the French romance, to which Berlioz's adherence is still clear. The first song, *Le coucher du soleil*, for tenor, has a dramatic introduction to two gentle strophes, with a strongly melodic vocal line. Berlioz is already confident in his insolent style of modulating:

Ex. 8

Hélène, no. 2 of the set, is for 'two hunters', either two male or two female voices, and extends to six verses of the ballad 'You remember Ellen, our hamlet's pride'. Its teasing rhythms invite a *marcato* style, but Berlioz specifically warns against it, regarding syncopation as something that should sound natural. He later arranged it for four male voices and small orchestra. William, the stranger who has made Ellen his bride, sounds his horn at intervals. The three choral songs in the set intersperse choral refrains with solo verses. In the *Chant guerrier* (no. 3) for men's chorus, reflective tenor and bass solos are heard between bursts of patriotic enthusiasm. In the *Chanson à boire* (no. 5), marked 'Allegro frenetico', the tenor soloist reminds the carousing chorus, in a melody of characteristically Berliozian span, that tears and laughter are never far apart. The *Chant sacré* (no. 6) is a six-part setting, its refrain being the solemn *Prière* from *Herminie*, the alternating solos being for soprano or tenor. In the first of these solos the evocation of the starry night draws high tremolos in the piano, strikingly prophetic of Aeneas in Dido's garden. For the second two verses the accompaniment is no longer apt, a mistake Berlioz realized in 1843 when he orchestrated it, for the two offending verses were omitted.

In *La belle voyageuse* (no. 4), for tenor and piano, not only are there four similar strophes; in each one the first eight bars are repeated a tone lower. But Berlioz varies the accompaniment subtly and at the end brings in a refined touch of counterpoint under the singer's plaintive 'La la lalerala'. Ferdinand Hiller, who was close to Berlioz at the time, tells the improbable story that he composed the song over two weeks, doing a few bars every morning like a counterpoint exercise. Various later versions exist, orchestrated and for chorus or larger vocal group. *L'origine de la harpe* (no. 7) has four verses with a characteristically expressive introduction to each, the harp of course being audible in the accompaniment. *Adieu Bessy* (no. 8) is also strophic, with four verses, at least in its A flat version. Its refrain 'Adieu Bessy!' alternating major and minor is touchingly effective. In 1849 Berlioz republished the song in G with its accompaniment and expression greatly intensified, perhaps to prepare the listener for the fervour of the last song *Elégie*, one of Berlioz's most passionate utterances and unique in French song for its dramatic intensity. The *Memoirs* imply that it was written under the first impact of Harriet Smithson: 'this is the sole occasion on which I was able to express a feeling of the sort directly in music while still under its active influence . . . I have rarely found a melody of such truth and poignancy, steeped in such a surge of sombre harmony.'[2] In fact it was written during some later crisis, at the end of 1829, and differs from the other eight songs not only in its emotional power but also in being a setting of prose rather than verse, abandoning strophic form. The text treats of a condemned man's undying love, and in the first editions Berlioz added an epigraph explaining how the dead man's lyre, placed on his tomb, was coaxed into sound by the wind on stormy nights, a reminder of the close of *La mort d'Orphée*. However, in 1847, when Berlioz was in London, he heard from Leigh Hunt the full history of Robert Emmet, the Irish patriot who inspired Moore's poem and whose defiant speech to his judges and passionate attachment to Sarah Curran lived on in Irish memories. Berlioz appended the text of Emmet's final speech to the music, and adapted his vocal line to Moore's original verse.

From the opening pianissimo tremolo the declamatory style is evident, and the twice-repeated monotone 'Car le ciel est témoin', bending into a strong cadential phrase, has great dramatic strength. It looks forward to Faust's 'Nature immense' in its cumulative harmonic growth and the finality of its cadence. The piano part, replete with tremolo and repeated notes, has been criticized for being un-pianistic, when this effect is precisely what gives the song its dramatic tension. This is his most ambitious example of piano writing and though quite different from the style of Chopin or Liszt, it is closer to the spirit of Beethoven; in good hands it is as impressive as any orchestration would have been, a task Berlioz began but never finished.

The emotional exaltation which gave birth to the *Elégie* was not exhausted, for the next work, released by a similar triggering after a long fermentation, was the great *Symphonie fantastique*, rapidly set down in the early months of 1830, and the climax of Berlioz's early music. It is still his best known work, a concert-hall classic and a favourite showpiece for symphony orchestras, yet it is distinctly an early and to some extent immature work for all its long strides forward into the modern orchestral world. It is essential to realize how self-consciously Berlioz has attempted to write his own version of a Beethoven symphony, there being at that time only the sketchiest tradition of symphony writing in France. To have seen that the emotional jungle in which he struggled for breath, the confused layers of passion for Harriet Smithson, Shakespeare, Goethe, Moore, Beethoven himself and possibly Camille Moke too, could be expressed in a five-movement dramatic symphony was an unmistakable stroke of genius. Such a plan required no sung words to articulate and so diminish the strength of feeling, it had the grand scale beyond the resources of a mere concert overture, and it had the variety of scene and mood, especially when expanded to five movements, to give expression to the multiplicity of his feelings. There were other remarkable ideas: the provision of dramatic continuity and musical unification at a single stroke by representing the beloved by a theme, the *idée fixe* (see above Ex. 5b) which reappears in different guises in every movement; and the evocation of many favourite romantic themes, such as the opium-derived dream, after the manner of De Quincey, the vision of the guillotine, ballroom music, shepherds' pipes, devilry and witchcraft, all touching a vital nerve in a year which more than any other, when we note literary and political events as well, marks the apogee of French romanticism.

The symphony has a programme which Berlioz distributed at performances of the work and which is as much part of its essence as the notes themselves. It tells of an artist's indefinable longing, à la Chateaubriand, for an unknown beloved, followed by the stormy passion he suffers once he meets her. This provides the slow and fast sections of the opening movement, her theme, the *idée fixe*, providing the main theme for development. In the second movement he attends a ball and catches heart-rending glimpses of her through the whirling dancers. By contrast the third movement is pastoral, and though she is not seen there, his obsessive thoughts and alarms about her give him no peace, and distant thunder symbolically deepens his suffering and solitude. Then, under opium, he dreams he has killed her in despair, is condemned to death and marched to the scaffold amid the jeers and roars of the crowd. The last movement protracts the dream into a nightmare of hellish spectres, an orgiastic dance of death to a parodied version of the Dies Irae. The beloved herself appears, distorted and bedevilled beyond recognition. The whole was entitled *Episode in an Artist's Life*, and subtitled *Symphonie fantastique*, a symphony of fantasies.

The first movement *Rêveries-Passions*, like his concert overtures, has a long expansive slow section, followed by an Allegro. The Largo uses a delicately scored version of a childhood melody, full of feeling, followed by mysterious horn-calls and violin arpeggios over a long held pedal A flat. This resolves into C major and a brisk tempo when the *idée fixe* appears on violins and flute scarcely accompanied and running to a length of thirty-eight bars. There is no second subject and the exposition, which is repeated, is short. So too is the development. Once he has started to recapitulate, Berlioz feels liberated from formal constraints and his imagination takes free wing. The recapitulation itself (bar 239) is in the dominant, requiring a further tutti restatement in the tonic later on, amid a series of codas of increasing energy and impulse. Finally, the movement drops to its knees for some *religioso* chords, a lamentable addition Berlioz made during revision.

Un Bal, in A major, opens with atmospheric suggestions of the salon as harps (at least four in number) parade their arpeggios before the waltz begins. The tune itself is pretty and four-square, though its second strain shows Berlioz's impulsively personal dynamics:

Ex. 9

With a mysterious shudder the key changes to F for the sudden appearance of the beloved against the continuing waltz. She appears dramatically again at the end just as the coda is hurtling the waltzers into a final spin round the floor.

The slow movement, *Scène aux champs*, in F, explores the artist's melancholy solitude. A shepherd's pipe (cor anglais) is echoed by its distant companion (off-stage oboe). Violins and flute, again almost unaccompanied, unfold a long, sad theme. The orchestration gradually fills out, rhythms sub-divide, counterthemes blossom, and a heavy cadence is reached in B flat. Stormy declarations by the bass instruments are answered by the *idée fixe*, plaintively stated by flute and oboe in octaves, and tension quickens to a volcanic outburst as the timpani break in. The long movement winds to a close with the restoration of calm; the sun sets, the wind caresses the trees and the shepherd is answered not by his own call in the distance, but by the rumble of thunder.

Then the horrific potential of Berlioz's orchestra begins to unfold, for the *Marche au supplice*, alternately sinister and brazen, with its blazing chromatic brass, deep snarling trombones, and carefully timed percussion. The movement had been a *Marche des gardes* in the 1829 revision of *Les francs-juges*, adapted for the *Symphonie fantastique* by simply inserting a piercing cry of the *idée fixe* from the clarinet followed by the crash of the guillotine.

The finale, *Songe d'une nuit de sabbat*, seems episodic but it presents its material in orderly fashion amid a welter of strange noises and convulsions. There is the *idée fixe* now distorted in rhythm and colour into a vulgarized 6/8 dance on the sneering E flat clarinet, then the plainchant *Dies irae* ponderously beaten out by four bassoons and two ophicleides (the ugliest noise Berlioz could think of) against the tolling of bells, and finally the round, a vigorous fugal dance in C major on which the weird and varied treatment is based, leading to a rousing combination of round and *Dies irae*, a final firework display of bizarre and unearthly sonorities and the thunderous C major of the close.

Conventional formal procedures in the symphony are swept away in the white-hot profusion of ideas much more often orchestral than thematic in origin. It would be impossible here to list the variety and resource of the rhythmic treatment, for instance, far more advanced than anything he had done hitherto, or of his orchestral virtuosity, which one can scarcely fail to observe. He is not just using novel instruments in a symphonic setting (harps, cor anglais and bells, for instance, previously familiar only in opera), he is requiring them to play in new combinations and in unexplored parts of their range. His capacity for conceiving new sounds was supported by a brilliant command of the technical resources of the orchestra without which he would have been a poet without a pen, a painter without a brush. Berlioz's achievement as an innovator is more striking here than in any later works, wherein, to a large extent, he set himself the task of consolidating this technical virtuosity while allowing the intellectual and emotional content of his music to reach more mature and less strident expression.

Berlioz declared himself drained by the composition of his symphony, which may be one reason why his Prix de Rome cantata that year (1830) was unambitious and restrained. The main reason was that he wanted to win, as he indeed did. He was not wholly ashamed of it, for he performed it four times in the next few years. The set text was an account of the death of Sardanapalus, king of Nineveh, a subject every bit as dramatic and fruitful as that of Cleopatra, as Delacroix had shown in his colossal canvas of 1827. The cantata called for tenor solo and men's chorus, like *La mort d'Orphée*, and was laid out in airs and recitative in the usual pattern. The only fragment to survive, however, is part of the Conflagration added after the judges had done their work. This reveals themes which later recur in *Roméo et Juliette* and in *Les Troyens*, again reinforcing the belief that some kind of *Roméo et Juliette* was already sketched out at this time; his friends recorded his continued obsession with the play, especially during his stay in Italy.

The arrangement of the *Marseillaise*, issuing from the turmoil of the July Days, has proved doughty enough to be heard on official occasions in France to this day. It sets the first four stanzas for unison voices in strophic fashion with recurrent fanfares in the wind. The fifth stanza starts gently, exhorting mercy for the vanquished, then rouses great fury against 'les complices de Bouillé' (a royalist general). The opening of the final stanza is even more restrained, holding back all accompaniment until the mighty refrain 'Aux armes, citoyens!' Berlioz's harmonization is already strikingly personal:

Ex. 10

Whatever his flirtation with *Romeo and Juliet*, his first direct confrontation with Shakespeare was with *The Tempest*, on which he based an overture, or 'dramatic fantasy', finished in October 1830 and later re-used as the finale of *Lélio*. It has a part for high chorus (no basses) singing in Italian and evokes events and characters in the play in a continuous patchwork, not the simple slow-fast form he had used in his overtures up to that point. At the opening Ariel's voice, in ethereal sounds of high solo violins, piccolo, flute, clarinet, and four-handed piano at the top of the keyboard, invites Miranda to find her destined husband.

Where should this music be? i' the air or the earth?

we might well ask, with Ferdinand. There follows the tempest itself, a passage of complex uncouth rhythms and wild orchestral fantasy rather like the stranger passages of *Les francs-juges* and *Waverley* overtures, building up to a storm of crashing thunder and teeming rain like the *Chasse royale et orage* in *Les Troyens*. At its height the spirits again call on Miranda. A new theme on violins and violas in octaves, full of espressivo rising ninths, represents 'young Ferdinand's shy passion':

Ex. 11

This quickly breaks off and modulates crudely into A flat for a long melodious theme intended to portray Miranda herself, based on a similar theme in *Cléopâtre*. Caliban's music breaks in, gruff and angular, in the basses. It falls in five-beat phrases, although Berlioz maintains the regular 6/4 notation. Miranda's theme replies, sweeter than before, in F major. Then the brass produce a new theme for Prospero's 'sinister magic', bold and boisterous. A sudden cry of 'O Caliban!' from the chorus leads back to Ferdinand's aspiring music which is followed by Miranda's theme now coloured by Ariel's ethereal trills. It fades to a long farewell and the chorus is silent, but the orchestra has an energetic coda in which Prospero, Alonso, Miranda and Ferdinand board their ship to the hurrahs of the crew.

The sequence of the music was expounded by Berlioz in a note for the press before the first performance.[3] Without it much of the music's content would be enigmatic and the sections would appear capricious in sequence; there is little pretence at dovetailing, nor is there any clear balance of keys. There is no obvious explanation why the text is in Italian, nor why it is so fragmentary, nor even who wrote it, though it is reasonable to guess the author to be Berlioz himself. Its strange structure can best be understood by regarding it as 'Scenes from *The Tempest*', selected much as they had been from *Faust* and here presented as a single movement rather than several. Its strictly illustrative passages are pointed and successful. The fading farewell would have made a fine ending, after the manner of *Herminie* or the *Ballet des ombres*, but perhaps Berlioz felt that an overture required something more decisive. *La tempête*, of all works, should have ended on a valedictory note.

6

The music 1831–1841

The stay in Italy was a distraction rather than an inspiration. Italian music, whether by Palestrina, Bellini or anyone else, had an entirely negative effect, for Berlioz disliked it all, and he devoted his fifteen months to walking and exploration more than to composition. The three-week interlude in Nice produced another Shakespeare work, the *Roi Lear* overture, inspired by his reading of *King Lear* in Florence, but it reverts to the model of the *Les francs-juges* overture, with a slow introduction and extended Allegro, rather than to the fantasy form of *La tempête*. Like the first movement of the *Symphonie fantastique* (which it closely resembles) it is in C major, but it gains an extra breadth in the opening Andante by slipping tacitly into 12/8. This is especially noticeable when the oboe's *dolce* C major melody is repeated on the trombones in E flat, a passage of almost Wagnerian grandeur. The opening theme itself looks forward more to Liszt, setting a fashion for emphatic rhetorical openings in the bass; Tchaikovsky's *Hamlet* is one such offshoot of *Roi Lear*. Whether it portrays Lear himself, and the oboe theme Cordelia, is not clear; all we can assert with confidence is that the mood and character of the play are contained in the music, and one passage – the timpani solos at the end of the introduction – is known, from one of Berlioz's letters, to depict the king's entry into his council chamber, in imitation of a similar drum signal used at the court of Charles X to announce the King's entrance.

The Allegro is rough and energetic, laying heavy demands on the strings, but the second subject is all tenderness, again given to an oboe solo, truly unusual in Berlioz to be so favoured. Its second strain is scored for violins and bassoon and has the highest breeding (Ex. 12). A stormy development is interrupted by the thunderous intrusion of the opening declarations of the Andante, not waiting for the coda as he had done in *Les francs-juges*, though it does happen there as well, followed by passages of increasing breathlessness, as well as some fragmentation of the theme, with forceful pizzicato chords suggest-

Ex. 12

ing the final unhinging of the poor king's brain. *Le roi Lear* is still an early work in that its raw vigour has not yet been tamed by the polish of his later music; but its strong conviction and well-ordered treatment of themes makes it a powerful orchestral work that holds its own with the best of his concert overtures. Certainly it has proved the most successful of many attempts to render in music Shakespeare's most recalcitrant tragedy.

With *Roi Lear* completed, he immediately embarked on another overture, this time on Scott's *Rob Roy*. Neither here nor in *Waverley* did Scott inspire his best, despite his real and lasting admiration. He described it as 'long and diffuse', which it is, and withdrew it after its only performance in 1833. As a new departure he had a long Allegro in 6/8, in the middle of which is heard an evocative slow melody on the cor anglais, later immortalized as Harold's theme in *Harold en Italie*. One of the Allegro themes was pillaged for the same work. The energetic rhythms, with suggestions of the scotch snap and quotations of 'Scots wha' hae', become quickly wearisome, particularly in the coda, where, as in *La tempête* he was trying to extract yet more energy from his material as a suitable way to close. There is plenty of contrast and vigour in *Rob Roy*, but except in the slow melody little feeling, and it is much easier to explain Berlioz's displeasure with this work than with the *Huit scènes de Faust* or the *Ballet des ombres* four years earlier.

At that point Berlioz's creative spring dried up, or had already done so, if we accept the self-judgment of *Rob Roy*. The rest of the Italian stay, admittedly less than twelve months, produced only small works and projects, and the only substantial work, *Lélio*, contained no new music at all. Circumstances had certainly changed from a year or two earlier, for although *Lélio* was the product of an emotional crisis turning into a creative force (as related in Chapter 2), these events generated the idea and the text of the work but none of its music. Whereas with the *Symphonie fantastique* Berlioz suddenly saw what frame his music should be set in, in the case of *Lélio* he was fired by recovery from emotional breakdown to realize that a group of earlier pieces could be the vehicle for an entirely new kind of dramatic work which would narrate his strange journey from imagined death (at the end of the symphony) to a reinvigorated will to live, largely for the benefit of his art.

The artist who appeared only in the title of the programme of the *Symphonie fantastique* now appears on the stage, in front of a curtain. He explains how the earlier 'episode' left him for dead, but in reality he has survived and, as one obsession after another passes through his mind, he hears, or thinks he hears, music (actually played by unseen musicians, singers and orchestra, behind a curtain). The beloved's image haunts him, but he recalls his friend Horatio and the song they wrote together 'five years ago'. It is a watery ballad, *Le pêcheur*, with the piano delicately suggesting the lake's surface, the reflection of the moon, the turbulence of the waves, the vanishing of the sprite, and – again! – a disappearing end, while the melody, similar in style to that of *Le coucher du soleil*, rises to its recurrent cadences, once even to high C sharp. From there the artist passes to *Hamlet* and his passion for Shakespeare. As he speaks he hears a setting of the ghost scene from *Hamlet* (a choral version of the *Méditation* from *Cléopâtre* of 1829). He decries the abuse and neglect Shakespeare once suffered and taunts the deathly hand of academic prejudice. Breaking out for freedom he invokes the idealist life of a brigand (*Chanson des pirates* to new words). He passes to more tranquil dreams (*Chant de bonheur*, based on the opening of *La mort d'Orphée*, and quite substantially elaborated therefrom). Over the graves of his Ophelia and himself the wind would caress his orphan harp (final *Tableau musical* from *La mort d'Orphée*, now entitled *Les derniers soupirs de la harpe*). But this is all illusion: he forces himself back to reality. Symbolically, the curtain is raised, and the artist proves himself ready and able to work as a musician and abandon dangerous brooding. He rouses his forces and gives the fantasy *La tempête* of 1830 as proof of his recovery and his determination to go forward.

It is quite impossible to judge *Lélio* simply as a work of music and it only makes sense when seen as an intimate document of Berlioz's inner life in 1831. The music was all worth recovering, even though *La tempête* could have been expected to lead an independent life, like *Le roi Lear*. In view of Berlioz's strong identity as Lélio and the burning passion of the text it is more than disappointing that he did not compose music specially for it. It is not the disunity and varied origins of the music that pose problems so much as the candour and immediacy of the text, appearing to lack the formal craftsmanship of high art. For Berlioz the disorder of his emotional life could be portrayed only in this way and its value as personal documentation is all the greater. There is certainly no comparable work of music from Berlioz's or any other time, with the consequence that modern performances to unknowing audiences have to be presented with extreme care.

Three small works survive from the Italian period and one or two others may be lost. In August 1831 he set a further Moore poem for chorus and seven wind instruments, and though the first version has vanished, it appears as *Méditation religieuse* at the beginning of the set *Tristia*, published in 1849. It is brief and heartfelt, similar to the *Chants de la fête de pâques*, held together by its one-line refrain (Ex. 13) and closing with a bleak horn solo on an expressive flattened sixth.

Ex. 13

The *Quartetto e coro dei maggi*, dated 1832 but very probably earlier (he referred to a *Marche religieuse des mages* in May 1828) has an Italian text, like *La tempête*, probably by Berlioz himself. For chorus and small orchestra, it is even more reminiscent of the *Chants de la fête de pâques* than the *Méditation religieuse*. It is a Christmas Hymn to match the earlier Easter Hymn, opening with a rising figure 'Il redentore e nato!' exactly parallel to 'Christ vient de ressusciter!' in the earlier work. There is some unorthodox fugal imitation and the whole satisfying design closes in a devotional halo of string sound.

La captive, on the other hand, most definitely was composed in Italy, though not in the elaborated version most often heard today.

What came out of Subiaco in February 1832 was just twenty-four bars of music, a heavenly melody for the first of Victor Hugo's stanzas. Three more verses were sung to the same music. The melody shows Berlioz's graceful introduction of a chromatic note in the third bar, the placid balance of first and second phrase, the long descent to low C sharp on 'sombre' and the closing sequence of three bars repeating the same pattern:

Ex. 14

No wonder this melody became the rage of the Villa Medici, especially allied to Hugo's evocation of the oriental harem. Soon after he added a cello obbligato, obviously to please a friend, and it was heard thus twice in Paris. In 1834 it was played with orchestral accompaniment, but whether it had then been extended is uncertain; probably not, or Berlioz would have featured it again during the 1830s. As it was, the full orchestral version emerged in London in 1848, sung by Pauline Viardot, and was published soon after in D major, a tone lower. By that time he had the most refined skill at his ready command, and in the five verses he exhibits as deft a show of subtle word-painting as you will find anywhere in his music. Verse one is unchanged; in verse two the melody is playfully compressed with staccato wind chords; the third is like the first; in the fourth the melody sinks to the muted cellos while singer and upper strings disport themselves in a bolero, to evoke the 'air espagnol' she sings. She can sing the words twice since the cellos take twice as long with it as she does, and they even need help from the basses (only in the D major version) when they sink too low on their instruments. Where the fifth verse evokes the moon-bathed night, the texture subsides to a shimmer, while the melody goes halting forward. By the end, when she recalls her opening lines, her melody is fragmented and she is lost in reverie. Poetry and music are here as one; it is one of the most beautiful of his songs, the equal of any of *Les nuits d'été*.

The full song grew out of a moment's inspiration in 1832. He had more success with this gem-like work than with the vast schemes with which he filled his notebooks and correspondence at this time: one about the Day of Judgment (*Le dernier jour du monde*), planned as an oratorio for enormous forces, another based on Napoleon's heroic return from his Italian campaign. Both ideas obviously needed time to ripen, and in the hectic life into which he plunged on returning to Paris there was little time for composition, and perhaps still little inclination: the year before his marriage was not a year of productive composition. 1834, however, produced a large new work, *Harold en Italie*, a second symphony, with a concertante part for solo viola. The novel idea of a viola concerto was due to Paganini, but the even more novel casting of the solo part as a personification of Harold, lost in reverie and contemplation amid diverse scenes of Italian life, was Berlioz's own, borrowing a protagonist from Byron's *Childe Harold* and a choice of scenes from his own recent memories. The symphony has no programme, though the movements have titles, opening with 'Harold in the Mountains, Scenes of Melancholy, Happiness and Joy'. As in *Waverley*, the slow section presents one mood (melancholy), the allegro another (joy), and in the opening Adagio we catch perhaps for the first time a glimpse of that wonderful world-weariness that recurs in the early scenes of *La damnation de Faust* and in parts of *L'enfance du Christ* with a downward-winding fugato, the epitome of romantic *Sehnsucht*. Harold's theme (which it is wrong to call *idée fixe*, since it is descriptive rather than obsessive) appears first in the minor and then, more plainly against a simple harp accompaniment, in the major on the solo viola. The theme is of perfect classical symmetry, yielding little development, and we are forced to see Harold as an outsider, even though his theme participates in each movement, as though Berlioz himself felt unable completely to identify with pilgrims, hillsmen or brigands, much though he would have liked to. For this reason *Harold* is a less personal work than the *Symphonie fantastique*, the parent, with Mendelssohn's Italian Symphony, of a vast literature of descriptive music of the late nineteenth century, most of it far more objective than Berlioz ever wished to be.

In the symphonic allegro the main theme is at first given in broken fragments, the opposite of his usual procedure, and the second subject fails to establish the dominant key, leaving the music still in the tonic at the repeat bar. Berlioz self-consciously develops and recapitulates, hurrying on to a series of codas where he can let the music and the mood of youthful exuberance expand in their own way; the orchestral style is here like that of *La tempête* and the *Scène de brigands* (both in *Lélio*), forceful, energetic and a little crude. The *Marche de pèlerins* is much more poetic, in a style unlike anything else in Berlioz. Soft chords on horns and harp (tolling evening bells) punctuate a melody of simple outline which proves capable of infinite variety and expansion as the procession of pilgrims approaches, especially rich as the bass instruments take it beneath the viola's musings. In the middle section basses plod, pilgrims chant and Harold quietly caresses his strings, and the end fades with widening silences as in so many other early pieces, including the *Sérénade* that follows. In this movement an Abruzzi hillsman (he is not a mountaineer) pipes to his mistress like the *pifferari* that so intrigued Berlioz in Italy (piccolo and oboe in octaves), then sings to her (cor anglais), to the strains of which Harold joins in with exquisite filigree decorations. Finally all three musical elements return together, the piping rhythm in swift 6/8, the serenade now on the viola solo in a 6/8 of half the speed and the watchful eye of Harold in long notes on flute and harp:

Ex. 15

Berlioz seems to have borrowed the idea from the first act finale of *Don Giovanni* (the Opéra's principal success of 1834), with its three on-stage bands playing in different time-signatures. It also shows how engrossed he was in rhythmic experiment at this time, for every page of *Harold en Italie* reveals rhythmic subtleties and novelties of all kinds, cross-rhythms, counter-rhythms, augmented and diminished rhythms, not to mention the sheer rhythmic energy which much more than thematic ideas propels the finale, the *Orgie de brigands*, to its noisy and brilliant conclusion. The scene he had in mind he had already described in the text in *Lélio*, a Byronic fantasy of the brigand's lawless life, free from the shackles of social propriety, a world in which Berlioz was truly a stranger by temperament for all his wishful imaginings. This is made clear by the viola's inability to contribute much to the movement, excepting a notable passage of nostalgia towards the end when the *Marche de pèlerins* is touchingly recalled on distant solo strings. At the beginning of the finale, when one by one the three earlier movements are cited as memories, it is not nostalgia this arouses, whatever Berlioz's intentions may have been, so much as a simple reminder that Beethoven's Choral Symphony was a shining example of symphonic genius which could not be ignored. Harold's principal theme, having been progressively elongated in each movement, is now stretched to four times its original note-values, and is so attenuated that it can manage only half its full course.

The part the viola plays throughout, so different from Paganini's conception of a concerto part, is as personal as that of the artist in *Lélio*; it speaks with Berlioz's own voice against the background of Italian scenery. The dark, melancholy colour of the instrument was for the first time fully exploited, and though balance and projection present problems in the concert hall that soloists are too often unwilling to face, *Harold en Italie* can strike the listener, especially in recording, as a colourful and moving evocation of a particular phase in Berlioz's career, not to mention the wider Romantic obsession with Italian landscape and life.

Before the next major work, six smaller pieces call for attention, all of them strophic songs on a small scale, like *La captive*, and all of them, also like *La captive*, elaborated and reworked at a later date, as though Berlioz eventually turned his back on their narrow outlook and modest scope. *Le jeune pâtre breton* is a setting of a poem by the Breton poet Brizeux, and its growth was almost the same as that of

La captive: originally (1833) a strophic song with piano, it acquired first an obbligato instrument (a horn), then a lost orchestral version, then (probably in 1835) a further orchestral elaboration which matches the last two verses of the poem with evocative orchestration. The image of voices answering one another across the valley is beautifully done, with clarinet and flute a bar apart, and in the final verse, marked *pppp*, the horn sounds in the distance, a ravishing piece of pastoral mood-making grafted on to a melody of great calm, anchored by an almost immobile bass and rising to an expressive chromatic climax in each verse.

Soon afterwards Berlioz set another Brizeux text, *Le chant des Bretons*, three strophes of vigorous Breton local patriotism for tenor

Ex. 16

(or male chorus) and piano. This too was elaborated at a later date in an attempt to disguise its repetitiveness. Another, *Les champs*, a romance which appeared in 1834, was similar to *Le jeune pâtre breton*. It is also in E flat, also in 6/8, and also rising to a high G flat at the climax of each verse. The poem, by Béranger, is a simple invitation to the pleasures of the country, including a farewell to 'Paris, where the arts achieve miracles'. In 1850 he refurbished it, cut three of the seven stanzas and gave the last two a new, richer setting with a certain passion and several touches of magic which cry out for orchestration (Ex. 16).

Sara la baigneuse, also from 1834, probably grew according to the same pattern as the rest of this group. We only have its final 1850 version for three choruses and small orchestra and the hint contained in a letter to Liszt of 1852: 'I am sending you the scores of *La captive* and *Sara la baigneuse*, which have grown since you knew them [i.e. in 1834]',[1] suggesting that the two pieces shared their evolution as well as their poetic source (Hugo's *Orientales*). So perhaps *Sara* was once a strophic song like the rest, its fourteen verses reduced to seven double verses, without all the elegant and subtle touches that make its final version so exquisite. The triple chorus gives not weight but intricacy and the orchestration is particularly delicate; the faintly erotic tale trips in a metre (3/8) and a key (A major) unusual to Berlioz, with a touch of vividness for the pair of oriental eyes peering at her in the darkness (they are actually not in Sara's thoughts, though Berlioz responds to them as if they were). He saves one of his loveliest phrases to the end, the refrain with which it closes:

Ex. 17

(Allegretto grazioso)

It is inexplicable that this beautiful piece is not better known. It loudly refutes the eternal *canard* that Berlioz was a composer of bombast.

In *Je crois en vous*, another strophic song, he plunged into D flat and produced, on commission, a melody of such tenderness that he used it later in *Benvenuto Cellini* for Harlequin's mimed song (and in the overture), a symbol of beauty because the boorish Balducci sleeps through it. The tune none the less has no clear focus until the last line,

when the refrain 'je crois en vous, je crois en vous' – hardly very
startling sentiments – subsides in a ravishing cadence; there are six
verses. Yet another strophic song of this period, *Chansonette*, was
also adapted for *Benvenuto Cellini*, becoming the *De profundis* at
the beginning of Act I.

After 1835 Berlioz was done with strophic song and he devoted
himself to longer works. The longest of all, the *Fête musicale
funèbre*, planned to contain seven movements, was never finished,
and the identity of the two movements which he reported as ready in
August 1835 can only be guessed. One was probably the funeral
march which opens the *Grande symphonie funèbre et triomphale* of
1840; the other may have been a setting of Béranger's poem on the
death of Napoléon, *Le cinq mai*, for bass solo, chorus and orchestra,
which later proved a useful item on his German tours despite its
sentimental attachment to 'le petit caporal'. It is by no means a
negligible work, full of imaginative touches of orchestration such as
galloping strings, brass fanfares, double basses divided into four
parts and distant cannon effects; there are no oboes. Although there
is a recurrent refrain, each verse is separately and very dramatically
set, and the refrain itself, 'Pauvre soldat', is strikingly intensified at
each return, with new counterpoints and new details in the accompaniment, and finally growing from the tenderest treatment on
muted strings to an immense clamourous tutti at the top of the final
phrase, then dying away to nothing. It is a noble tribute to the hero
that Berlioz, for all his mocking cynicism, could not help admiring.

The four large works which preoccupied him in the next five
years were an opera, a choral work and two symphonies, alternating
from the dramatic to the monumental in such a way that his
approach is radically readjusted for each. *Benvenuto Cellini* and the
Requiem present a vivid contrast; *Roméo et Juliette* and the *Grande
symphonie funèbre et triomphale*, though both symphonies, have
little more than their genre in common.

The genesis of *Benvenuto Cellini* has been outlined in Chapter
2. Whether it originated as a serious or a comic opera, the result, in
all its many versions, is a compound, a characteristic blend of idealism and farce, grandeur and wit, breadth and vivacity. Berlioz
poured into it every drop of invention and feeling at his command in
a torrent of notes that make up a long and very lively opera, and its
heterogeneity, so baffling to Parisians in 1838 and Londoners in
1853, is one of its main virtues.

The libretto is a fanciful expansion of various unconnected episodes in Benvenuto Cellini's *Life*: the commission of the statue of Perseus by Cosimo de' Medici (the libretto makes it a papal commission), the street-fight in which Cellini kills Pompeo, and the conflict with the papal treasurer Balducci (originally a dispute in which Cellini was accused of forging coins). The young craftsman Ascanio is in Cellini's text, so are Francesco and Bernardino, both doctors. There are two rivals, Michelotto and Bandinello, conflated by the libretto into a single figure, Fieramosca, whose name was probably taken as a humorous tribute to Berlioz from a best-seller of 1833 entitled *Hector Fieramosca*, a biography by Massimo d'Azeglio of the Italian nobleman who won a notable victory against the French in 1503. The pantomime of Harlequin and Pasquarello is borrowed from *Signor Formica*, a story by E.T.A. Hoffmann, and perhaps indirectly from *Hamlet*. The carnival was based on Berlioz's experience in Rome in 1831. The rest, including the role of Teresa, was newly invented, neatly bringing Cellini, Fieramosca, Balducci, Teresa and the Pope together in a web of intrigue and rivalry, and giving full expression to artistic idealism.

In its full original version the action is as follows: the curtain rises on the apartments of Balducci, treasurer to Pope Clement VII, on the eve of Mardi Gras. Balducci, in a hurry for an appointment with the Pope, chides his daughter Teresa for gazing out of the window and grumbles that the Pope should employ the hothead Cellini (who is also Teresa's lover) as his sculptor and not Fieramosca, a rival for Teresa's hand. Cellini and his friends are heard serenading in the street; Balducci goes furiously to the window and is showered in confetti. He storms out in a rage. Teresa, on the other hand, has a bouquet of flowers thrown to her, and she sings a light-hearted cavatina on the joys of young love. Cellini runs in and they sing a rapturous duet during which Fieramosca creeps stealthily in and hides. He then overhears Cellini's plans to elope with Teresa the following night during the Mardi Gras carnival. As Balducci's returning steps are heard, Fieramosca hides in Teresa's room and Cellini hides behind the door. To aid his escape Teresa directs her father into her own room with the tale that she has seen a man there — which is precisely what Balducci finds. Cellini slips away and Fieramosca, discomfited, is given a good drubbing.

The second scene of Act I takes place in the Piazza Colonna on Mardi Gras. Cellini, alone, sings of his love. His companions gather at the tavern and order wine, singing the Goldsmiths' Chorus, the hymn to their trade. When the wine runs out the innkeeper refuses to serve more until they pay, but an unruly argument is avoided by the arrival of Ascanio with papal money to pay for the great statue of Perseus which the Pope has commissioned Cellini to fashion. The purse is quickly emptied, and Cellini leads his companions off to prepare the little comedy they have in mind for the humiliation of Balducci. Fieramosca steps forward and boasts to his henchman Pompeo of his skilled swordsmanship. They plan to preempt Cellini's elopement plot by themselves assuming the disguise (of monks) which Cellini and Ascanio will wear. Balducci and Teresa arrive for the carnival, followed by Cellini and Ascanio in their monks' disguise. The dance begins and the stage is quickly filled with animation and movement. Then the crowds pause to watch a dumb-show in which a figure dressed as Balducci with asses' ears yawns through Harlequin's beautiful song but beats time lustily when Pasquarello dances to a grotesque thumping rhythm. The real Balducci's rage is diverted by maskers entering with candles, among them Fieramosca and Pompeo, also now dressed as monks. Cellini, finding another dressed as he is, draws his sword, and kills Pompeo when he springs to Fieramosca's defence. The crowd gasps that a monk should commit such a deed, but their horror is curtailed when the cannon of Sant' Angelo sounds, the candles go out, and Cellini seizes the moment to escape in the darkness. Fieramosca is mistakenly apprehended instead.

Act II is set in Cellini's atelier the following day. Teresa and Ascanio anxiously await news of Cellini, and offer a prayer for his safety. He rushes in, having used his disguise to slip in with a procession of monks. His only thought is of flight with Teresa and he sends Ascanio off to find a horse. They sing a long love duet. Ascanio returns not with a horse but with news of the arrival of Balducci and Fieramosca demanding Teresa's return. Worse yet, there soon arrives the Pope himself demanding his statue, and a big ensemble develops. Cellini is given the rest of the day in which to complete the work, on pain of death.

The final scene is set in the Colosseum where Cellini has set up his foundry. It is four o'clock and Ascanio sings facetiously of the dramatic events earlier that day. Cellini's thoughts, in contrast, are more sombre in an air in which he longs for the pastoral life. Offstage his workmen sing a plaintive sailors' song, and Cellini and Ascanio are preparing to urge them on to faster action when Fieramosca appears with two heavily armed cronies challenging Cellini to a duel. A rendezvous is agreed; Ascanio goes to fetch Cellini's sword. Teresa enters, in flight from her father, and gasps when Ascanio brings in the sword. She fails to prevent Cellini from going to fight, and her alarm redoubles when the discontented workmen lay down their tools. Fieramosca has in fact lured Cellini away in order to stir his workmen up against him. Teresa, unaware of that, sees Fieramosca arrive and assumes Cellini to be dead. The workmen think the same and despite Fieramosca's offer of money prepare to hurl him in the furnace. Cellini and Ascanio return, enraged at being duped, but instead of despatching Fieramosca they force him to assist in the foundry.

The Pope duly arrives to witness the casting. The foundry is revealed at full heat, but as the moment of casting approaches the metal runs out. Cellini is in despair; Balducci relishes the hope he may fail. But at the last moment Cellini orders every finished work in the atelier, no matter how precious, to be thrown into the mould. The statue is thus cast, emerging whole and perfect. The Pope gives his blessing, Balducci gives his daughter, Fieramosca congratulates his rival, the lovers embrace and the chorus sing their Goldsmiths' Chorus.

This summary of the action will, I hope, convey the variety and pace of the drama, as well as its clever construction. It is by no means an inept libretto, except that it too often presupposes continuous action and allows too little occasion for lyrical expansion. Berlioz filled his score with both, writing many numbers in which a scene is elaborated on the musical plane only, as well as a great deal of swift-moving action conveyed in highly developed recitative, extremely complex in rhythm and scoring and dauntingly difficult to perform. Instead of the breadth and essential simplicity of sentiment and contrast which Meyerbeer and Scribe strove for in their big pageant operas, Berlioz here generates a vivacity of colour and pace that he never equalled. His rhythmic ingenuity is even more pronounced than in *Harold en Italie*; the brilliance of the scoring, for example in the carnival scene or the overture, is dazzling. The opera is *sui generis*, being quite remote from Weber's romantic world and a deliberate reaction against Scribe's style of historical opera. It has many elements of comedy (Balducci, Fieramosca and the Pope are all comic figures) and many of high seriousness (the Goldsmiths' devotion to their art, Cellini's capacity for reflection as well as intemperate action), it has thinly-veiled declarations about modern art and modern taste, and it takes a youthful delight in mixing all these diverse elements into a single finished whole, just as all the knick-knacks of the studio go to the casting of the finished Perseus.

Balducci, a buffo bass, has a grumbling leitmotif, heard at the end of the first scene and many times thereafter:

Ex. 18

The Pope, also a bass, always enters to the same grandiose sound of trombones in broad triple time. The innkeeper is sharply sketched as a high, whining tenor. Teresa perhaps of all the leading characters is the least clearly defined in musical terms and her main solo, the cavatina in Act I, is strangely uninspired, especially in the Allegro section: Berlioz wrote it in a hurry to replace the original aria (later converted into the *Rêverie et Caprice* for violin). Ascanio's lively narrative aria in the last act is much more strongly characterized; so too is Fieramosca's aria, with its rapidly changing time-signatures to simulate the cut and thrust of swordplay. Of Cellini's two arias, the first, 'La gloire était ma seule idole', is a case where Berlioz yields wholly to the lure of line, the two verses depending entirely on the singer's melodic instinct and scarcely at all on accompaniment. The second, 'Sur les monts les plus sauvages', is more complex, anticipating the reflective style of *L'enfance du Christ*, and offering a superbly handled return to the tonic via the obligatory top C. Here, as in the few cadenzas scattered about the opera, he was conceding to contemporary taste, but one should observe how much more vital are the ensembles in this work than the solos, ranging from the unrivalled zest of the carnival scene (better known in its later adaptation as the *Carnaval romain* overture) to the nimble Act I trio in which Fieramosca overhears the lovers plotting and tries to repeat their words. Berlioz was so proud of it that he dreamed up an excuse to repeat it, Fieramosca this time picking up a little more of the plot. One of the most impressive ensembles brings the company on stage in the carnival scene, each character singing his or her own music in turn (Balducci leads off with 'Vous voyez, j'espère') and then combining in a grand 'réunion des thèmes', which adds up to much more than the sum of its parts. Berlioz was right to see in the opera 'a variety of ideas, an energy and exuberance and a brilliance of colour such as I may perhaps never find again, and which deserved a better fate'.[2]

The opera's dramatic vitality is self-evident, but its acceptance is still hindered by the same misconceptions as those that contributed to the disastrous failure of the Paris production of 1838. These were the comparatively racy language of the libretto, the difficulty of the music, its unfamiliar idiom even in its own day (what contemporary critics always called Berlioz's 'lack of melody'), the merciless mixture of comic and serious, and the unwillingness of singers and management to put faith in the work. The Pope had already been replaced by a cardinal to satisfy the censors. Now Berlioz began to revise the opera, removing much of the opening scene between Balducci and Teresa, the extensive intrigue early in the last scene and many shorter passages. This did not save it, and after its revival in Weimar in March 1852 Liszt and von Bülow suggested to Berlioz some radical revision. More cuts were made, Fieramosca became a baritone, not a tenor, and the two scenes of Act II were compressed and reordered so that an hour, not the best part of a day, passes between the Pope's ultimatum and the casting. The three surviving scenes became three acts. Ascanio's aria now tells of the events during the carnival, not of the Pope's ultimatum. The worst anomaly of the revised 'Weimar' version is Cellini's leisure to long for a shepherd's existence ('Sur les monts') while under threat of death if he does not complete the statue within an hour, and it also deprives the work of much sharp-edged music which still, as a consequence, remains unpublished. The London production of 1853 was another failure, although the opera's success in Weimar led to its publication in 1856 in the later version. Berlioz spoke also of revising it with dialogue in place of some of the recitative, but nothing came of this beyond the omission of the recitative from the French (Choudens) edition of the vocal score.[3] *Benvenuto Cellini* is a work that still awaits the vindication of posterity.

We pass now to the *Grande messe des morts*, or *Requiem*, composed in the summer of 1837 and as different a work from *Benvenuto Cellini* as can be imagined. He was drawing on concepts and material that had been in his mind for some years and in some cases, notably the famous *Tuba mirum*, already written down. He was not an orthodox believer, and the Christian significance of the Requiem text meant less to him than its dramatic interest, the potential for grand spatial design and the tradition of Gossec and Lesueur which he aspired to follow. As befits a religious work, counterpoint played a greater part than in his music hitherto, though it was deliberately not modelled on Cherubini and Handel, whose style he warns against imitating in the *Sanctus*. The austerely devotional character of two movements, *Quid sum miser* and *Quaerens me* – the first for male voices, cor anglais, bassoons and lower strings, the second for unaccompanied chorus – introduce a quite new facet of his music, unless it had already surfaced in the lost portions of the 1824 *Mass*. In these movements the texture is spare and the dynamic subdued, and the *Quaerens me* deliberately evokes the penitential modal counterpoint of the sixteenth century. In contrast the larger movements explode with force and excitement, aided by the massive orchestra with its quadruple wind, twelve horns, sixteen timpani, and four separate brass choirs to be placed at the four corners of the orchestra. Berlioz's vision of apocalypse was here overwhelmingly realized, though it is not merely loudness that these huge forces generate, they combine with the vast space that the work needs to immerse the listener in sound coming from no particular direction, as if he were himself within the very source of the music. It thus compels involvement and response.

The opening *Requiem et Kyrie* is subdued and full of premonition, the firm lines of each fugato entry answered by a halting, chromatic figure first heard in the tenors which persists to the end of the movement. At the words 'et lux perpetua luceat eis' Berlioz paints the glare of eternal light with soaring violins (Ex. 19). The *Kyrie eleison* is muttered on a cowering unison and the movement fades to *pppp*. For the *Dies irae* the traditional explosion of wrath is prefaced by a series of quasi-modal fragments in A minor, thinly scored, which combine simultaneously before a sudden chromatic surge raises the tempo and the pitch for the basses to intone the same melody as before to new, more angular and dramatic counterpoints. The pitch rises again, now to D minor, the tenor's line becomes more frantic, and the moment approaches for the revelation of all the trumpets of heaven after another rise of pitch to the mighty E flat chord on which the *Tuba mirum* sounds. The four bands' fanfares are scored with overlapping rhythms that demand breadth of tempo, cadencing on to the thunderous entry of the massed timpani, an

Ex. 19

overwhelming moment which even the most powerful choruses have difficulty in sustaining once the voices enter. The first grand outburst is sharply contrasted with the abject humility of 'mors stupebit', the second with a meek statement of 'judicanti responsura' to close the movement in a mood of contrition. The extreme contrasts of the movement are as striking as the force of its climaxes, and before the next summit the quiet *Quid sum miser* is heard, echoing fragments of the *Dies irae* material. The *Rex tremendae* adds energy to grandeur, with a particularly effective setting of 'confutatis maledictis' and a climactic *écroulement*, such as were heard in *Sardanapale* and *Le cinq mai*, for 'ne cadam in obscurum'. The end is dominated by the imploring snatches of 'salva me' passed from voice to voice.

From the unaccompanied *Quaerens me*, the fifth movement, Berlioz made a few cuts in later editions: it shows his contrapuntal style at its most severe, in anticipation of the close of *L'enfance du Christ*, with a fondness for quasi-parlando repeated notes in the lower voices. The *Lacrymosa* brings out the full cohorts again in a broad 9/8 given a curious swing by the off-beat interjections of wind and upper strings. The eleven-bar theme, spanning an octave and a half, is treated as the exposition of a fugue, followed by an expressive section in the relative major, still to the same words, whose theme is neatly foreshadowed in the preceding few bars. The fugue returns, then the second section returns in the tonic so that Berlioz can get on with the coda, a tremendous discharge of energy, perhaps the most powerful in the whole work, the last contribution that the full brass groups make.

The next three movements are distinct in character and dignified in style, each exploiting technical features as aids to expressive elaboration. In the *Offertorium*, no. 7, it is the persistent chanting of the unison chorus on just two notes, swaying back and forth while the orchestra weaves a fugato around them: the final cadence is beautifully drawn out as if the two notes had at last broken their confinement. In the *Hostias* it is the famous passage where the men's chorus hears the final chord of each phrase echoed as if from the firmament itself by the unearthly sound of three high flutes and eight low trombones. The root-position major chords – that is to say the first, third and seventh – sound magnificent, but the others are in practice marred by dissonant overtones, especially the B flat minor chord in which a prominent D natural can always be heard in performance or recording; the last chord of the movement is one of these.

For the *Sanctus* Berlioz applies the celestial sound of flute, high solo violins and divided tremolo violas, while the solo tenor sings a melody of great sweetness at the top of his range. The female chorus echo each line, often transposing his music with artless subtlety to suit their own more modest range. The *Hosanna* provides contrapuntal contrast, one of Berlioz's most straightforward fugues, directed to be sung without heavy accents. The *Sanctus* then returns with the addition of a cello line and majestic punctuation from bass drum and cymbals, pianissimo, and the *Hosanna* too is repeated against the continuing celestial violins (often inaudible). A noble unison 'hosanna in excelsis' ends the movement.

The closing *Agnus dei* introduces another orchestral effect with a deliberately acoustical purpose: slow detached woodwind chords are given the artificial echo of divided violas, mingling imperceptibly with the building's real echo. Hence the notion of 'architectural' music is given explicit meaning. The movement otherwise recapitulates both the *Hostias* and the opening *Requiem*, drawing together the most devotional passages of the work and preparing for the final series of six Amens, the 'A-' set successively to different triadic harmonies, the '-men' always to chords of G:

Ex. 20

The bare harmony is telling enough, but with string arpeggios weaving round each cadence and eight timpanists marking a solemn ostinato, the close attains a miraculous sense of peace appropriate to the public solemnity which Berlioz sought to celebrate.

1838 was an unproductive year, largely because of the Opéra's production of *Benvenuto Cellini* amid the usual torrent of feuilletons, but 1839 gave birth to *Roméo et Juliette*. As we saw earlier, Berlioz was clearly planning this work in the late 1820s, perhaps even immediately after his first hearing of the play in 1827. Whatever form it would have taken at that time, his response to Paganini's famous gift in December 1838 was to compose a 'dramatic choral symphony' for concert performance. It is striking how different the result is from either the opera or the choral work which had preceded it, for although there are operatic and choral scenes in the symphony, it is still a drama of the imagination with clear links back through the *Symphonie fantastique* to Beethoven, especially to the Choral Symphony. The outer sections are more theatrical, the inner sections (where voices have little part) more symphonic, and the result is a compelling work even if strictly hybrid by traditional measures. As always with Berlioz, however, the treatment was dictated by the material, and he shaped the symphony in such a way as to present the many external events of the drama in semi-operatic manner, leaving the heart of the tragedy to instruments alone. This is clearly explained in his preface:

> If the celebrated garden and cemetery scenes, the lovers' dialogue, Juliet's asides and Romeo's passionate declarations are not sung, if the duets of love and despair are entrusted to the orchestra, the reasons are numerous and easily grasped: first – and this would fully justify the composer's procedure on its own – because he is writing a symphony, not an opera. Second, sung duets of this kind have been composed a thousand times over by the great masters, making it prudent as well as interesting to try a new approach. Furthermore, since the very sublimity of this love opens pitfalls for any composer

who attempts to paint it, he has had to give his imagination greater freedom than the precise meaning of sung words would allow, turning instead to the language of instruments, a language richer, more varied, more flexible and by its very imprecision incomparably more powerful in such circumstances.

There are seven movements of which nos. 2, 3, and 4 resemble the first movement (with slow introduction), slow movement and scherzo of a traditional symphony and are frequently extracted for concert performance for this reason. The first movement and the last three are vocal and un-symphonic, and the whole work is bound together by the drama and by thematic reference, for example to the quarrel of Montagues and Capulets, to the lovers, and to Queen Mab. Apart from the B minor of the opening and the B major of the close, and the use of F major for two movements, there is little tonal gravity.

Berlioz's preface stipulates precisely how the chorus and soloists are to be placed on the platform. It also hints at his deviations from Shakespeare's sequence. Later in the score a note warns against performing the work before audiences who are not familiar with Garrick's version of the play and who have no refined poetic sensibility, 'that is to say 99 times out of 100'. At that time Garrick's version was indeed more familiar than the original. Harriet Smithson acted it in 1827; Berlioz set the reconciliation scene as his finale despite Garrick's omission of it, claiming: 'This scene has never been performed on any stage since Shakespeare's time. But it is too fine, too musical, and it crowns a work such as this too fittingly for a composer to consider any other [i.e. Garrick's] treatment.' Garrick suppressed Romeo's original love for Rosaline, so that from his first entry he is in love with Juliet, and he altered the scene in the Capulets' vault so that Juliet wakes before, not after, Romeo's death, allowing a final passionate but desperate farewell. This alteration is crucial to our understanding of the sixth movement.

Berlioz's vocal resources are alto, tenor and bass soloists, of which only the last represents a Shakespearean character (Friar Laurence); the other two are commentators. The double chorus represents the warring families and a semi-chorus of thirteen voices (altos, tenors, and basses only) plays the part of narrator in the opening movement, an unusual and strangely impersonal device.

The opening movement 'Introduction' has two parts, the first a vivid taste of dramatic action, the second a detached summary of the plot and its background. The symphony plunges at once into the strife-torn streets of Verona with a fiery fugato in B minor quickly growing into an energetic orchestral scene. The intervention of the prince is presented in stark recitative by trombones, ophicleides and horns, in a transformed version of the fugato. This has a musical if not a dramatic purpose:

Ex. 21

The skirmishing bands scatter in broken snatches of fugato. Only now does the semi-chorus inform us, in sculptured rhymed verse set as choral recitative, of the city's ancient feud and of Romeo and Juliet's star-cross'd love. This Prologue is a musical Table of Contents, giving a foretaste of nearly every movement and outlining the connecting action. It serves to release Berlioz from un-symphonic explanatory matter in the main body of the work and to set out his main thematic material. The feud music has already been heard as a dramatic curtain-raiser; in turn now we hear fragments of the Ball (second movement), Romeo alone (also second movement, cello phrases), the love scene (third movement), and the Queen Mab scherzo (fourth movement). After the manner of Shakespeare's two choral prologues, Berlioz originally wrote a second prologue later in the work to resume the summary narrative, but when he abandoned that he only added the briefest conclusion to the first prologue, prefiguring Juliet's funeral procession (fifth movement). The final reconciliation is mentioned but not annotated with music. The prologue is thus incomplete, emphasizing its already curious invention. Furthermore the foretasted scherzo is not the same as the fourth movement (except the final flourish); it is a 'scherzino' or 'scherzetto' (Berlioz used both titles) in 2/4, with the tenor soloist and semi-chorus giving a deliciously light picture of the Queen of Dreams, who

gallops night by night
Through lovers' brains, and then they dream of love.

This is the most delicate music Berlioz ever penned, scored only for piccolo, flute, violas and pizzicato cellos. The other oddity – a very beautiful oddity – is the two-verse song 'Premiers transports' sung by the contralto soloist as commentary at the mention of the lovers' passion. With the calmest detachment she sings of young love beneath the azure skies of Italy, even mentioning Shakespeare's name as the supreme poet who alone can penetrate its mystery. The harp is prominent in the accompaniment and in the second verse the cellos add expressive counterpoint.

It is plain that thus far the work is neither symphony nor opera, but Berlioz has set forth his dramatic *donnée*, unveiled his main musical ideas and proclaimed his adulation of Shakespeare. On that basis he can now dig deeper into the emotional substance of the drama and allow symphonic forces to take over. The second movement is also in two sections, the first being a slow introduction describing Romeo alone in a state of melancholy longing, the second evoking the Capulets' ball. A bare violin line, punctuated by light chords, similar to the *Scène aux champs* in the *Symphonie fantastique* but more chromatic and thus more expressive, pictures the solitary, pensive Romeo. A broader, less chromatic theme follows, then yet another on the oboe against pizzicato cellos, set against the approaching rhythms of the *fête*. The allegro finally breaks out in a forceful F major, sneakingly reminiscent in its rhythmic vivacity of the brigands' orgy in *Harold*, but Berlioz makes no pretence of sonata form. He hurries on to bring back the oboe theme (now on full brass) in combination with the main allegro theme and then to a long series of brilliant codas.

There follows the *Scène d'amour*, justly the most famous part of the work, and the music which Berlioz himself felt most deeply for; for him it represented the deepest imaginable expression of human emotion. It is a long movement in A major, rich in melody and atmosphere, with the sublime calm of the 'blessed, blessed night' interspersed with more agitated sections, the swing from serenity to palpitation and back providing the formal movement. Berlioz's inspiration takes wing the moment he is immersed in the scene. When writing *Les Troyens* in 1856 he looked back at the fervour of composing this love scene and recalled that he could barely summon up the iron discipline required to muster material of such enervating intensity.

The Adagio is preceded by some scattered fragments sung by the departing Capulets over slow, still harmonies, with their tra-la-las throwing an ironic shadow over the coming love scene. At first it is not by melody that Berlioz casts his spell but by a murmuring string texture of muted violas and divided cellos and occasional sighs from the wind. The main declaration comes on cellos and horns after a slight increase in speed:

Ex. 22

The cellos constantly articulate Romeo's words, with Juliet's whispered responses usually in the woodwind, the whole orchestra providing warmth and passion in generous measure. The final statement of the melody, which Berlioz has lovingly repeated many times, is put haltingly together (the *Eroica* again) and the fading farewells are beautifully suggested by a drooping cadence ('a thousand times goodnight') which shows Berlioz as unwilling to close the scene as Romeo and Juliet are to part.

The scherzo (*La reine Mab*) which follows is Berlioz's supreme exercise in light orchestral texture, *prestissimo* and *pianissimo* almost without pause. The scoring is extraordinarily inventive, using string harmonics, the high-pitched tuned 'antique' cymbals which he had discovered in Pompeii, horns and percussion in original combinations and feathery strings throughout. He even at one point evokes a genial snore on horn and bassoons:

> Athwart men's noses as they lie asleep.

Instead of a symphonic finale Berlioz devised a series of tableaux reverting to the more theatrical sphere of words and action. At this point the second prologue originally set out the remaining scenes, and without it we need to be aware of Garrick's hand in the sequence. The *Convoi funèbre*, for instance, the fifth movement, was a feature of Garrick's version, and it allows Berlioz to take the basic musical idea of the *Offertorium* in the *Requiem* one stage further: the chorus lament over Juliet's body on a monotone while the orchestra weaves a mournful, angular fugato around it. No better illustration could be found of Berlioz's belief in the superior expressive power of instruments, made plain when chorus and orchestra reverse roles and the emotional density of the music is lowered.

The sixth movement, *Roméo au tombeau des Capulets*, is unintelligible without reference to Garrick's version of Shakespeare's Act V Scene 3, for every step is reproduced in the music. This is the most literally programmatic music Berlioz ever wrote, and maybe he was unhappy with the result, since he never again relied so heavily on his audience's sympathetic understanding. He was predictably cautious about offering it in public. In brief, the action is as follows: Romeo arrives at the Capulets' vault in a state of wild desperation, confronts Paris and strikes him dead. Solemn chords suggest the awe of the place and in a curiously scored melody he contemplates Juliet's beauty for the last time. He takes the poison (descending tremolo cellos, an effect borrowed by Wagner for Tristan's drinking of the potion), but before he dies Juliet stirs (clarinet solo) and wakes. They share a frenzied few moments with their love theme, Ex. 22, wildly speeded up before Romeo collapses. His death agony is fragmented and deranged. Juliet stabs herself (a pair of high, dissonant chords) and dies.

Garrick's version ended there, but Berlioz retrieved the reconciliation scene and made of it a grand finale which is the most operatic section of the work. For the first time one of the characters, Friar Laurence, sings, and the two choral bodies enact their horror and continued feuding. The musical styles are very mixed: the repetitive rhythms of Friar Laurence's 'Mais vous avez repris la guerre de famille' and his 'Silence, malheureux!' to the factious chorus both recall Berlioz's music from the 1820s and may belong to his first plans for a setting of the play. The *Air* 'Pauvres enfants' on the other hand looks forward to the more tender pages of *Béatrice et Bénédict*, while the *Serment* approaches the colossal manner of Meyerbeer and the Italians, with its broad 9/8 pulse and big tune. It is forcefully echoed in the overture to *Tannhäuser*, composed four years later.

In the symphonic movements Berlioz's style and assurance had advanced considerably, and at its best the work stands, with *La damnation de Faust* and *Les Troyens*, as one of his greatest works. He had taken a decisive step in loosening the symphonic bond, drawing into his plan the same heterogeneous elements as in the *Huit scènes de Faust* or *Lélio*. Again one must observe Berlioz's fondness for picking on a single striking image in his source and making a self-contained movement out of it regardless of dramatic wholeness and continuity. The *Fête* movement and the *Reine Mab* scherzo are examples which have musical, even symphonic justification, but are less dramatic, in the strict sense, than the death scene or the finale, both of which work on the imagination in a different way. The *Scène d'amour* is symphonically and dramatically essential; it drew out Berlioz's highest genius and thus reposes at the heart of the symphony.

The *Grande symphonie funèbre et triomphale* of 1840 reveals a quite different world. It is in no sense a continuation of Berlioz's symphonic ambitions but a commissioned work composed for a specific occasion largely from pre-existing material. The large military band and the monumental manner were dictated by the occasion and by the tradition of public ceremonial which had flourished in France since the Revolution. Composed originally for a large wind band of 200 players, it was enlarged two years later to include optional strings and, soon after, a chorus. Neither strings nor chorus contribute much to its effect, the strings having no independent music and the chorus being too awkwardly placed in tessitura to sing the stirring refrain of the finale, a fact acknowledged by Berlioz when he later issued a piano version of the movement transposed up a fourth. As wind music the symphony holds a unique place in that uneven repertory, for although Mendelssohn, Wagner, Gounod and other leading composers of the period wrote for wind band, there are no substantial symphonic works to equal Berlioz's. It must be said that it is not itself an evenly impressive work, the first movement (which may be a relic from the incomplete project from the mid-1830s mentioned earlier) being by far the strongest. Its cumulative breadth and massive sonority rest on a magnificent sense of line, sustained over a heavy, mournful pulse. Eight side-drums, alternating with horns and trumpets, lay down a relentless slow march and the long melody unwinds. For the first and last time in a symphony Berlioz has a second subject which behaves 'correctly' in key, character and placing, but there is no development section. In its place the bass instruments introduce a new elephantine theme in the remote key of E major forced back to the tonic F minor after only ten bars; the process is repeated, then the regular recapitulation proceeds. There is a wealth of interesting detail within the solid blocks of sound, of which perhaps the most forceful example is the harmonic clash over irresistible rhythms:

Ex. 23

(Moderato un poco lento)

The opening *Marche funèbre* is followed by an *Oraison funèbre* for which Berlioz borrowed a scene from his abandoned opera *Les francs-juges*, transcribing the voice part for solo trombone. There is a touching simplicity in this movement, in G major, with its lighter scoring and slow harmonic rhythm. It leads directly into the fanfares which proclaim the final *Apothéose*, a triumphal march of brutal obviousness in the key of B flat major. Probably because the movements already existed independently in different keys, Berlioz nonchalantly overturned the convention of beginning and ending symphonies in the same key. The final key certainly sounds triumphant after the deep mourning of the first movement, perhaps emphasized by the breathtaking coda in which the whole massive army swings into A major before the final return to B flat. Otherwise the movement is disappointing, an obviously occasional piece which fails to live up to the grandeur of the opening movement; mourning has always inspired finer music than triumph.

In 1840 Berlioz at last returned to smaller forms, even though opera plans continued, unfruitfully, to preoccupy him. In March of that year he set Théophile Gautier's love poem *Villanelle* for voice and piano, though what or who persuaded him to do so is not known. Was it for publication, for a performer or out of enchantment with the poem? It was his prettiest song yet, with its three verses delicately varied after the manner of the *Chanson de Méphistophélès*, and teasing counterpoints added in the left hand while the right hand has lightly repeated chords whose origin in the second movement of Beethoven's Eighth Symphony is clear from Berlioz's article of February 1838: 'The wind accompanies the violins' and basses' dialogue with eight *pianissimo* chords in each bar, like two children picking flowers in a field one spring morning.' There soon followed five more songs from the same collection (*La comédie de la mort*) and they were published in 1841 under the title *Les nuits d'été*. All were later orchestrated with such skill that the piano version is now rarely heard; originally all six songs were for mezzo-soprano or tenor, suggesting performances of the set as a cycle. In the orchestral version, two songs were transposed for other voices.

Le spectre de la rose, originally in D, was transposed down to B when it was orchestrated and given a majestic eight-bar introduction. The haunting mystery of Gautier's poem is dramatically evoked not in a neat formal setting but with continuously evolving music. The shapely melody of the opening is never fully repeated, and the last page dissolves in tremolos, followed by a new graceful line. The final recitative could not be more simple or more affecting. The setting is greatly enhanced in its orchestral version. *Sur les lagunes* (no. 3) also has tremolos that ill suit the piano version (in G minor; the orchestration is a tone lower, for baritone). It is a mournful necromantic piece: 'Ma belle amie est morte', with an expressive motive confined not only to the accompaniment but also to its pitch no matter where the music has modulated:

Ex. 24

(d)

Tolling like a bell the D and E flat refer always to G minor, a powerful picture of obsessive grief. The voice has its own refrain, a long falling figure at the end of each verse to the words: 'Ah! sans amour s'en aller sur la mer!' The last verse takes the voice into a passionate climax of great intensity as he recalls the reality of his love, but then realizing he is now alone, his own refrain gives way to a rocking figure as the boat sways across the lagoon, and for the first time he shares the accompaniment's two-note figure, Ex. 24. The music closes impotently on the dominant, unable to reach any finality. The whole song is an impassioned cry of grief, worthy of comparison with Dido's despair, in *Les Troyens*.

Absence (no. 4) is equally melancholy. F sharp major symbolizes remoteness and profundity to the romantic mind, and the lingering refrain (again conveying obsessive longing, as in *Sur les lagunes*) is a full melodic statement, complete and whole in fifteen bars. The eleven-bar episode which twice intervenes is bare and plaintive, the second one a variation of the first. *Au cimetière* (no. 5) provides no emotional relief, on the contrary the poet's despair deepens, set against the graveyard's ghostly shadows. Plain repeated chords stand immobile as gravestones while the singer 'à un quart de voix' recalls the solitary dove in the yew-tree's branches. This evokes memories and the music quickens, rising once to a sweet memory quickly dampened by a passing ghost, represented by clashing harmonies and string harmonics. The return of the opening melody has an additional drooping counterpoint in the orchestrated version, and the persistent bitter-sweet flattened sixth persists almost to the end.

With *L'île inconnue* we emerge from the gloom into a world of hope and fantasy. The music is accordingly more extrovert and tuneful. What exotic shore would you like to visit? The Baltic? The Pacific? Java? Norway? Berlioz too longed to travel to such places, and though there is a touch of irony in the poem, Berlioz ends with the wind filling his sails and a new beginning ahead.

Most of the songs in *Les nuits d'été* profit greatly from their orchestral setting; the use of restrained forces and lightly applied touches of colour are masterly. Above all the songs show a complete maturity of style, based on the achievement of *Roméo et Juliette*. He is no longer concerned with simple strophic setting; he finds drama and expression in each poem; and his command of harmony is now completely assured, indeed there are few works where one may more profitably study his idiosyncratic methods and their close dependence on verbal expression. Though the set of six songs is not necessarily to be considered a cycle, the four songs of despair framed by two songs of hope make a satisfying and complete exploration of romantic love. It is one of Berlioz's works to treasure most.

7

The music 1841–1849

In the years 1841 to 1846 the disorder of Berlioz's home life and his frequent absences from Paris are immediately reflected in the fragmentation of his work as a composer. It is painful to reflect on the larger works that might have been written at this time if he had found stability and tranquillity; the preceding years had demonstrated that his invention had never been more fertile or his technique more assured; the range of styles and subjects open to him was vast, his response as full-blooded as ever. But until *La damnation de Faust* emerged miraculously from his itinerant workshop in 1846, his genius is only fitfully active. Any period which produced such moving and diverse works as the *Hymne à la France*, the *Corsaire* overture, and the *Hamlet* march cannot be considered fallow, but the slackening in pace and the uncertainty of direction are none the less evident. Two symptoms of this slackening may be identified: one is his repeated turning to his own and others' works to make arrangements from them; the other is his inability to find an opera subject or libretto which suited him.

The opera he devoted most effort to at this time was *La nonne sanglante*, a libretto concocted by Scribe from Lewis's popular success of 1795, *The Monk*. Its subject had much in common with Meyerbeer's *Robert le diable* and was thus calculated to gratify the Opéra audience's taste for dark dealings in the cloister. Berlioz had no objection to Satanic subjects but his poor relations with Scribe and the lack of any personal commitment condemned the project from the beginning. In addition, the mechanical doggerel of Scribe's rhymed verses worked against all Berlioz's musical instincts. By 1847 composer and librettist had abandoned each other, and the libretto was finally set by Gounod in 1854.

A substantial quantity of music survives from Act II, still unpublished: two airs, an incomplete duet and an incomplete *Légende*. There is enough to identify the two principal male characters, the hermit Hubert (bass) and the hero Rodolphe (tenor), the former relating closely to the Pope in *Benvenuto Cellini* and Narbal in *Les Troyens*, the latter looking forward strikingly to Bénédict and even Aeneas. The recitatives in particular provide an interesting link between Spontini and *Les Troyens*. The heroine, Agnès, appears in the duet, and the *Légende* tells the story of the bleeding nun herself, supposed to appear on the castle walls at midnight. Berlioz was happy to abandon his repetitive score; there is no evidence that he used up any pieces in later works. Some of his disillusionment was reflected in his great reluctance to embark on *Les Troyens* ten years later.

As a songwriter Berlioz was still mining a valuable vein. Eight new pieces belong to this decade, beginning with *La mort d'Ophélie* in 1842. Like so many of his songs it was later orchestrated, with the solo part arranged for female chorus. The style is very close to that of *Les nuits d'été*, the poem by Legouvé paraphrasing the Queen's speech in *Hamlet* 'There is a willow grows aslant a brook'. The song repays the closest study, for the various fragments of melody and refrain recur many times, but never the same twice. Berlioz is incessantly varying his ideas, no matter how simple, and the melodic line itself is as graceful as can be. The endless floating repetitions of the refrain itself provide a beautiful coda to each verse, and the brook murmurs almost to the end:

Ex. 25

(Andantino con moto quasi allegretto)

La belle Isabeau appeared in December 1843. There are three verses, again displaying Berlioz's device of continuously evolving material so that the third is only remotely related to the first. It is a setting of a poem by Alexandre Dumas about the lovely Isabeau imprisoned by her father to keep her from her knightly lover. The real protagonist is the storm, suggested by isolated rain-drops and surging chromatic scales, like the *William Tell* overture, with some effective piano writing and the intervention of a chorus, of all things, with the words 'Prions Dieu!' at the end of each verse.

Le chasseur danois and *Zaïde* were both composed for Berlioz's concerts in Vienna at the end of 1845, respectively for bass and soprano voices with piano; both were orchestrated also. The first is a reversion to the simpler ballad style of *Hélène* and the noisy 6/8 of the *Choeur de brigands* (in *Lélio*). Only in the fourth verse, where de Leuven's poem finds the huntsman dead, does the music pause for a dramatic hush. *Zaïde* is much more rewarding: three verses (variations of each other) interleave four repetitions of a stirring rhythmic refrain in bolero rhythm and with castanet accompaniment, even in the piano version. Like all French composers Berlioz responded warmly to an exotic picture of Spain and to the story of Zaïde captivated by her love of Granada, also by the knight who carries her off. The poet was Roger de Beauvoir. The accompaniment figures in the three verses are especially absorbing, more so in the orchestral version.

Four further songs are hard to give precise dates, though two of them were first listed in a catalogue issued with the libretto of *La damnation de Faust* in November 1846. *Prière du matin*, for children's voices in two parts, is a delicate strophic setting of a poem by Lamartine, viewing the world through a child's wondering eyes. The touching simplicity of the tune looks back to Berlioz's earliest songs, the subtlety of the harmony forward to Anna's music in *Les Troyens*. *Le trébuchet*, a scherzo for two voices, has a curious history worth recounting. It was a romance by the eighteenth-century poet Antoine de Bertin, a sentimental tableau in a strophic setting similar in key and jumpy accompaniment to the *Chanson de Méphistophélès* about the flea and possibly dating from the 1820s. In 1849 Berlioz unearthed it for publication but could find only the first verse of the text, so he persuaded Emile Deschamps (the librettist of *Roméo et Juliette*) to supply two further verses, a task of literary pastiche he undertook with great skill. Berlioz thanked him with characteristic exuberance:

> Mon cher poète, je vous remercie forty thousand times; la vostra canzonetta is very charming, and perfectly taillata per la musica. Your poetry sur les folies socialistes is magnificently true and truly magnificent. Inveni quatuor amicos inter ces beaux vers . . . you understand? . . . (Et Dieu qui tient en main, etc . . .) Je vous enverrai le recueil dès qu'il aura paru.
>
> Good morning   Schiav![1]

So once again Berlioz turned a strophic song into a through-composed piece with subtle variations of accompaniment and vocal line in the later verses wedded to the tiny drama of the words, and the result is a masterpiece in miniature. The two voices should be two women's or two men's voices, not one of each.

Two further songs probably belong to the period 1847 to 1849, both settings of the same words, by Adolphe de Bouclon. Why Berlioz should have set the same light-hearted poem twice and published them side by side is a mystery. The two pieces are very different. *Petit oiseau* is strophic and a little sombre, with a modal flavour; *Le matin* sets one more verse and is more sharply coloured, against a roughly strophic background. It has a tender entreaty to the poet's aged mother to listen to the bird's early morning song, and the warblings themselves become more and more prominent until at the end trills take over completely:

Ex. 26

The remaining five compositions of the period are oddly miscellaneous. First we must consider the *Hymne à la France*, a patriotic work for large chorus and orchestra composed for Berlioz's colossal Paris concerts of 1844. In 1849 it was coupled with *La menace des Francs* under the title *Vox populi*. The text was by Auguste Barbier, librettist of *Benvenuto Cellini*. Even to non-Frenchmen it is a stirring piece, the superb refrain 'Dieu protège la France!' returning at the end of each of the four verses. The technique is now familiar: the melody is broadly similar each time, the voices taking turns to sing it, but the accompaniment is newly composed for each verse. Both melody and accompaniment have Berlioz's individual stamp, and the final refrain is overwhelming, suggesting the *Chœur national* in Act III of *Les Troyens*. A fifth verse was deleted after the early performances.

Soon afterwards Berlioz wrote his only solo keyboard music, three short pieces for the new 'orgue-mélodium' (something similar to a harmonium) commissioned by the manufacturer Jacob Alexandre, whose son Edouard became one of Berlioz's close friends. Both Berlioz and Liszt took an interest in the instrument, and promoted it actively. The first of Berlioz's pieces is a *Sérénade agreste à la madone* based on a melody of the *pifferari* he had heard in Italy. The opening has a churchy, almost Handelian flavour, and it alternates with the pipers' music over a drone bass. The second is a *Toccata*, with a left-hand perpetuum mobile. Without any title, dynamics, tempo marking or expression marks of any kind, it is Berlioz's only venture into abstract composition, a single oddity in his whole œuvre, but strikingly successful on its own modest terms. The only comparable music is the fugal passage for the Ishmaelites in *L'enfance du Christ*. Indeed all three works look forward strikingly to that work, including the third, *Hymne pour l'élévation*, a somewhat sanctimonious fugue.

Berlioz's holiday in Nice in August 1844 saw the composition of the *Corsaire* overture. It was first played in Paris in 1845 under the title *La tour de Nice*, then revised and retitled *Le corsaire rouge*, after Fenimore Cooper's *The Red Rover*, and finally issued as *Le corsaire*, suggesting Byron. It is one of his most spirited and characteristic works, immediately suggestive of the city and the sea which inspired it, with memories of his stormy sea voyage of 1831 still doubtless in his mind. Like the overture to *Benvenuto Cellini*, it opens with a rush of energy before presenting the slow section, a ravishing melody in A flat, which always seems too short even though the last six bars are repeated. Notice Berlioz's obsession with the note D flat in the bass, a recurrent booming that magnetizes the harmony.

The allegro theme is truly swashbuckling, and Berlioz immediately inverts it:

Ex. 27

He treats it also in canon, and uses it in the dominant as a subsidiary theme. Main contrast is provided however by a speeded up version of the Adagio theme, now in C major, and as usual Berlioz hurries ahead to the coda, one of the most infectious and powerful of any of his codas. The tension comes from relentless harmonic movement and constant syncopation (perhaps derived from Beethoven's third *Leonora* overture), and the grandeur from the long series of declarations in the brass against swirling rising scales in the strings. Four bars from the end, when the pace finally slackens for a moment, a fortissimo A flat chord reminds us of the Adagio before plunging on to the final C. The overture's zest has a curious resemblance to that of the overture to Glinka's opera *Ruslan and Lyudmila*. Since Glinka (who had first met Berlioz in Italy) arrived in Paris in July 1844, Berlioz may have seen a score of *Ruslan* before his departure for Nice. The two composers saw much of each other that autumn, although Berlioz admitted that he did not at first fully appreciate Glinka's work.

If the magnificent *Marche pour la dernière scène d'Hamlet* was definitely written in the autumn of 1844 for a Paris production of the play which never took place, it makes those months seem volcanically active in comparison with the rest of this period. Where *Le corsaire* perfected Berlioz's capacity for speed, movement and atmosphere, the *Hamlet* march is his ultimate funeral utterance, even more telling than his other three notable pieces of the same type: Juliet's funeral procession, the first movement of the *Grande symphonie funèbre et triomphale* and the closing scene of *Les Troyens*. The *Hamlet* march seems to convey the whole tragic burden of Shakespeare's play in a single movement of only twenty pages, in which the effect is of culminating an enormous work; it has a truly epic sense of scale and solemn grandeur. With a wordless chorus intoning 'Ah!' from time to time, the dry colour in the orchestration

and the persistent Schubertian rhythm

Ex. 28

(Allegretto moderato)

the march generates tremendous tension which can only be released with the discharge of a 'peloton', Berlioz's orchestral equivalent of Shakespeare's 'peal of ordnance'. Thereafter the music is pathetically weakened. Double basses tentatively break the hollow silence and the music creeps back to life for one of the most heart-rending dismissals in musical literature. Soft reverberations rise from the tam-tam, and Berlioz's miraculous falling chromatics intertwine:

Ex. 29

(Allegretto moderato)

The last word is given to the chorus holding a unison C long after A minor has faded to nothing.

The notion of a 'Railway Cantata' may seem frivolous in our down-to-earth age, but as each new line was opened up between the capitals of Europe the railway seemed to fulfil romantic dreams of brotherhood and progress. It is difficult to imagine that either Jules Janin, one of Paris's leading literary figures who wrote the text, or Berlioz shared the portentous acclamations of peace, the monarchy, the workers, the fatherland, or the wonders of science which fill the many verses of the *Chant des chemins de fer*, commissioned in 1846 for the Chemin de Fer du Nord. The music is decidedly laboured, partly because it was written for outdoor performance and therefore had no space for subtlety of scoring or word-setting, partly because it was hurriedly written, and certainly because Berlioz felt no personal commitment. The key of B major is unusual for a public work of this kind. The main refrain is heard no less than six times, with a tenor soloist leading the male chorus. The fifth refrain is curtailed, leading into a strange, devotional hymn of thanksgiving where the women's voices join in (an octave above the tenors). The one passage which must win our admiration is the third verse section, telling of the old men's pride in the new railway. It is such a beautifully moulded melody, and the string accompaniment so refined, like a pre-echo of Chorebus's air in Act I of *Les Troyens*, that it must be quoted in full:

Ex. 30

We must turn now to the arrangements which proliferate in this period. As usual Berlioz was anxious not to waste music which deserved to be rescued from abandoned or neglected works. The first of this group is the *Rêverie et caprice*, a romance for violin and orchestra. It was arranged in 1841 from the cavatina in Act I of *Benvenuto Cellini* which had evidently displeased the singer Madame Dorus-Gras in 1838 and been replaced. It is rather more awkward for violin than for voice and has never won many admirers. Its impulsive changes of mood and speed need the support of words (originally 'Ah, que l'amour une fois dans le cœur') and the brief development section is abandoned after nine bars just when both the harmonic direction and the violin writing are generating some interest. The accompaniment was also arranged for the piano.

Berlioz would disdain the suggestion that his recitatives for Weber's *Der Freischütz* should be subject to critical scrutiny. He was self-effacing about their musical value and felt unhappy about accepting the task at all. He would certainly have been aware how pointless and damaging it was to provide notes for Kaspar's melodramatically spoken words in the Wolf's Glen scene, speech being at that time forbidden on the Opéra stage. For the snatches of dialogue between verses of songs or for the more extended dialogue between scenes the recitatives are harmless and effective, given the exigences of the French stage in 1841. Berlioz occasionally picks up Weber's motivic ideas and incorporates them in purely chordal recitative; at times his own manner creeps in uninvited, with harmony such as the following:

Ex. 31

But generally the style is as faceless as recitative usually is. There are some twelve stretches of recitative added to the opera. A more disquieting interpolation in the 1841 revival was Weber's popular piano piece *Aufforderung zum Tanz*, orchestrated by Berlioz for use as the obligatory *divertissement* in the last act. He transposed the piece up from D flat to D and used his normal French orchestra, whose four bassoons, two cornets and two trumpets differ from Weber's usual forces. In addition he uses two harps to brilliant effect. But anyone who hopes to find here the key to Berlioz's command of orchestration will be disappointed. There are few imaginative effects or individual touches, efficient and effective though the scoring is. Berlioz was taking the utmost pains not to impose his own personality on Weber's music.

His next arrangement was of his own music and so permitted him the greatest display of orchestral skill. Convinced (correctly) that Paris would never see a revival of *Benvenuto Cellini*, he gathered some of its more striking ideas into a new concert overture, *Le carnaval romain*, first played in 1844. The form is much the same as that of the opera's real overture: a burst of fast music, a slow passage in 3/4, then the main allegro of brilliant energy. Two scenes from the opera are used, the carnival chorus from Act I Scene 2 (Act II in the revised version) and the love duet between Cellini and Teresa in the first scene of Act I, arranged as the contrasting slow passage of the overture. The re-writing is complete; it is much more than an orchestral arrangement of vocal music, in fact one would scarcely suspect that the fast section at least was vocal in origin at all, so swiftly and neatly do the violins and wind pass the themes back and forth. In the slow section the first statement is given first to the cor anglais in C major. A diminished seventh twists the tonality into E major where the theme is exactly repeated, now in the violas, with a graceful countermelody in the wind and a more lively rhythm in the accompaniment. There is yet another statement, now in A involving the full orchestra at different rhythmic and dynamic levels, carefully superimposed. Not only is the melody answered in canon, at one beat's distance, by the upper wind and strings; its slow and serene pace is thrown into sharp relief by the chattering, dancing rhythms underneath.

This superbly controlled balance of forces is apt to be forgotten when the Allegro begins, sweeping everything aside in its headlong exhilaration. The phrase-lengths vary, the tonality keeps shifting, but the momentum is irresistible. A curious fugue is buried in the midst of all this activity, recalling the melody of the slow section in the key of F on four bassoons. But this brief attempt at integration is swiftly swept aside. Just as the revelries seem finally to be closing, a series of overwhelming chords on the brass add a final flourish. Strings and percussion leave the last pause to the wind, a simple but stunning effect, used again in the *Marche de Rákóczy*. Berlioz's reputation as a brilliant master of orchestral effect rests largely on the eternal impact the *Carnaval romain* overture makes in the concert hall, and that reputation is solidly based. It is only a pity that the original, equally brilliant version of this music in its operatic context is not more often seen and heard.

In 1845 Berlioz took to arranging popular marches for orchestra, a lowering of his artistic sights explained only by his need for concert material and hard to accommodate within our preferred picture of an idealist in musical taste. He who had only recently mocked Musard's transcriptions of Mozart was himself providing the kind of music mid-century audiences were flocking to hear. It began with Léopold de Meyer's piano piece *Marche marocaine*, a jaunty evocation of Morocco which Berlioz heard the composer play in February 1845. He immediately scored it for large orchestra including two piccolos, two pairs of timpani and much 'Turkish' percussion, including the Pavillon chinois, or Turkish crescent. The last five pages of score are a rousing coda by Berlioz himself. Here, much more than in Weber's *Invitation à la valse*, can Berlioz's extrovert orchestral style be observed. A few months later he did the same to de Meyer's *Marche triomphale d'Isly*, although no performances are known and the surviving score (in the library of the Paris Opéra) cannot be proved to be Berlioz's work. This was followed in February 1846 by the same treatment for the famous Hungarian melody *Rákóczy-Indulo*, hurriedly written to win his concert audiences in Budapest. Its lively energy and bright orchestration succeeded beyond his wildest dreams and it has won immortality in the unlikely context of *La damnation de Faust*, into the opening scene of which he incorporated it by placing Faust arbitrarily in the plains of Hungary. The arrangement is more than a simple exercise in orchestration, for the theme is developed and expanded, and in its second version (as found in *La damnation*) there is an additional coda of great brilliance. Two years later, in London, he planned to write arrangements of Rouget de Lisle's *Mourons pour la patrie*, Méhul's popular *Chant du départ*, and another of *God Save the Queen*, but these were probably never made.

Only a composer of Berlioz's range could have dared to put a piece of so obviously popular a purpose as the Rákóczy March into a large-scale choral setting of Goethe's *Faust*. Indeed its popular origins contrast sharply with Berlioz's sudden exertion towards reflective music written in the difficult circumstances of a busy central European tour. His aspirations had not declined after all, nor had his inspiration. *La damnation de Faust*, completed in October 1846, takes the *Huit scènes de Faust* of 1828–9 as the set pieces round which the fabric of a larger treatment is woven; it draws on the style and outlook of *Roméo et Juliette* moving yet further away from symphony and nearer to opera, and it provides a bridge to the final period with glimpses of the classical serenity so fully expressed in *Les Troyens*. He planned it as a concert opera in four parts, something larger than a dramatic cantata and more operatic than a dramatic symphony, but never intended for the stage. It was finally entitled 'Dramatic Legend' and filled with explicit directions of setting and action which serve only to guide the imagination; changes of scene are too abrupt and inconsequential for a staged spectacle, often though this has been attempted, sometimes with considerable success; the technique is closer perhaps to that of the cinema, yet still relying, as Berlioz always does, on the inner vision of the imagination's eye.

His approach to Goethe's masterpiece was still selective, as it had been in 1828. Some notable scenes and characters are omitted (and the Hungarian setting inserted). Furthermore Berlioz consigns Faust firmly to Hell, mindless of his later redemption in Goethe's Part Two, providing a strong and colourful contrast between Pandaemonium and Heaven and a simpler resolution of Faust's tainted strivings. Obviously the character has less breadth than in the poetic drama, but at times – for example in the opening pages of Parts I and II and Part IV's *Invocation à la nature* – Berlioz's Faust approaches closer to Goethe's fathomless embodiment of human aspiration than any other Faust work, even against such distinguished competition as Liszt and Busoni. Spohr, Wagner, Schumann, Gounod and Boito, in their various Faust works all fall short of Berlioz's profoundly characterized blend of poetry and drama, vitality and reflection.

Part I finds Faust in the plains of Hungary rejoicing in the spring, with fugal textures that spread into a calm vista of nature at peace (see Ex. 59, p. 192). Into this untroubled landscape steal the sounds of peasants merrymaking and of military bugle calls, prefiguring (as in the Prologue of *Roméo et Juliette*) the two scenes which follow. The carefree *Ronde de paysans* (from 1828) excites Faust's jealousy; the brazen confidence of the *March hongroise* leaves his heart unmoved. Part II also begins with a dense fugato, now minor and chromatic to express Faust's deepening malaise, with the fugue broken only by an outburst of feeling:

Ex. 32

Recitative carries forward the tension as he takes the cup to his lips, interrupted by the sound of bells (cellos and basses pizzicato) and the singing of the *Chant de la fête de Pâques* in a nearby church. Many details were tidied up in this reworking of the first of the 1828 scenes, and Faust's stunned response, 'O souvenirs . . .', adds a dramatic dimension. More recitative (see below, Ex. 60) then seals his rediscovery of faith, and all would end there were it not for Mephistopheles' sudden appearance in a flash of piccolo and trombones. Faust, bewildered, accepts his offer of pleasure and happiness with no more reflection than a long pause and they proceed instantly, with some violent changes of key, to Auerbach's cellar in Leipzig. The *Chœur de buveurs*, with its coarse orchestration and spirited choral writing, was newly composed, but the two songs sung by Brander and Mephistopheles in turn were taken unchanged from the 1828 collection. In between there is much dramatic recitative and the famous Amen Chorus, in which Berlioz treats the theme of Brander's song to an ironic fugue, composed (as he imagined) like a Handel chorus and scored like a drinking song. The humour is heavy and the technique less clumsy than Berlioz probably intended, so performance is always problematical. At least he shows within the same work how fugue can be used either for expressive or for academic purposes and leaves us in no doubt as to which he prefers.

Another swift transformation takes Faust and Mephistopheles to the banks of the Elbe where placid textures and a long focus on D major brings calm (illusory, of course) to Faust's soul. Mephistopheles' beautifully moulded air 'Voici des roses' provides a fine example of Berlioz's gift for a long, freely expanding melody which never repeats itself. The accompaniment of cornets, trombones and bassoons is again fully in the spirit of irony. Without a break the *Chœur de gnomes et de sylphes*, a much revised version of the 1828 *Concert de sylphes*, follows, with Mephistopheles and Faust participating. Faust sleeps, and for the first time sees Marguerite in his dream, against choral harmony of delicious density:

Ex. 33

The end of the scene is the most protracted of Berlioz's fading endings, the final cadence being, as it were, decorated by a waltz on a transformed version of the sylphs' theme, even though the bass line has reached the tonic D where it remains throughout. The feathery scoring, with harps prominent, leaves the melody almost entirely to the first violins. Extracted from its context, this *Ballet de sylphes* loses all its magic.

Faust wakes with a start, demanding to know when he can find her. Mephistopheles obliges and offers to take him at once to her chamber. At that moment, with sublime irrelevance, there passes a contingent of soldiers followed by a crowd of students, both intent on the pursuit of the girls of the town. Faust and Mephistopheles sing along with the students, 'Gaudeamus igitur', although Berlioz's real reason for introducing the scene is to offer a musical *tour de force* as the close of Part II. The soldiers sing in B flat, in 6/8, and in French, the tune heard at the end of Marguerite's *Romance* in the 1828 *Huit scènes*; the students sing in D minor, in 2/4 and in Latin, and both choruses unite in stirring counterpoint, the whole framed at the beginning and end by a long winding melody on four bassoons in unison.

At the opening of Part III the retreat is still heard in the distance, off-stage brass echoing the orchestra's call. The dramatic thrust is now more continuous with a solo each for Faust and Marguerite, a love duet and a final trio with Mephistopheles and the chorus. In the centre of the scene Mephistopheles' diversionary entertainment consists of an *Evocation*, the *Menuet des follets* and his *Sérénade*. Part III is certainly closer than the rest to operatic structure, with two numbers, Marguerite's *Ballade* and Mephistopheles' *Sérénade*, retrieved from the 1828 scenes. Faust's *Air* is yet another long self-generating melody, the tender 3/4 Andante rising to impassioned expressions of gratitude and joy as he finds himself actually in her chamber. To a long ambling line on the violins he explores the room, as the flute helpfully explains, repeating the figure to which Faust has just sung 'Que j'aime à contempler ton chevet virginal'. Mephistopheles reappears (in a flash less violent than the first) and urges Faust to hide as Marguerite approaches. She too is troubled by a dream (in Goethe's *Faust* the lovers first see each other in a street, not in dreams), and sings by way of distraction her *Chanson gothique* about the King of Thule, now transposed down from G to F and with the addition of some delicate sighs in the second and third verses. The viola solo and low, dense chords perfectly capture her melancholy mood. Faust, we are to assume, is on the point of stepping out of his hiding place, but first we are taken (in imagination) outside into the street where Mephistopheles summons his spirit helpers to cast a spell over the scene within. This *divertissement* is pure wizardry, with Mephistopheles' stern, distorted summons represented by bizarre chromatics:

Ex. 34

The 'follets' respond in glittering woodwind runs, three demonic piccolos chasing each other. Ordered to dance, they perform the *Menuet des follets*, a feast of orchestral skill, couched in the courtly rhythms of the old minuet. Eventually the piccolos take off at full speed with a dazzling display which, after a few reminders of the minuet, closes the dance. Their theme is a speeded-up version of Mephistopheles' sardonic *Sérénade*, in 1828 a simple guitar song, but now a greatly enriched version with rolling string pizzicatos and boisterous interjections from the chorus. The follets are dismissed, their work done, and the scene dissolves.

Back within the chamber the *Chanson gothique* is still lingering in the air as Faust and Marguerite come face to face. They plunge straight into a love duet supported by muted strings and light woodwind. Passion glows in every bar, proving that Berlioz could convey amorous intensity as well with words as without them. The form of the duet suggests that the main melody would have returned a second time, were it not for Marguerite's languorous collapse ('Je meurs . . .') and the sudden arrival of Mephistopheles urging a hasty departure. The music rides on a theme in the violas and cellos never shared by the voices and never exactly repeated:

Ex. 35

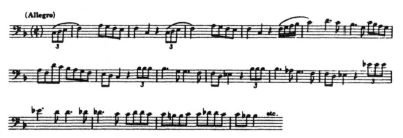

Faust bids farewell, the chorus threateningly invade, and the brilliant *Trio* closes Part III, tension and energy mounting inexorably to the very end.

In Part IV one grand scene succeeds the next. First Marguerite, alone, sings her desolate *Romance*, almost unchanged from 1828. Then Faust, also alone, invokes the majesty of nature in a piece unique in Berlioz's music for its harmonic breadth and for a visionary quality remote from any other music with which comparison might be made. The sentiment of the words – the deference of the soul to nature – is common enough in romantic poetry, nobly expressed in Berlioz's poem though it is, but the quality of restless striving in the music, embodied in strange unexpected progressions, the inexorable rumblings in the bass, and the majestic shape of the vocal line, owes nothing to any other music and is uniquely Berliozian. In these pages Faust's eternal quest and the hunger of his soul are definitively portrayed.

A macabre dialogue with Mephistopheles ensues, against interjections from huntsmen's horns. Faust is persuaded to sign the contract to serve Mephistopheles' will and thereby save Marguerite. His doom is now sealed and two black horses are summoned on which to ride to hell. The ride itself is a spectacular piece of tone-painting, with galloping hooves in the violins, the inexorable tread of cellos and basses and a plaintive wandering melody on the oboe. Scenes of horror confront them: peasants kneeling at a wayside cross who flee in terror, a hideous monster in pursuit (low trombones, tuba and ophicleide), giant nocturnal birds (flapping woodwind). Mephistopheles offers to turn back and the ride halts, but Faust, more determined than ever to save Marguerite, rides on with redoubled energy, past grinning skeletons, over quaking ground, through raining blood, to the abyss itself into which with a bloodcurdling cry he falls. Hell is the violent opposition of F major and B major chords with the grotesque cries of the damned singing an 'infernal language' invented by Berlioz once before in an earlier version of *Lélio*. The music is violent and shapeless, changing speed and tonality at will. The orchestration is impressively resourceful, but hell, like heaven, was too beset with clichés in romantic imagery to yield its secret easily to this abundant ingenuity, and heaven, to which Marguerite now ascends, was equally taxing on the composer's pen. Berlioz predictably relies on harp, high violins and women's voices, less of a cliché in 1846 than it later became, and leaves us in a state of serenity in D flat major. Still, the finality of Faust's damnation and Marguerite's salvation was more satisfactory than in Goethe's questioning close, especially in a concert work to which no sequel was intended.

As in *Roméo et Juliette*, the dramatic focus of *La damnation de Faust* shifts from tableau to tableau, extending the original eight scenes to some twenty-five. But continuity is equally Berlioz's concern, much more so than in the symphony, and the recitatives and free linking passages, deriving from the technique evolved in *Benvenuto Cellini*, merit particular study for their dramatic immediacy and for their concern with control of pace and tonality. The contrast with the *Freischütz* recitatives is extreme. Here every bar has character, often with no structural component, yet often too with reference to passages still to be heard. This technique is the opposite of the 'reminiscence motive' since it always prefigures a motive in advance. The prologue to *Roméo et Juliette* had already explored these 'anticipation motives'; interesting examples in *La damnation de Faust* are the transformations of the *Chœur de paysans* and the *Marche hongroise* within the opening scene (already mentioned), snatches of the *Chanson gothique* and the *Sérénade* after Mephistopheles' entrance in Part III, and Marguerite's dreamy anticipation of her own *Romance* when she first mentions her 'futur amant . . . Qu'il était beau'. The rich scoring in this last case can only be appreciated when we know the later passage to which it refers. Mephistopheles' *Sérénade* is also given advance airing at the end of the *Menuet*. There are no leitmotives associated with individual characters, simply a regular escort of trombones for Mephistopheles, who, unlike in some *Faust* works, does not have all the best tunes, nor does he steal centre stage. It is curious to note that when in 1847 Berlioz fruitlessly discussed a staged adaptation of the work with Scribe, its title was to have been changed to *Méphistophélès* and the balance of character shifted. In the work as we have it Faust remains our prime concern: the opening two scenes of Parts I and II and the *Invocation à la nature*, carefully matched in mood and vocal style, ensure that. Marguerite is naïve in Part III, her character deepening rapidly to the profound loneliness of her *Romance*. In the *Huit scènes* she simply had two personalities; here the growth from one to the other is made plain.

Before we come to the *Te deum*, a single piece of massive choral writing, *La menace des Francs*, is found. Composed at an unknown date before 1848 for an unknown purpose to words by an unknown author, it is a ponderous exercise for chorus, male-voice semi-chorus and large orchestra, proclaiming defiance against tyranny. The main stretch of music is repeated without variation of the words or orchestration and there is much doubling at the octave of the male and female voices, with crude effect. One only hopes that Berlioz found some reward (paid by the author of the text?) for setting it.

The *Te deum*, completed in 1849, is as enigmatic in origin but greatly superior in quality. It is a noble companion-piece to the *Requiem* of 1837. It derives in part from the grand Napoleonic plans of 1832–5 and in part from discussions with Stasov in Russia in 1847 about using the organ in antiphony with an orchestra. It was not commissioned and was not performed until 1855, but it clearly absorbed Berlioz's closest attention and aroused his pride: 'colossal, Babylonian, Ninivite' he called it, borrowing imagery from Heine. It is architectural in spirit, relying on space and distance as an integral element, and the concluding *Marche* provides an occasion for ceremonial, rather like the lengthy ballets at the end of Lully's or Lesueur's operas. Chorus and orchestra are both large, with quadruple wind and correspondingly augmented strings. The organ is required to be placed at a great distance, as it is in the church of St-Eustache where Berlioz gave the only complete performance in his lifetime. There are two three-part choruses and an additional choir of 600 children's voices inserted as an afterthought in 1851 when Berlioz heard the Charity Children in St Paul's Cathedral; they are directed to be separate from the main chorus.

The style of the music is diverse, varying sharply from each of the seven movements to the next. Some parts refer back to the old Revolutionary style of broad, massed effects (and part of the *Christe, rex gloriae* is borrowed from the 1824 *Mass*), some have a tenderness close to that of *L'enfance du Christ*. In structure, too, he adopts a different approach in each movement. As in the *Requiem*, there is much contrapuntal writing, but since this is true equally of *La damnation de Faust* and *L'enfance du Christ* it is not especially remarkable. The most traditional type of choral counterpoint is found in the opening movement after a series of grandiose chords flung from one end of the building to the other, and though the first choral entries are discouragingly obvious, a number of dramatic events occur in succession. The grand descending scale first announced by the organ begins to assume greater importance as a countersubject; homophonic writing intrudes suddenly for 'omnis terra veneratur'; a climax is built out of overlapping cries of

Ex. 36

(Allegro moderato)

Te de-um lau-da-mus

and the hushed ending modulates suddenly and surprisingly towards B major.

This is the key of the second movement, *Tibi omnes*, one of the finest pieces in the work, for it grows to colossal strength from the tamest opening, a subdued four-part passage on the organ of devotional character. The structure is the same as that of the *Hymne à la France*, successive verses being given to different voices with different accompaniment, the third and final verse being extended with a powerful coda; the devotional music, now made expressive by being scored for strings, provides the last word. Within each verse there is simple statement, long crescendo and climax, the crescendos being built on the triple 'Sanctus' and the climax being the firmest of tonic cadences. No other music has so directly represented the power of prayer to lead to the heavenly vision of angels in glory.

In the autograph manuscript there follows a brief *Prélude* which reverses the modulation of the opening movement, back from B to F. It makes further chromatic discussion of the fugal material and prepares in its turn for the definitive No. 3, the *Dignare*. Berlioz omitted it from the published score since it was for ceremonial purposes only and full of 'doubtful modulations' – a useful guide to Berlioz's harmonic values.

The *Dignare* is unique in Berlioz's music using a structural principle of great simplicity and originality. After a brief introduction it is based on a series of bass pedals, rising in thirds from D to E flat, up a semitone to E natural, then down in thirds again to D:

Ex. 37

no. of bars: (14) (10) (7) (8) (11) (4) (9) (8) (12) (5)

The duration of each pedal is different and the textures built on them are constantly in flux. Two strong effects which result are the brief central climax in the unusual key of E and the eventual return to D with the overpowering sense of cyclic return largely because the tonic key has played so little part in the main body of the movement. The weaving of choral lines is itself a source of abundant interest and the supplicatory tone of 'Miserere nostri' is delicately established.

Christe, rex gloriae, no. 4, recalls the *Rex tremendae* of the *Requiem*, as the opening words would obviously suggest. The downward scale is again prominent. A softer middle section with the tenors leading 'Ad liberandum' yields a climax of energy sustained right to the end. The scoring is mostly full and the choral writing magnificent. No. 5, *Te ergo quaesumus*, is in gentle contrast. Its melody is examined later, in Chapter 9 (see pp. 189–90). One curious feature is the chorus's monotone 'Fiat super nos' against soft shifting brass chords; another is the melismatic passage in the major leading to the last choral statement, with the melody now in the bass.

For the chorus's last participation, the *Judex crederis*, Berlioz builds one of his mightiest movements. 'The *Judex* surpasses all the enormities of which I have been guilty up to now', he wrote in 1855. One enormity is the striking open fifth on which the full organ ('Jeu de trompettes') states the pervasive rhythm of the movement; another is the bizarre modulating fugue with which the basses enter, an eight-bar subject in lumbering 9/8 metre slipping almost unperceived from B flat to B natural for the soprano entry; next the tenors come in on C. The first climax falls on a chord of D, yet the B flat major/minor tonality is never threatened. The contrasting section, the 'Prière', in D flat, is another variant of the descending scale. The descending figure turns into a monotonously repeated accompaniment and gradually the opening 9/8 rhythm returns in menacingly repeated fragments. The tonal control is ingenious: the D flat passage allows Berlioz to bring the full restatement of the fugue back on the note A flat. Chromatically rising entries, as before, thus conclude in B flat, which, though constantly diverted in breathtaking shifts through remote keys, ultimately draws the overlapping series of climaxes, each mightier than the last, to a resplendent close.

Many performances end with this overwhelming statement of B flat major, with good reason, for it is a hard movement to follow. Berlioz concludes the whole work with an orchestral march for the presentation of the colours, recalling the hollow military style of the *Apothéose* of the *Grande symphonie funèbre et triomphale*. Its origin may well be an earlier march for military band on to which Berlioz has grafted string parts and some reference to the fugal entries of the first movement. A passage which again reintroduced the broad descending scale and gave brilliant prominence to the newly invented soprano saxhorn was cut before the first performance.

Berlioz passed sober judgment on his *Te deum* when he prepared a publicity note for the first performance: 'A *Te deum* is generally thought to be a ceremonial hymn of thanksgiving. Ceremony is indeed its principal character, but several verses of the text are actually prayers whose humility and melancholy offer contrast to the majesty of the hymns. There is even a *Miserere* in the *Te deum*. The composer has therefore attempted to reproduce these quite different moods.'[2] Contrast and veracity of expression again dominate his approach to the words, not tonal balance nor even thematic reference, despite the unusual frequency of a single theme, the descending scale. It is significant that he was quite content to make cuts which severely weaken the structural purpose of this theme. His passion for contrast accords with his recurrently stated beliefs about art, and the dramatic results are magnificent; it is also responsible for a variety of styles which we now recognize as a habitual feature of his larger works, most of which draw music of many origins and periods together into a composite, finely woven whole.

8

The music 1850–1869

The early 1850s were exceptionally active years in Berlioz's public life. He was incessantly conducting, travelling and writing prose without apparently rediscovering the creative pressure that put *La damnation de Faust* together in similar conditions. His musical output was consequently slight, and it is tempting (though largely unfounded) to see the gap as a pause in which to prepare for the three great works of his last years: *L'enfance du Christ, Les Troyens* and *Béatrice et Bénédict*. The operas were of course the outcome of long years of contemplation, but *L'enfance du Christ* came into being in a quite unplanned way. Most of it was composed in 1853 and 1854, while the three movements which make up the central part of the trilogy, *La fuite en Égypte*, had been written three years earlier. In the interim he seems to have composed nothing. He was more concerned with retrieving some of his forgotten songs and choruses and publishing them in new collections. *Tristia* and *Vox populi* appeared in 1849, *Feuillets d'album* and *Fleurs des landes* in 1850; very little in any of these collections was new.

His earlier preoccupation with composing operas had faded after the failure of *La nonne sanglante*, the only exception being a libretto for *Béatrice et Bénédict* planned and abandoned in 1852, like the symphony in A minor which Berlioz tells us in the *Memoirs* he had to *refrain* from writing. His fear of the commitment of composition was increasing in these years. He would not have embarked on the full *L'enfance du Christ* as a deliberately planned work had an accident not thrown a pebble in the pool spreading ripples outwards from the centre. *L'adieu des bergers* (the 'Shepherds' Farewell') was originally an organ piece written in a friend's album at a party in 1850. 'I thought it had a certain pastoral, naive mysticism about it, so I decided to put appropriate words to it. The organ piece disappeared and became the chorus of shepherds in Bethlehem bidding farewell to the baby Jesus as the Holy Family depart for Egypt.'[1] A few days later he added the movement for tenor which follows, *Le repos de la sainte famille*, taking the Holy Family on their journey to Egypt, and an overture in modal F sharp minor, all three pieces being for very small orchestra: just two flutes, two oboes, two clarinets and strings. Since *La damnation de Faust*, for which he had by necessity to contribute much of the sung text himself, writing his own words was taken for granted. He proved to be an adept versifier.

He thus had an unusual choral piece which he entitled *La fuite en Égypte* ('The Flight into Egypt'), 'Fragments of a Mystery in ancient style', and published in 1852. Compared with *La damnation de Faust* or the *Te deum* it is indeed restrained, containing no heavy orchestration and no violent rhythms. But to anyone familiar with Berlioz's songs and with those parts of his larger works which deliberately offer subdued contrast there is nothing in *La fuite en Égypte* to generate surprise. Fugal writing had been an essential element of his style from the beginning; modal scales were beginning to attract him more, not out of any sympathy with folk music but for the simple archaism they evoked. A scene of touching simplicity such as this offered him scope for expressive music, and that, in his view, was sufficient justification.

All three movements are in triple metre, befitting the tenderness of the subject. The fugue of the overture has two expositions, one for strings, one for wind, and a series of apt ideas introduced later on with some whole passages repeated. The leading note of the scale is kept flattened as often as possible. The three verses of *L'adieu des bergers* follow on naturally, for the overture has set the scene of crib and stable familiar from devotional painting. The third verse is slightly modified by being marked *ppp* with extra interjections from the rustic-sounding wind. Berlioz's characteristic capacity to produce harmonic surprise and deceptive enharmonic change over a bass line that is always melodic is perfectly illustrated (Ex. 38).

Le repos de la sainte famille (Légende et pantomime) takes the melody of bars 4 to 5 of Ex. 38 as its starting point for a delicate dialogue between wind and strings. This is unquestionably one of Berlioz's most beautiful movements, major and minor modes being treated as equals and the flow of line being as graceful for flute as for tenor as for strings. Even the donkey is affecting, and at the end two Alleluias from an unseen chorus of angels close the scene. A similar angel chorus, invisible, was heard in Gossec's oratorio *La nativité* of 1774, with which Berlioz may well have been acquainted.

Ex. 38

For the next three years he wrote no music at all, an extraordinary period of silence. The full *La fuite en Égypte* was not performed until December 1853, in Leipzig, and it was there that his friends urged him to extend it with *La sainte famille en Egypte*, for which they were later rewarded with its dedication. The idea may even have come from Brahms, whom Berlioz met there. He composed this new part at once, the title actually changed to *L'arrivée à Saïs*, and it turned out to be twice as long as *La fuite* and much more complex in structure, introducing Mary and Joseph as soloists as well as the Ishmaelite father. Furthermore, although for its opening movement he retained the themes of the earlier overture transformed into *alla breve* time and the very restrained orchestration, thereafter he adds bassoons and timpani and treats the subject in more dramatic, less contemplative fashion, much closer in method to *La damnation de Faust*. It opens with 'Scene I', even though no further divisions of scenes are marked. It is pictorial drama, as Joseph and Mary seek shelter in the inhospitable city. Tremolo cellos and basses in thick harmony, high wailing violas and knocking timpani support their pleading, twice rudely spurned by voices within. A third time, after their prolonged pleading in duet, an Ishmaelite opens his humble door and welcomes them in. The violas continue to symbolize the Holy Family's distress, while the Ishmaelite father, the nearest Berlioz ever came to portraying a good Victorian churchman, greets his guests with recitative and counterpoint. He is pious and even at times unctuous. For all the clean textures and cross-rhythms of the choral writing, the busy orchestral fugato which portrays the young Ishmaelites and their servants scurrying about the house yields the most fascinating music. For *divertissement* Berlioz inserts a trio for two flutes and harp, instruments used in Gounod's *Sapho*, of 1851, to evoke classical antiquity and purity as they were to do many times again in later French music. There are touches of modality, exoticism and virtuosity, looking forward to the ballets in Act IV of *Les Troyens*, and the cadence which clumsily takes the tonality into F for a further chorus of good will and benediction leads Berlioz near to sentimentality.

Fortunately he did not close his work there. A series of long isolated notes help the listener to draw back from the domestic scene and contemplate its larger meaning, and for this, although Berlioz still relied on the traditionally devotional tone of choral counterpoint, he is not found wanting. The Narrator's recitative leads sublimely into his invocation in E major, 'O mon âme', which the chorus take up, and the calmly floating unaccompanied lines suggest, paradoxically, the deepest sincerity in Christian faith – which we know Berlioz did not experience. But as a composer he is equal to the task; this concluding section is one of Berlioz's most sublime and unexpected inspirations and the eight off-stage voices singing the last drooping Amens remind us of the closing Alleluias of *La fuite en Egypte*.

Aware perhaps of the imbalance in scale and dramatic style between the two parts of his work, Berlioz immediately planned another, to be placed first, in order to recount the events that drove the Holy Family from Bethlehem. This opening part, *Le songe d'Hérode*, is even more dramatic than *L'arrivée à Saïs*, and more heavily orchestrated. There are stage directions and obviously theatrical incidents, but it is still directed to the imagination, not to the eye. The strength of this part is the remarkable creation of Herod as a tyrant who suffers the torment of power, and his solo scene and air 'O misère des rois!' is Shakespearian in its depth of character. Berlioz may have had in mind the famous lines of Henry VI (Part III Act II Scene 5):

> O God! methinks it were a happy life,
> To be no better than a homely swain;
> Ah! what a life were this; how sweet! how lovely!
> Gives not the hawthorn bush a sweeter shade
> To shepherds looking on their silly sheep,
> Than doth a rich embroider'd canopy
> To Kings that fear their subjects treachery?

These were sentiments already expressed by Cellini under the stress of crisis.

The *Marche nocturne*, after the opening narration, evokes the streets of Jerusalem at night (another fugue) patrolled by Roman soldiers. It seems to be modelled on a similar *Marche nocturne* in Berton's *Virginie* of 1823, with perhaps a memory of the *Marche des pèlerins* in *Harold en Italie* when the steps fade gradually away into the distance, a favourite device he had not used for many years (if we exclude the very different *Ballet des sylphes*). Herod, like Mephistopheles, is supported by trombones, and the intense agony of his soul, already vividly painted in his *Air*, becomes yet more oppressive when he describes his dream to the soothsayers, lower divided strings supporting snatches from the *Air* on a solo clarinet:

Ex. 39

The soothsayers' cabalistic dance is a pungent exercise in 7/4 time, written throughout as 3/4 and 4/4 in alternation and craftily orchestrated. It is much more than a mere *divertissement* and it never reaches a full cadence; the soothsayers break in to read their divination to the king in music which inverts Ex. 39, the three unison trombones taking the clarinet line, inverted, beneath sustained wind chords. They unleash the king's wrath in a movement of grim violence. At the climax trumpets and cornets (a latter addition) join in with manic, distorted fanfares and still no cadence is reached. The music simply collapses from a climactic diminished seventh, a typically Berliozian discharge of energy, and a long measured silence joins directly into the next scene, in the stable, where Mary and Joseph are tending their child. The contrast is complete. The style, metre and orchestration revert to (or rather, in the sequence of the work, anticipate) *Le repos de la sainte famille* with episodes describing the lambs at play. With hindsight from Act IV of *Les Troyens* we may read this movement as the purest of love duets for Mary and Joseph. Invisible angels with harmonium accompaniment warn them of danger and urge them to depart, concluding with Hosannas fading into nothing. For this fade Berlioz contrived a 'sourdine vocale' by which a door is gradually closed, shutting off the choir from the audience, a beautiful effect if well managed, and spoiled only by the three plain chords with which the orchestra has to close.

Tracing *L'enfance du Christ* thus in order of composition gives insights denied to the listener who hears it in the correct published sequence. In the end it became a balanced trilogy, the two outer panels framing a more static and reflective central part like an interlude in the drama, and the hazards of an unplanned structure were overcome. Berlioz ran the risk of treading on two varieties of dangerous ground and did not entirely escape either. One was the picturesque orientalism made popular by Félicien David's *Le désert* in 1844 followed by other David works and by Reyer's *Le sélam* which Berlioz had warmly praised in 1850. The other was sentimentality, the besetting sin of mid-nineteenth-century sacred music which Berlioz had hitherto avoided. Both failings may be observed in the third part, *L'arrivée à Saïs*, but the end of the work, Herod's music and *Le repos de la sainte famille* may be reckoned among the finest things he had done, giving more than a hint of the yet greater achievement of *Les Troyens*. Berlioz liked to compare *L'enfance du Christ* to the illuminations in medieval missals, an apt parallel which conveys the mixture of devotion and craftsmanship of which he was rightly proud.

In the summer of 1854, before *L'enfance du Christ* was finished, Berlioz hurriedly composed a cantata for double chorus and large orchestra, *L'impériale*, in expectation of a performance for the Emperor's birthday on 15th August. In the event it had to wait a year for an occasion to put it on, during the closing ceremonies of the 1855 Exposition Universelle. The text, by one Captain Lafont, is a grossly fawning encomium of the Emperor, as obsequious as anything ever offered to Louis XIV, in praise of a man whose personal qualities Berlioz knew full well to be imperfect, especially as regards his nation's culture. In a passage of recitative, for example, the revival of the Bonaparte dynasty is compared to the coming of the Messiah.

For the music it is hard to be enthusiastic. The style is the solid wind-based sonority of the French Revolution, chordal and sonorous, with some varying contrast in the verses. The opening broad theme supplies the first two verses, in the second of which a striking counterpoint is heard on eight trombones, three ophicleides and two tubas, leading to a short but resplendent passage borrowed from *Sardanapale*, of 1830. There follows the abject recitative, then five alternations of a new broad hymn with varying verses, the second of which was later cut. The third, 'O race révérée', has a fine effect of imitation; for the fifth a tremendous cry of 'Vive l'Empereur!' is accompanied by the powerful dotted rhythms that crowned the *Tibi omnes* in the *Te deum*, and for the final return of the opening strain the full army of brass is unleashed in furious triplets that make the cantata an exciting experience however hollow the musical invention.

1854 was thus a very productive year after a long silence, and if it was followed by another gap in output of nearly two years it was no longer because he had lost the will to compose. On the contrary, he seems to have made up his mind to embark on the greatest challenge of his life and needed only some outward prompting to begin, drawing confidence from the immediate wide success of *L'enfance du Christ*. Astute readers of the *Journal des débats* might have noticed more frequent references to Virgil, and his closer friends had already received hints of this new – or more accurately, old – preoccupation when he visited Weimar in January 1855. Carolyne Sayn-Wittgenstein there diagnosed his true intentions and a second visit a year later confirmed them: to compose *Les Troyens*, a grand opera in five acts, the outcome of a lifetime's love both of Virgil and of opera. The libretto was begun in April 1856 and finished two months later. The music then followed in the order Acts I, IV, II, III and V, the last page of score being dated 12th April 1858, almost exactly two years' work. We have more information about the composition of *Les Troyens* than about any other of his works, since he wrote freely and fully to the Princess Sayn-Wittgenstein about progress on the work, and consulted both her and (later) Pauline Viardot about details of structure. Furthermore, a substantial body of sketches for the opera has survived, especially rich in tracing the growth of the Act IV love duet, the first music of the opera to be composed.

A brief synopsis must serve to outline the action of the opera. After ten years of war the Trojans are rejoicing that the Greeks have departed, apparently defeated, leaving an enormous wooden horse outside the city. Cassandra, daughter of Troy's King Priam, is alone in foretelling disaster, while everyone else, including the young prince Chorebus who is in love with her, sees the horse as a favourable portent from the Gods. Despite her pleas and despite ominous noises from within it, the horse is dragged into the city.

In Act II disaster has struck. Aeneas, the Trojan hero, is visited by the ghost of the slain Hector and urged to flee while there is still time. He must carry the Trojan destiny to Italy. The city is in flames, and the Trojan women huddle in terror in the Temple of Vesta. When the Greeks arrive Cassandra leads them in a mass suicide rather than face captivity and dishonour. They die with the word 'Italy!' on their lips.

Many years have passed when Act III opens at the court of Queen Dido of Carthage. Her sister Anna suggests a new marriage for her to assure the city's future, but Dido swears loyalty to her husband Sichaeus's memory. The arrival of a strange fleet is reported and the remnants of the Trojan army, driven ashore by a storm, are welcomed. Next, news of Numidian hordes invading Carthage prompts Aeneas to throw off his disguise and to offer his army in the Queen's defence.

The Numidians are defeated, and in the opening tableau of Act IV, Aeneas and Dido are hunting in the forest. The Gods conspire to bring them fatally together by sending a storm. They take refuge in a cave. In the second scene, festivities and entertainment deepen the bond that now holds Dido and Aeneas. Mercury warns Aeneas that his destiny commands him to voyage on to Italy.

In Act V Aeneas has decided to leave. His own men are disgruntled at the news; Dido is in despair. She begs him to stay, but destiny drives him on. Left alone she bids farewell to her own city. A funeral pyre is built, and on it, in austere ceremonial, she kills herself, as her people cast a curse on the race of Aeneas, soon to become the Romans and the founders of a mighty empire.

This libretto, based on Book II (for Acts I and II) and Books I and IV (for Acts III to V) of the *Aeneid*, is striking for its epic span, conveying both a huge era of time and the whole of the Mediterranean, from Troy to Carthage to Rome. Just as Virgil's declared purpose was to honour the Emperor Augustus by tracing his origins to the royal line of Troy, Berlioz's first plan was to pay tribute to Virgil in a closing scene which predicted the coming of Hannibal, Scipio, Caesar and finally Virgil himself. The key to his ideas lies in this closing scene of the opera, where in the original version time symbolically passes and Clio, the muse of history, parades the march of centuries and the great leaders and artists of the future. Berlioz rejected it, on Pauline Viardot's advice, rightly – we may suppose – since at the end of a long opera of action and drama an audience cannot be asked to contemplate a vision essentially seen by the mind rather than the eye. Characteristically Berlioz had allowed the reality of stage action to be blurred by the leaping ideas of his imagination. The ending which replaced it is, alas, one of the least satisfactory parts of the score. Dido dies with predictions of Hannibal's vengeance on her lips, but the closing statement of the *Marche troyenne* is asked to round off the opera in ringing tones and also to convey the Carthaginians' hatred since it has (symbolically) become the Roman March, emphasized by the Roman legions who are seen parading before the Capitol in Rome. In musical terms the unison choral line is supposed to be in *opposition* to the March, a difficult contrapuntal concept with unconvincing results.

It is as well to confront at once the single flaw in this great work, worthy to stand beside the masterpieces of Wagner and Verdi as one of the monuments of nineteenth-century music. It is the culmination of his life's work, his longest and greatest composition, drawing on all the resources at his command, reaching back to the tradition of Gluck and Spontini which he had admired since his first days in Paris and fulfilling a love of Virgil implanted by his father in early childhood. Wagner's incomprehension when he heard Berlioz read him the libretto in 1859 was due to his failure to grasp the strength of the French tradition to which *Les Troyens* unquestionably belongs. Its length, once unjustly notorious and often misrepresented, is about four hours of music, the same as the operas of Rameau, Rossini (*William Tell*), Meyerbeer, Wagner, and many others that had been performed in Paris for generations. Its historical emphasis and its epic title may be compared to *Les Huguenots* or *I Lombardi*; its five-act structure, its use of rhymed verse and its inclusion of generous *divertissements* may be attributed to the well-recognized practice of the Paris Opéra. On the other hand, Berlioz stands apart from the tradition in his unusual identification with its epic purpose, creating historical scenes not because they are attractive on stage but because he loved the characters and their background and because he felt he 'had known them all his life'. He brought a new Shakespearean quality to the opera by endowing his characters with the reality of passion, not its semblance, by diversifying the setting, by devising purposeful contrasts of mood and pace, and by imitating the technique of the historical plays with appearances of ghosts and rapid shifts of scene at moments of strong action. The literal debt to Shakespeare is found in the Act IV love duet, 'O nuit d'ivresse', where Dido and Aeneas borrow the words of Jessica and Lorenzo in Act V of *The Merchant of Venice*: 'In such a night as this, when the sweet wind did gently kiss the trees'. 'Virgil Shakespeareanized' was Berlioz's own accurate and succinct summary.

For many years the work was regarded as two separate operas, *La prise de Troie* and *Les Troyens à Carthage*, a division forced on Berlioz by the exigencies of 1863 and perpetuated in the published scores. It is all the more important to stress the oneness of his conception and to realize that he himself had a vocal score printed in 1861 which set out the full and original version as a single five-act grand opera; the great scarcity of this score has encouraged the two-opera myth, so too has the fact that the two heroines, Cassandra and Dido, die at their own hands at the ends of Act II and Act V respectively. But the wholeness of the work is plain both in the libretto and the music. The persistence of the theme of destiny driving Aeneas on, forcing him to abandon both Troy and Carthage, is self-evident, represented musically by the cry of 'Italie!' that recurs at the crucial moments of decision in Acts II, IV and V. The *Marche troyenne* also serves as a recurrent musical reminder of the Trojans' epic purpose, being heard in Acts I, III and V. With the exception of Cassandra, Berlioz does not identify individuals with characteristic motives or keys, nor is there any systematic musical structure. His technique is, as it always was, the committed response to individual scenes, actions and situations with music of the clearest and deepest expressive power. Time and again he emphasized the 'expressive veracity' of his score, and no sensitive ear can fail to respond to it. No other work illustrates this fundamental aesthetic attitude as well as *Les Troyens*, especially the last three acts where inspiration and expression join hands.

In Acts I and II Berlioz has created the character of Cassandra from the slender suggestions of her role given by Virgil, and the strength of her feelings is represented at her first appearance. With no overture (an innovation in the history of opera) and an opening choral scene scored for wind and hectically high in pitch to portray the Trojans' hollow joy, Cassandra's rapid rising scale – the nearest thing to a personal motive in the work – introduces the weight of strings as portentous commentary on her sense of doom. Her recitative is unrelievedly sombre, her *Air* shot through with glimpses of the happiness she will never know. In the long scene with Chorebus her mood never softens, and in his own blind love he never believes her. His entreaties (a *Cavatine* in E) are rather bland, and her response, structured as the middle section of his solo, is some violent recitative built out of her own rushing rising scale and dotted rhythms and from a foretaste of the main theme of the *Duo*, still to come, using the *Damnation de Faust*'s anticipation technique:

Ex. 40

After her horrifying vision of a river of blood, Chorebus's renewed avowals are ineffective. So too is his beautiful evocation of the peace of nature to which he calls her, another self-generating melodic line of great length and firmness in which only the last few bars are repetitions of what has come before. Chorebus's music, being almost all in triple metre, gives no hint of his heroism, for all his devotion. Their duet is tense and energetic, the bass line made up entirely of her rising scales, interrupted once by some recitative and leading to the final dramatic point where she abandons hope of persuading him to flee: 'Jealous death prepares our marriage bed for tomorrow!' rings out with her top B, and they rush off together.

A new key, C, is quickly established for the approach of King Priam and his court to a stirring military rhythm, with much percussion. An invocation to the gods of earth and sea brings in the full company: Ascanius (Aeneas' son), then Hecuba, Aeneas and Priam, with trains of warriors, priests and people. The first of the many ballets follows, an ingenious and sprightly *Combat de ceste* for wrestlers and athletes, brilliantly scored. The middle section is in 5/8 metre, a reminder of Fieramosca's fencing air in *Benvenuto Cellini*. A sudden and dramatic change heralds the *Pantomime*, a scene in dumb-show where Andromache, Hector's widow, leads her son Astyanax to receive Priam's blessing. There is no more moving music of mourning than this. One need not assume that Berlioz felt revulsion from war and its slaughter in order to perceive how agonisingly sad the solo clarinet line is, one of his magisterial melodies of great span over calm, characteristic harmony. The symbolism of Andromache's silence and the fact of great emotion being bestowed on an instrument, not on the voice, confirm Berlioz's faith in wordless music, as if *Les Troyens* still upheld the symphonic ideas of *Roméo et Juliette*. Soon after composing this scene, in February 1857, he wrote: 'Its importance terrified me . . . But there it is, done, and I feel it is the most successful piece in the whole act. I have wept over it like eighteen calves.'[2]

The scene has two middle episodes. In the first the clarinet turns to the major key while still sustaining the tone of lamentation, as Gluck was wont to do; the second represents Priam's blessing, solemnly sanctified by harps, trombones and cymbals, like the Pope's music in *Benvenuto Cellini* and the *Sanctus* in the *Requiem*. When the first clarinet melody returns it is now a minor third lower than before, with a few forlorn comments from Cassandra, half-heard from the back of the stage.

In Berlioz's original plan there followed a scene, based on Virgil, where Sinon, the Greek spy, is dragged in by the Trojans demanding his death. Cassandra never trusts him; Priam, on the other hand, believes his story that he has escaped from the Greeks when they demanded his sacrifice and has fled to Troy. He says the wooden horse is an offering to Pallas Athene which will cause the destruction of Troy unless it is brought within the walls. Musically it is a mixture of recitative and arioso with interjections from the chorus and some amplifications of Priam's otherwise sketchy character, but it was expendable since only the scene that follows, Aeneas' account of Laocoon's death, was needed to convince the Trojans that something must be done about the horse. So the hush at Andromache's departure is in fact broken by Aeneas' cry of alarm. The music is fast and furious, with graphic representation of the two monstrous serpents that devour Laocoon on trombone pedals, and a tremendous cadence:

Ex. 41

The shock that this news causes generates a huge, static ensemble for the whole company, like a moment of horror expanded to five minutes or more. It begins as a Reicha-style fugue, the voices entering respectively on F sharp, E and D, each entry rising and falling a full span. When F sharp minor is re-established, the chorus basses mutter 'un frisson de terreur' on a low pedal while the upper voices build up to a vast unaccompanied descending unison. This might have closed the movement, but Berlioz again uses the major key to extend a scene of lamentation, and the 12/8 pulse and long flowing lines build a big ensemble as they do in Meyerbeer or Verdi, although instead of repeating diminishing units of music as they habitually do, Berlioz only repeats the main statement with fuller scoring, and closes with stunned murmurings: 'Laocoon, un prêtre!' 'Horreur!'

A decision is quickly taken to appease the gods by bringing in the horse. Aeneas summons the Trojans to action and they all go off to fetch it, leaving Cassandra to bewail the fate of her city unheard.

Her *Air* is of the developing type with violent changes of key and theme, taking on more and more impassioned character and dissolving in audible tears as the procession is heard in the distance. The finale is a grand processional march, based on a similar one in Spontini's *Olympie*. It introduces the *Marche troyenne* whose outline rhythm is stamped out by distant trumpets at the beginning after the manner of the *Marche hongroise* and the full melody is first played by the farthest of the three off-stage bands before the chorus, also well in the distance, take it up. The tune is one of Berlioz's most stirring inspirations with a daring plunge from B flat into A flat after only four bars and a shifting alternation by which it finds its way back:

Ex. 42

Gradually the chorus comes nearer, yet leaving Cassandra for a long while alone on stage, as the nearer bands are brought into action. The main orchestra only supports Cassandra and contributes very little to the build-up. Although at the climax the chorus crowds on stage, the wooden horse itself is not seen in Berlioz's final version. No modern production can resist the staging of anything so theatrical, yet Berlioz himself seems to have conceived it as monstrously huge, better imagined than seen, like so much else in his stage works. When a clash of armour is heard within, the procession pauses, but instead of sanity the people's madness grips them even more fervently and they press on with greater resolve. The off-stage bands are heard as if receding into the distance, leaving Cassandra to a final outburst of despair.

Act I is the longest of the five, but it is replete with action and its major involvement of the chorus puts the Trojan people at the centre of the drama. Act II recounts the destruction of Troy, and in the opening scene Aeneas's role in saving the race is made plain. A descriptive opening with sounds of war in the distance finds Aeneas asleep. Ascanius dashes in to music almost identical to some given to his near-namesake Ascanio in *Benvenuto Cellini*, but he does not wake his father. Four stopped horns and heavy pizzicatos mark the spectral tread of Hector's ghost; a pause . . . a deep sigh . . . another pause . . . then a huge crash wakes Aeneas, who questions the ghost in tense recitative with trombones pulsing in the background. Hector's reply descends chromatically through a full octave against a texture like that of Ex. 39, with dense chromatic chords in the lower strings and occasional soft comment from the trombones. He commands Aeneas to flee and seek his hero's destiny in Italy, then solemnly withdraws. The reality of catastrophe instantly intrudes. Pantheus and some soldiers rush in and against hectically energetic music they hurl defiant shouts at the enemy. Aeneas declares himself ready to die, mindless of Hector's words, and leads his son and soldiers into the fray.

The scene changes over a held tremolo to the Temple of Vesta where the Trojan women have taken refuge. Their wailing is portrayed by a droopy 9/8 pulse and a modal scale rising from G to G in the key of A flat. Cassandra's own rising scale, when she enters, is more tonal, more purposeful and more abrupt. She calls them to their fate, knowing that Aeneas has saved the city's treasure and escaped. She knows too that Italy is his eventual destination, so cares nothing for the deaths of Priam and Chorebus, which she had foreseen, nor even for her own. Two motives dominate the scene, both heard only on unison strings, the first containing her rising scale, and both constantly varied in pitch and shape:

Ex. 43

(a)

(b)

Against these motives Cassandra rouses the women to sing their great *Hymne*, a heroic tune in A flat, against whirling harps (lyres), 'Complices de sa gloire'. She then turns on the weak-willed few who shun death and drives them out of the temple, 'Vous n'êtes pas Troyennes!' The remainder affirm their steadfast resolution in a reprise of the hymn, now in A and now forcefully extended as the Greek soldiers break in. The music has a fury, almost fanaticism, which dumbfounds the intruders who can only look helplessly on as Cassandra and the women stab themselves. Their dying word is 'Italie!' and the city perishes in flames.

Act III transports us across great distances and the passage of many years to Dido's Carthage, and after the chaotic, battle-worn music of Act II, the sound is instantly ordered and peaceful. Clearly defined numbers replace continuous action, and the sun of Africa replaces the smoke of Troy. Berlioz seems to convey all these contrasts in his score with an act full of formality and grandeur befitting a queen's court. This act belongs most securely to the classic French tradition of choruses and ballets as main pillars of the *spectacle*. Apart from the quiet scene for Dido and her sister Anna, and the surge of action at the end, rejoicing and ceremony fill the stage. Berlioz asks for a huge supplementary chorus to add weight to the *Chœur national* with which Dido is greeted. Its likeness to *God Save the Queen* has often been observed, originally by Berlioz himself, and it frames a scene in which Dido greets her loyal subjects and makes presentations to worthy servants of the state, in turn builders, sailors and farmers. First we should note how Berlioz characteristically amplifies her brief lines with additional expressive responses in the violins:

Ex. 44

163

Then, in the *entrées*, each group of workers has its own colour and character, the builders strangely like Mephistopheles' 'Follets', the sailors jaunty with bassoons and two piccolos, the farmers plaintive and rustic, the melody always in pairs of woodwind an octave apart. Eventually the stage empties, and Dido confesses to her sister in a scene of wonderful expressive intimacy wherein the instruments never cease to give point to every uttered phrase, that sorrow clouds her soul. Again the motive is instrumental, not vocal, and when Dido and Anna do share a melodic line (at the 6/8) their contrasting voices are delicately woven into textures and modulation as Mozart might have done. Anna gently urges her sister to forget Sichaeus and seek a new love.

Iopas, the court bard who is also used as message-bearer, intrudes with news of a strange fleet in port. Without hesitation Dido offers them hospitality, and in a brief scene which is easily overlooked, 'Errante sur les mers', she elaborates Virgil's sentiment that those who know suffering can more easily understand the suffering of others. She too has known years of wandering at sea, and we at once glimpse the basis of her feelings for Aeneas. This little *Air* of some forty bars exemplifies the sheer quality of inspiration in these final acts of *Les Troyens*; not a note is out of place, not a note is routine or obvious, voice and orchestra, harmony and line, chromatics and diatonics are all in perfect balance; furthermore vocal line, bass line and orchestral colour are all markedly Berlioz's own. He wrote at the time of composition:

> I am at present staying with friends in Saint-Germain. They have given me a room facing the sun, opening on to a garden looking over the Marly valley, the aqueduct, woods, vineyards and the Seine; the house is isolated; peace and quiet all around; and I work on my score with inexpressible joy, without a thought for the agony it is bound to bring me later on. The view of the countryside seems to intensify my Virgilian passion. I feel I knew Virgil, I feel he knows my passion for him. Yesterday I wrote an Air for Dido which is merely a paraphrase of the famous line: 'Haud ignara mali miseris succurrere disco'. After I had sung it once to myself I was naïve enough to say aloud: 'That's it, isn't it, cher maître? Sunt lacrymae rerum?' as if Virgil had been there.[3]

Aeneas (in disguise) and his men enter to a minor version of the *Marche troyenne*, naively but effectively suggesting their forlorn condition. Ascanius is left to announce their identity and origin.

'Notre chef est Enée' he proudly declares, 'je suis son fils.' Over a bare fifth in a remote key Dido reflects 'Étrange destinée', already glimpsing the course of fate. No sooner have the newcomers been welcomed than Narbal, the chief minister, rushes in with news of invasion by the Numidians under Iarbas, Dido's savage suitor. The headlong pace is carried, again, on a main orchestral motive, the urgency of which should be compared with Ex. 35:

Ex. 45

At the height of general distress, the brass rap out a repeated A flat, and on a colossal chord of E major Aeneas steps forward, throwing off his disguise, one of the most stirring moments in the opera. With tremendous dignity against persistent fragments of Ex. 45 he offers his services to the queen and the full chorus prepares for war with ringing cries. Before they leave, however, Aeneas must take leave of his son. Against the predominant B major of the war-cry, his heartfelt farewell, in E flat, holds the company spellbound with a magnificent line and climax that will be quoted as Ex. 58, below. B major returns, the chorus closes with a rousing 'Aux armes!' and the music fades as they set out to war (though without any stage directions to say so).

These closing few bars of Act III, with their long diminuendo and falling chromatic line, actually foreshadow the opening bars of Act IV – another 'anticipation-motive' – although the atmosphere is quite different. The first tableau of the new Act is the famous *Chasse royale et orage*, a mimed 'Intermède', with stage action and unseen chorus. Like Andromache's scene in Act I, it transfers the emotional weight from voices to instruments, emphasizing Berlioz's eternal belief in the power of the orchestra for great utterances of this kind; at the same time it is firmly visual in effect: the audience is to watch the play of naiads in the African forest, the arrival of hunters on foot and on horseback, the darkening sky, the entry of Dido dressed as Diana and Aeneas as a warrior, the crash of lightning, their entry into the cave, Satyrs, Sylvans and Fauns dancing with flaming branches, the return of calm. The only vocal sounds are distraught cries of 'o-a-o-a-o' as part of the storm (like the chorus aiding the

storm in *Rigoletto*) and cries of 'Italie!' to remind Aeneas of his
destiny. Although it is often played as a concert piece, giving it the
status of a symphonic poem, it is the most theatrical movement in the
whole opera, requiring elaborate effects and the traditional French
panoply of ballet and spectacle. With uncanny judgment Berlioz
gives the coming together of Dido and Aeneas great symbolic significance by enacting it in mime, and at the same time displays his
musical powers at their fullest and most imaginative. The movement
begins and ends in C, but has no formal tonal scheme. The introduction treats the falling theme (from the close of Act III) as a strange
fugato, against magical wind writing and softly shifting harmony.
When the hunt begins, the first fanfare is heard on a solo saxhorn
off-stage, echoed by another, further away, leading in the galloping
hunters. A second fanfare is heard on three distant trombones,

Ex. 46

before the rain begins to torrent down. A third fanfare, more urgent, is again on saxhorns, but now near at hand, and a fourth follows quickly after. The storm rises to its climax as the fanfares return in resplendent counterpoint, their motifs and rhythms clashing like an avalanche of rocks and stones (Ex. 46). This E flat climax, with the full orchestra in contest with the offstage fanfares, is followed by another in D flat and finally a long passage of subsiding chromatics until the return of the opening C major and a final memory (stretched out) of the first fanfare, now played by the orchestral first horn.

It is marvellously evocative music, perfectly designed and executed, and it sets the seal on the whole of the act. Small wonder that Berlioz composed this act before Acts II and III, eagerly rushing ahead to the heart of his great love story. The *Chasse royale et orage* was played only once in the 1863 run of performances and then cut. Even then Berlioz had reorchestrated it incorporating all the off-stage instruments except the two pairs of timpani in the main orchestra. It is doubtful if it has ever been staged as he conceived it, but then he would not have been surprised:

> If the theatre is not large enough for a lively and spectacular staging of this tableau, if it is hard to get the women of the chorus to run across the stage with hair flying and the men of the chorus to dress as Fauns and Satyrs and indulge in grotesque antics crying 'Italie!', if the firemen are afraid of fire, if the stage crew are afraid of water, if the director is afraid of everything, and especially if no quick scene change can be made before the next tableau, then this symphony should be omitted.[4]

Dido's gardens by the sea are the setting for the rest of the act. Dido and Aeneas are now lovers, and the serenity of the scene is marred only by Narbal's unease, by Dido's impatience until she is alone with Aeneas, and, at the end, by the insistent call of destiny. The scene is a succession of beautiful numbers, with the love duet as its climax. First, we find Anna and Narbal discussing affairs of state. Her rather shallow delight contrasts sharply with his portentous gloom, a contrast made audible in the quite different musical styles of their solos; Berlioz inevitably combines the two at the end of the duet, so that her swift-moving cavatina becomes a decorative run over the solemn chords and firm line of his solo. His fine melody, another long self-generating span, is deftly anticipated in the orches-tral introduction to the scene.

A fairylike version of the *Chœur national*, with muted violins and harp harmonics, brings Dido and Aeneas on stage with a group of courtiers. They are to be entertained by some *divertissement*, the third set in the opera, three dances of strongly contrasted character, as in the previous act. The moods are here languorous, energetic and exotic. Berlioz left the composition of ballets to the end as a tiresome chore, but these are nevertheless done with lively invention. The wind runs in the first ballet, the vigorous string writing of the second, and the brilliant eastern inflections of the third dance, the *Pas d'esclaves nubiennes*, give each dance strong individual character. The Nubian dance is quite unlike anything Berlioz had attempted before, being modal, non-harmonic and very strangely scored. The slaves intone more of his make-believe 'South Seas' language used in *Lélio* and *La damnation de Faust*.

Dido is bored with the dancing, so she commands the poet Iopas to sing. He does so, to the accompaniment of a Theban harp. His song to Ceres is elegantly pastoral, three short verses interspersed with two episodes, the second of which prettily evokes birds and lambs. With an extended final cadence and a carefully placed high C, Iopas hopes to impress his queen, but she is again impatient. (In the first draft she actually interrupts his song as he embarks on a fresh episode about butterflies.) She now wants Aeneas to conclude the story of his wanderings – the device by which Virgil recounted the sack of Troy after telling of the arrival of the Trojans in Carthage. As soon as he mentions Andromache's second marriage to the King of Epirus she breaks in with doubts about the strength of her own resolve. Her sudden flight into melody turns into a quintet of surpassing beauty, the gentle pulse and delicate scoring enhanced by the warm sonority of D flat major. An instrumental motif again plays a part:

Ex. 47

Ascanius deftly draws the ring off Dido's finger – a scene suggested by a painting, now in the Louvre, by Pierre-Narcisse Guérin, whom Berlioz probably met in Rome in 1831. Guérin was at that time at work on another canvas *La dernière nuit de Troie* which

Berlioz may also have known. The stage-direction is particularly precise here. Since Aeneas's part was a late addition to what was originally a quartet, four voices alone will convey something of the music's elegance, even without showing the accompaniment:

Ex. 48

Aeneas then invokes the night sky to the celestial sounds of the *Sanctus* of the *Requiem*, and this rather abruptly modulates into F for the *Septuor*. This was originally a sextet with Dido silent (corresponding to Aeneas' silence in the quintet). It is an invocation to the sky and the sea, stabilized by the incessant upper pedal in piccolo, flute and clarinet on repeated C's occasionally touching on D flat and back. Another hypnotic effect is created by the recurrent breaking of waves (low horns, lower strings and bass drum) at irregular intervals, seemingly regardless of the melodic pattern. The high shimmering strings, representing starlight, is likewise heard at differently irregular intervals throughout the piece. A simple melodic ensemble is thus transformed into a piece of magical atmosphere. Having pictured the billow of the sea in *Le corsaire*, he now presents its obverse – the calm of the Mediterranean night, a setting he was to come back to in *Béatrice et Bénédict*.

The occasional D flat in the upper pedal is used to steer the music from F major up a semitone to the G flat where the love duet must be. Berlioz was proud of this modulation (he should have been unsure of the previous one), and the new key was essential since, for one thing, the love duet was already finished, having been the first music of the opera to be composed, and also because G flat was the inescapable key for love duets in mid-nineteenth-century opera owing to its symbolic profundity and emotional warmth. Since Meyerbeer established the practice in *Les Huguenots* with 'Tu l'as dit', the character of such a key, whether love duets or not, whether in *Die Meistersinger* or *Aida*, was not to be misunderstood.

The stage is now empty but for the two lovers; the stage direction is 'clair de lune'. Formally the duet has a refrain, heard three times, and two episodes, and is thus, and in other respects also, similar to Iopas's song. But where he was timid and formal, the lovers are now swathed in passion, and the greater intensity of the music, the richer tonality and orchestration, all support them. In the refrain the two voices seem closely linked together in a divine flow of melody over soft muted strings, whereas in the episodes each voice comes forward with the famous borrowings from *The Merchant of Venice*. While the refrain is merely intensified on each return (each time delayed with false returns), the episodes are more adventurous. When Dido sings of Venus and Anchises (Aeneas' parents), he responds with a decorative variation of her line, telling of Troilus and Cressida. In the second episode Aeneas first has a passage of magical, sliding chords and delicate scoring, in reference to Diana and Endymion, then a repeat of the pattern in which Dido's melody is immediately varied in Aeneas' response. The lovers are thus an indivisible pair in the refrain and inter-responsive individuals in the episodes; for once Berlioz reserves no special musical material for the orchestra but vests it all in the voices. He is being whole-heartedly operatic, and though the duet is easily performable on its own, it has only rarely been extracted. In the last resort he was prouder of his voiceless love-duet in *Roméo et Juliette*, but here he was still displaying his highest powers in a medium which needed no apology nor explanation and for which audiences need no wooing.

The larger plan could not allow this act of gloriously serene music to end here. Originally Berlioz called up the shades of Cassandra (which explains the quick rising scale) and Hector, but moved them to Act V after attending Ambroise Thomas's opera *Psyché* in

January 1857. In his notice for the *Débats* Berlioz showered mockery on Thomas's leading character Mercury, but at the same moment he slipped the same character – also present in Virgil – into the end of Act IV to remind Aeneas of the call of destiny. The musical effect, heavy chords of E minor while the G flat of the love duet still lingers in the mind, is brutally disquieting.

Act V continues the cellular construction, scene by scene, of the two previous acts, but with more dramatic momentum as the unfolding tragedy demands. The song of the young sailor Hylas at the opening of the act may not affect or concern the crisis between Dido and Aeneas, but it carries the woes of the Trojan people with a depth of nostalgia unequalled in any other music. A simple refrain, light orchestration, a swaying rhythm – these are enough to express the tears of the race. For Berlioz himself it called to mind his beloved sailor son: 'I thought of you, dear Louis, as I wrote it . . .'.[5] There are three strophes: in the second a brief squall stirs up the waves, in the third he falls asleep at the masthead, his song heart-rendingly unfinished.

Pantheus and the soldiers enter with some startling harmony (Ex. 49) and heavy syncopations that are to feature in the next two scenes. Haste and alarm emerge as fugato and imitation, and an unseen chorus of shades intones 'Italie!' They rush off to busy themselves with their now inevitable departure, leaving two sentinels to grumble in vulgar fashion at their master's quixotic urge to sail on. It is not a cry on behalf of oppressed soldiery of all ages so much as a simple comic scene inserted, as Berlioz explained, to heighten the impact of Aeneas's great monologue which follows – as indeed it does. Berlioz invoked *Macbeth* and *King Lear* as his precedents, remaining loyal to Romanticism's profound belief in the productive contrast of opposites. The music is distinctive for its jaunty pulse, its

Ex. 49

colour (cor anglais, clarinets and bassoons) and its casual modulation from G minor at the start to F minor at the end.

Aeneas's solo scene presents the classic conflict of love and duty. Where his obedience to unseen laws sweeps the music along with restless energy and incessant syncopation, his dread of saying farewell to Dido produces yet another self-generating melodic span, a full 31 bars in a tender but intense 6/8. The words here are equal to the music:

> Ah! quand viendra l'instant des suprêmes adieux,
> Heure d'angoisse et de larmes baignée,
> Comment subir l'aspect affreux
> De cette douleur indignée?
>
> Lutter contre moi-même et contre toi, Didon!
> En déchirant ton cœur implorer mon pardon!
> En serai-je capable?[6]

This Andante's dolorous harmonies end with a disarming major cadence, and the return of the Allegro, relentless in its urgency and sweep, seals his determination to see her once more. The final cadence, once again, is of the heroic mould. An extreme and sudden contrast of tonality and sonority raises the shades of Priam, Chorebus, Hector and Cassandra, to shore up his weakening spirit. Dramatically, the scene also raises the shade of Shakespeare. The bass clarinet's sombre colour, later to darken Dido's final scenes also, makes itself strongly felt.

Aeneas no longer wavers; his resolve is firm, and the galloping strings piece together the *Marche troyenne* as his men prepare for departure. The pace slackens from dotted notes to chattering triplets as he turns towards the palace for his adieu. At this point a full declaration of the March and a high B flat would have seen Aeneas off the stage for the last time, but Berlioz's resolve was less firm than his hero's. As a late addition to his plan, he decided to bring on Dido at this point for the confrontation that Aeneas longed for but had decided not to face. Written some two years later than the rest of the opera, the duet gives a foretaste of the manic derangement that Dido suffers in her final scenes. Aeneas's pleas and protestations have no effect on her, nor is his character anywhere defined in the music. There is a binding rhythm in the strings, but little else of shape or strength except her strident curse as she sweeps offstage. Aeneas and the fleet leave for Italy and the curtain falls on a colossal roll of drums, originally intended, like similarly held chords in Acts I and II, to cover the scene change.

Yielding to practical necessity Berlioz made a clean start for the new scene, in Dido's apartments as dawn breaks. The insertion of the duet in the previous scene here produced some dramatic dislocation since Dido tells her sister Anna to implore Aeneas to stay, as if she had never confronted him on the quayside. The vocal line of this scene would on its own give no impression whatever of the intricacy and expressiveness of the music, completely entrusted to the orchestra. The subtle placing of accents, discreet wind chords, a gentle pulse and above all the cello melody convey Dido's last glimmer of hope. The melody embodies the very spirit of the cello:

Ex. 50

Five times it is heard, each time one step higher than before. When it enters on high B, at the fifth time, it falters, and the scene continues without it, drained of life, like the queen it portrays. Iopas's news that the Trojan fleet has sailed induces sudden despair and, with it, desperation. The long scene that ensues encompasses every mood, from madness to nostalgia and resignation, making heroic demands on the singer. The derangement of the music recalls the final moments of his first two great heroines, Cleopatra and Juliet, although here the dramatic span is wider and the calmness and resignation of Dido's end are all the more profound. There are sudden shifts from fury to impotent despair and from cries of vengeance to confessions of lingering love. Virgil seems very close to Berlioz's elbow as he takes Dido forward to her immolation. The bass clarinet and cor anglais respond in funereal phrases as she gives orders for the pyre to be raised, and the same dark colours accompany the stately recitative 'Je vais mourir . . .' Her cry to Venus 'give me back your son!' is heart-rending but vain. She sings her farewell to Carthage and her people in the most solemn of the slow 6/8 movements that mark moments of high emotion throughout his music. Violas join the clarinets, and soon after her brief, rapt memories of the love duet, they even steal the climax of the aria:

Ex. 51

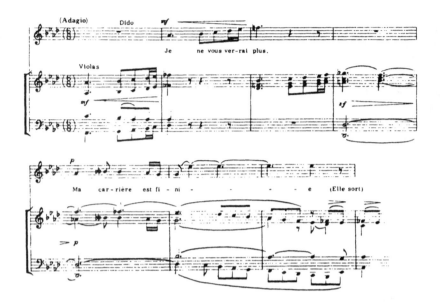

(As in the slow section of *Le corsaire*, also in A flat, the bass note D flat has a mesmeric booming effect.) 'Of all the passionately sad music that I have ever written, I know of none to compare with Dido's in this scene, except for Cassandra's . . .'[7]

The *Air* concludes with soft pulsing trombones – possibly a symbol of death in Berlioz's mind, as Hector's scene in Act II suggests – in the key of A flat, and thence resolves with calm inevitability on to C sharp minor for the final scene. A funeral pyre has been erected in the palace gardens overlooking the sea, where priests and priestesses are gathered as might be in any opera by Lully or Gluck. A solemn *pompe funèbre* unfolds to the steady tread of timpani and pizzicato basses, cornet and trombones intoning the chant. With pagan malice they call upon the gods of darkness to bring Aeneas and his people to destruction. Berlioz carefully authenticates his stage directions with lines from Virgil, Ovid and Horace as Dido prepares herself for sacrifice. Fatal destiny is plucked out of a slowly descending chromatic scale, as it had been for Herod and Hector. Having mounted the pyre she foretells the coming of an avenger, Hannibal, and in music of violent convulsion she draws Aeneas's sword and plunges it into her breast. Anna rushes to her side and with her dying words Dido pronounces not Hannibal's name but that of his bitter enemy, Rome; she has seen yet further into the future to the immortal glory of Rome. The *Marche troyenne*, symbolically transformed into a Roman March, rings out in triumph, the emperor's court is viewed in the distance and the feeble curses of the Carthaginians are overwhelmed in a blaze of B flat major.

To evaluate the qualities of this great opera in a few words is no easy task. Yet it should be stressed they are not qualities which any attentive musician in the 1850s would have found innovatory or disturbing; they were the traditional virtues of classical French opera animated by a romantic faith in feeling and expression In technique Berlioz was at the height of his powers: his feeling for the human voice was that of a natural composer of opera, with his personal attachment to the mezzo-soprano voice lovingly defined, even with the role of Béatrice yet to come. His command of the orchestra is exemplary in its restraint and sensitivity. He makes none of the audacious errors we find in his early music. The two most striking methods of approach which attain perfection in *Les Troyens* are the gift of long, naturally extensible melody, and the very personal use of orchestral motives to construct individual scenes. The latter device reflects his fundamental belief that instruments were the equal of the human voice in range and force of expression, a belief which, when his whole output is viewed, threatens his standing as a supreme composer of opera. Against the comparison of Verdi, for example, Berlioz's methods were too wide-ranging, too un-vocal and too personal to compete; they were also too retrospective, belonging more to the world of Gluck and Spontini. Nevertheless, when these idiosyncratic aspects of *Les Troyens* are understood in their wider context and when Berlioz's love for Virgil's and Shakespeare's worlds are accepted, together with his explicit faith in the power of music to express the highest passion, one can only acclaim this as his supreme score. For a hundred years the opera was little known and universally mis-judged. Today it takes its rightful place as an honoured masterpiece. On May 3rd 1861, Berlioz wrote with unerring certainty: 'I am sure I have written a great work, greater and nobler than anything done hitherto'.[8]

In 1863, in order to see even part of the work staged, he allowed its division into two, and the production of Acts III to V as *Les Troyens à Carthage* necessitated a prologue to explain the previous action. It opens with a *Lamento* consisting mainly of a slow and ponderously scored transformation of the theme of Cassandra's duet with Chorebus in Act I (Ex. 40b), concluding with some solemn chords. A Rhapsode then recites in formal verse the account of the sack of Troy, and the full *Marche troyenne* is played before the curtain rises. A similar version of the *Marche troyenne*, but without chorus, was made in 1864 for concert use but not played in Berlioz's lifetime.

Before moving on to *Béatrice et Bénédict*, Berlioz's last major work, some attention must be given to the handful of smaller works which belong to the later years. There were four short religious works, using the word in its widest sense, especially to describe the *Hymne pour la consécration du nouveau tabernacle*. This seems to have been Berlioz's way of thanking a curious individual named J. H. Vries, widely known as Docteur Noir, for attending him in 1859 when his illness was particularly acute. Vries dreamed of a universal religion that would unite all nations, to be sanctified in a new temple to be built in the Champs-Elysées. The fantastic background of the piece and its author is a great deal more interesting than the music, which consists of eight verses of a plain 16-bar hymn; sopranos and tenors are in octaves throughout, as in the *Ballet des ombres*, the *Chant des chemins de fer* and *La menace des Francs*. *Le temple universel*, which Berlioz originally intended for two large choruses, French and English, singing in their own languages in the Crystal Palace, is a much finer piece, composed early in 1861. The idea appealed to him even though it was not his own, but it was never performed and it survives only in French. It asserts the triumph of right, liberty and brotherhood in an optimistic F major, with the two male-voice choirs in balance. Since it proclaims the unity of Europe and has two contrasting sections providing some bracing dramatic interest, it would merit more frequent revival today. The writing is shapely and accomplished. Two sacred pieces for women's voices belong, without any certain date, to the last years: *Veni creator spiritus*, with or without organ accompaniment, alternates between solo and full groups and is simple and affecting, without any Berliozian signature. *Tantum ergo* is more recognizably his work; the organ part is essential and the chromatic part-writing nicely judged. If this happens to be his last work, there would be no greater irony than for him to have ended with a contrapuntal Amen, the one form of music he had most consistently vilified.

There are also three arrangements, oddly miscellaneous. In 1859 he scored Martini's famous *Plaisir d'amour* for voice and small orchestra. He probably knew the piece from childhood, or at least knew Florian's sentimental text, and thus went about his task with evident affection. There are even reminiscences of 'Nuit d'ivresse', the love-duet in *Les Troyens*, Act IV. The orchestration was evidently made for a Baden-Baden concert in 1859, and for the 1860 season there he scored Schubert's even more famous *Erlkönig*. Berlioz probably shared the contemporary view that Schubert's dauntingly difficult piano part was best transferred to the orchestra, whereas the modern listener enjoys the pianist's sufferings as essential to the music. In Berlioz's version we may admire his confident addition of tender descending phrases at the father's words, 'Du lieber Kind, komm' geh' mit mir' and 'Ich liebe dich'. On the other hand it is odd to find the unmistakably pianistic figures at 'Willst, feiner Knabe, du mit mir gehn?' transferred to the violins unchanged. Both these orchestrations are worth reviving. The third of these arrangements is the movement *Sœur Monique: Rondeau* from Couperin's *18ᵉ Ordre*, arranged for female voices and piano, the words from an eighteenth-century adaptation, 'Adressons nos vers'. Its new title was *Invitation à louer Dieu*.

For his last opera, *Béatrice et Bénédict*, Berlioz once again went back to a subject he had pondered for many years. The original Baden-Baden commission was for an opera on a historical text, set in the Thirty Years' War, by Edouard Plouvier. He hesitated for a full year before realizing this would never do. He went back to an idea first hatched in 1833 and worked out in collaboration with Legouvé in some detail in 1852: for a comic opera on Shakespeare's *Much Ado About Nothing*. He never saw the play on the stage and can only have admired it from reading; even then it is unusual in that the comedies attracted him much less than the great tragedies. By 1860 he knew that he could provide his own libretto, using Benjamin Laroche's translation of 1839, and compressing the play into one act by removing much of the 'ado', reducing the parts of Hero and Claudio and omitting the villainous Don John. He preferred to focus on the war of wits between Beatrice and Benedick, exploiting the symmetry of this abbreviated plot. As a critic Berlioz's most tormented hours had been spent listening to the flood of comic operas produced in Paris every year, so he would have been fully conscious of the trivial style he most wanted to avoid. In this he succeeded, without any doubt, but in creating the part of Somarone, the *Maître de chapelle* of clumsy wit and topical absurdity, he accepted the Opéra-comique's stock requirement of a figure of fun. Somarone (which means 'big donkey') is in fact derived from Shakespeare's Balthasar, but the jokes were Berlioz's own. Being opéra-comique, the action is couched in spoken dialogue.

Most of the music was composed in the autumn of 1860 with a second burst of work on it a year later. He started with nine numbers, then expanded to twelve; then he decided to divide it into two acts[9] and added the drinking scene to open the second act. In this form, with a very short second act, it was played in Baden-Baden in 1862. In response to a critic's suggestion he expanded the second act with the *Trio* and *Chœur lointain*, and with these final additions the vocal score was published; the opera was revived in Weimar in 1863 and again in that year in Baden-Baden. It was a success in both cities, and it gave Berlioz the highest pleasure in that he never once doubted the good faith of his audience or his artists; the contrast with the habitual hostility of Paris was all too plain.

Writing the score had been a pleasure and a relaxation to him. It rarely plumbs the depths of *Les Troyens* but it is always accomplished and has the experienced composer's polish and refinement. It is both simple and subtle and he aptly described it as 'a caprice written with the point of a needle' which 'needs the utmost delicacy of execution' – nowhere more plainly than in the overture, where speed, lightness and ingenious scoring conceal the skill with which some half-dozen references to the opera are woven together. It is rightly a concert favourite, though not to be lightly undertaken. As in his earlier overtures, an Andante section provides affecting contrast.

The action of the first act takes place in the gardens of Leonato (a spoken role), governor of Messina, in Sicily. The people are rejoicing at Don Pedro's victory over the Moors in a lively but conventional chorus. A large section of Shakespeare's Act I Scene 1 tells us of Benedick's return with the victorious army and of Beatrice's scorn of his heroism and wit. When the chorus resumes, she impatiently mocks the hollow rhymes (*gloire-victoire, guerriers-lauriers*) that Berlioz himself had endured a thousand times at the Opéra-comique, and had let slip in his own verse. So she leaves them to sing it out and then dance a *Sicilienne* whose quasi-modal line is adapted from, of all things, *Le dépit de la bergère* of 1819, his first published work. There had been very little self-borrowing in *Les*

Troyens and only this instance in *Béatrice et Bénédict*, so it is tempting to suppose that the melody was excavated unconsciously from a depth of forty years (see Ex. 2, p. 4). The style is similar to the *Troyens* ballets, though scored with unusual solidity, the whole woodwind section intoning a melody which runs for seventy bars with scarcely a rest.

Hero, Leonato's daughter and Beatrice's cousin, now sings a formal *Air* of delight at her lover Claudio's return from the wars. The Andante section belongs to the group of such triple-metre pieces familiar since *Roméo et Juliette* and highly characteristic of Berlioz's tender mood. The Allegro, on the other hand, is dangerously showy, leading to a big vocal cadenza, comparable to Teresa's *Cavatine* in Act I of *Cellini*. The best feature is a martial tune given out first by the trumpets, which has already provided stirring impetus in the overture. The *Air* is the first of a sequence of numbers of increasing complexity and ingenuity. Its burden is a girl's unclouded rejoicing, but the *Duo* and *Trio* which follow present much more subtle characterization. Clearly in the *Duo* Berlioz enjoyed making musical capital of the duel of wits between Beatrice and Benedick; the instruments chortle with delight at the cut-and-thrust dialogue with all manner of trills, syncopations and fluttering figures. In the middle of the Allegro section, where the voices move more closely together while railing even more fiercely at each other, they offer a mock-lugubrious prayer to heaven not to be stricken with a spouse such as the other; the wind cannot resist churchy contrapuntal comment.

In the *Trio* Don Pedro and Claudio attempt to persuade Benedick that his horror of marriage is absurd. It has a recurrent refrain and a number of episodes, in the first of which Benedick discourses to the lightest imaginable accompaniment on Shakespeare's line 'That a woman conceived me, I thank her'. In the second the tempo quickens and the exchanges become briefer and less polite. A nimble snatch in the violins reveals the character of the episode:

Ex. 52

The refrain saves the argument from bitterness, and Benedick then takes a solemn oath that if ever he falls prey to a woman he will accept a sign over his door 'Here you may see Benedick the married man'. The coda resumes the brilliant animation of the overture, with such irresistible comedy as the following:

Ex. 53

They withdraw, and we see Somarone coming forward to rehearse his musicians for the coming marriage of Hero and Claudio. There is certainly humour in this scene, though after the deft wit of the previous two numbers it can only seem lumbering except in the most skilled hands. Somarone is a private joke on Berlioz's part. The bumbling musician with a taste for terrible music is gently satirized, and is given the equivalent of Beecham or Barbirolli jokes in his dialogues, well-known sayings by Gluck or Spontini (both of whom Berlioz of course hugely admired). The staging of the scene is straight-forward comedy, but the music they rehearse, a 'Grotesque Epithalamium' which appeals to the happy pair to 'die of joy, why survive such sweet moments?', is a ponderous exercise in the type of textbook counterpoint Berlioz most detested. It is more painful than amusing, especially when Somarone lovingly composes an oboe obbligato and runs it through all over again. A long stretch of Shakespeare's dialogue (from Act II Scene 3) brings relief and advances the plot. Knowing Benedick to be concealed, Don Pedro and Claudio discourse with feigned astonishment on Beatrice's secret love for him. When they leave he leaps forward with instant resolution to fall in love. His *Rondo* takes up the key, metre and colour of the *Trio*, only this time his feelings are reversed. He even splutters with fortissimo rage at the thought that his informants might have been lying.

There follows the *Duo-Nocturne* for Hero and her attendant Ursula, which is scarcely functional to the action but has become the most acclaimed movement of the opera for its subdued, atmospheric beauty. Hero, the happy bride-to-be, basks in tender emotion as the light fades and the long melody unwinds against murmuring string accompaniment. The style is similar to that of the duet for Dido and Anna in Act III of *Les Troyens*, with touches of tone-painting in the wind instruments. It makes a magnificent close to the first act, the last few bars after the voices are silent (a late addition to the scene) fading in a shimmer as night closes.

A reprise of the *Sicilienne* provides an entr'acte, then the curtain rises and for the greater part of the opening scene of the second act nothing is seen except various servants coming in and out of the banqueting hall on the left of the stage. Somarone and the chorus are drinking and singing lustily off-stage in admiration of their Sicilian wine to the accompaniment of trumpets and guitar. The guitar rhythm is precisely the same as in 'Bienheureux les matelots' in the last scene of *Benvenuto Cellini*, almost certainly a rhythm Berlioz habitually strummed himself in his guitar-playing days:

Ex. 54

Allegretto

| 3 ♪♪♩ ♩ | ♪♪♩ ♩ |

They only come on stage for the last verse, another case where Berlioz finds it easier to imagine the action in his mind's eye than most audiences do. The song has some charm, although Somarone, drunk, is even duller in his wits than when he is sober, and it also has considerable dramatic point, being carefully placed, like the sentinels' scene in Act V of *Les Troyens*, to heighten the monologue which follows. In this case it is Beatrice, entering in great confusion having overheard the contrived news that Benedick is secretly in love with her. Shakespeare had staged the scene where she overhears it (Act III Scene 1) but Berlioz was able to omit it and bring her on in a high state of emotional tension. Unlike Benedick she does not instantly resolve to fall in love; she is instead aware of 'fire in her ears' and now understands her earlier feelings when the army left for the war. She reveals her horrified dream that Benedick had fallen in battle, and now for the first time admits the love she has never before acknowledged. This self-discovery provides the finest music of the opera in a dramatic *scena* which transcends the world of opéra-comique and recalls the stronger accents of Cassandra's and Dido's music. For the first time since the overture the trombones are heard again, and the Andante, far from being a mere prelude to an exuberant allegro, is a rounded section of strongly contrasting moods. At the end she takes wing in something close to coloratura. This fine *Air* puts Beatrice firmly at the centre of dramatic attention.

Hero and Ursula enter and join in a *Trio* which recalls rather too closely the murmuring 6/8 of the *Duo-Nocturne*, although the middle section is a scene of more dramatic than musical interest. They lure Beatrice into reasserting her bitter resistance to marriage, but when Hero is overcome by jealousy at the thought of an unfaithful Claudio, Beatrice is tricked into raging with fury too. 'Could jealousy affect you so?' mocks Hero. It was primarily to fill out the second act and give the ladies a trio to balance that of the men that this movement was written, and perhaps for this reason it scarcely equals theirs in invention and subtlety. The other late addition to the score, the *Chœur lointain*, on the other hand, is uniquely inventive, a hymn for chorus (without basses) and guitar accompaniment, calling the bride to the altar. It brings to mind the *Ciel* scene at the end of *La damnation de Faust* and is again a piece for which Berlioz imagined some idealized setting, for it is sung off-stage while Beatrice, on stage, listens with growing emotion.

There follows a precious scene in dialogue between Beatrice and Benedick both floundering between their declared indifference and their hidden love. It is not taken from Shakespeare but passes well as if it were. The wedding procession arrives, with harps gracing the chorus of welcome. Hero and Claudio give their signatures and the notary asks for the second couple to come forward. Here we are in Shakespeare's Act V Scene 4 wherein the conspiracy is uncovered and the quarrelsome lovers are united. Benedick now faces the humiliation of seeing the threatened signboards carried on, to heavy chords from the full orchestra.

For his finale Berlioz writes the most feathery, witty music of the whole opera, used for exactly that effect as the main material of the overture. Beatrice and Benedick lead off in a sparkling duet about the elusiveness and folly of love: today the truce is signed, but tomorrow they will be enemies once again. 'Tomorrow, tomorrow!' the chorus cry as the curtain falls.

Any opera that leans heavily on Shakespeare and retains much of it in spoken dialogue runs the risk of seeming to be half in the dramatist's world, half in the composer's. This has certainly been the fate of *Béatrice et Bénédict*, only rarely welcomed into the operatic repertory because of its essential requirement of fine acting singers and because Berlioz's contribution is, if anything, too self-effacing. He captures Shakespeare's pace and wit with especial mastery in those scenes where he offers a real musical equivalent to a scene from the play, as for example in the *Duo* for Beatrice et Benedick, the men's *Trio*, and Beatrice's solo scene. These have the best music in the opera. When he adds his own glosses on the comedy, as in Samarone's scenes or the women's *Trio*, his invention is strikingly weaker. But encased in an overture and finale of such brilliance and with the beautiful *Nocturne* at its heart this short opera is anything but problematical or puzzling. It can be as much a source of delight and satisfaction as we know it to have been for the composer himself.

9

Berlioz's style

To ears brought up on the German classics, as most still are, Berlioz's music strikes a strange and sometimes jarring note. It is immediately obvious that his procedures and sonorities are not those of Bach or Mozart, nor even of Schumann or Chopin, and this will either estrange or fascinate the newcomer to his world. It is often said that his music is like nobody else's, but no composer is entirely without debts to his traditions; even allowing Berlioz full measure of originality as an inventor, we must recognize that it is the tradition as a whole that is strange and not this one member of it. Since the music to which he was first introduced and which aroused his earliest admiration is now rarely heard, we have to make special efforts to unearth the roots of style.

The French tradition, to which Berlioz squarely belonged, was very different from the much better known German and Italian traditions, but for him it was of recent date. He paid little heed to composers as early as Lully and Rameau, regarding the art in their time as in too backward a state to merit very serious attention, but he inherited indirectly from them a feeling for dramatic space and pace which is unmistakably French in its statuesque grandeur, expression, colour and vocal dignity. Berlioz wrote at length about Rameau's *Castor et Pollux* but whereas the modern listener readily perceives common ground with Berlioz's music, he himself was more conscious of the gap that separated them. The close affinity between Rameau and Berlioz is most clearly embodied in the work of Gluck, who, though not a Frenchman by birth, combined classical dramatic values with a feeling for intense musical expression, especially in *Orfeo* (1762), *Iphigénie en Aulide* (1774) and *Iphigénie en Tauride* (1779). Berlioz adored Gluck all his life and lovingly revived his operas; though he came to know and admire Mozart, he would never acknowledge him as Gluck's equal as a dramatist. Gluck's gift for unadorned melody and simple unaffected accompaniment made a deep impression on him, and he devoted numerous articles to his music. Many of them were collected in *A travers chants*, but many more were not reprinted, stretching from his first encounter with Gluck in 1821 to the revival of *Alceste* in 1866. Many examples of Gluck's expressive orchestration are given in the *Traité*. There was a fundamental affinity between the two composers, for although Gluck did not equal Berlioz's range or vitality, they both believed in the supremacy of dramatic expression. Berlioz did not, it should be said, accept Gluck's apparent subjection of music to poetry (promulgated in the famous preface to *Alceste*), and in a crucial letter written as he embarked on the composition of *Les Troyens*, he stated his position thus:

> The hardest task is to find the musical *form*, this form without which music does not exist, or is only the craven servant of speech. That is Wagner's crime; he would like to dethrone music and reduce it to 'expressive accents', exaggerating the system of Gluck, who, fortunately, did not succeed in carrying out his ungodly theory. I am in favour of the kind of music you call *free*. Yes, free and proud and sovereign and triumphant, I want it to grasp and assimilate everything, and have no Alps nor Pyrenees to block its way; but to make conquests music must fight in person, and not merely by its lieutenants; I should like music if possible to have free verses ranged in battle order, but it must itself lead the attack like Napoleon, it must march in the front rank of the phalanx like Alexander.[1]

Gluck's mantle fell upon Spontini (1774–1851) who perhaps stood second after Gluck in Berlioz's pantheon. Berlioz knew Spontini personally, won his praise, and drew from his music all kinds of mannerisms which we would acknowledge more freely if Spontini's three great operas *La vestale* (1807), *Fernand Cortez* (1809) and *Olympie* (1819) were more than occasionally revived today. Spontini's dramatic recitative affected Berlioz strongly, as can be seen from the second of these two brief passages from *La vestale*, with a premonition of one of Cassandra's themes, Ex. 43a (p. 162) (Ex. 55a and b). Spontini's bold expressive orchestration also impressed the young Berlioz, indeed the whole school of French opera which grew out of the Revolution developed the resources of old and new instruments. Both in orchestration and dramatic style the opéra-comique of Cherubini and Méhul, as unfamiliar today as Spontini's music, cut new paths in European music, becoming swiftly popular in Germany. Both composers can be said to live more vividly today in their disciples, Beethoven and Berlioz, than by their own lights. Méhul's

Ex. 55

(a)

(b)

style is especially prophetic of early Berlioz, energetic in movement and stark in harmonic style; he was also, like Berlioz, a great orchestral innovator, using new combinations of instruments in the opera house, and he also contributed to the patriotic repertory of hymns and marches which celebrated the Revolution. These pieces were broad and popular in style and many were scored for massed forces of wind and percussion for open-air ceremonies and processions. Both the *Requiem* and the *Te deum* hark back to this tradition and the *Grande symphonie funèbre et triomphale* belongs wholly to it, bearing an uncanny resemblance, in its first movement, to Gossec's sombre *Marche lugubre* of 1790. A link with French revolutionary opera is apparent also in the impulsive dynamics and surging phrases found in much of Berlioz's early music (see Exx. 5, 9 and 11 on pp. 82, 91 and 94, for instance), although it has an intensity not found elsewhere.

Melodies from opéras-comiques by Dalayrac, Boieldieu and others reached Berlioz before he left La Côte. In Paris it was the current operatic repertory that widened his conception of style, especially Gluck. He also picked up ideas from Berton's *Virginie* of 1823, though his opinion of Berton was low. Rossini in Berlioz's view discredited Italian opera for his slavish bowing to vocal display, noisy orchestration and empty melody, though for his handling of large choral scenes in *Moïse* (1827) and *William Tell* (1829) he won his admiration. The mass suicide of women in *Le siège de Corinthe* (1826) may even have suggested the similar scene in Act II of *Les Troyens*.[2]

In addition Berlioz paid both his teachers, Lesueur and Reicha, the tribute of imitation. Lesueur's style was too unsophisticated to appeal strongly to Berlioz, but his doggedly experimental outlook and his preoccupation with the significance and meaning of everything he wrote stirred his pupil as much as the warmth of his personality. He was a careful and highly imaginative orchestrator. His habit of footnoting and annotating his scores reappears as Latin quotations from Virgil strewn over the last few acts of *Les Troyens*. His church music and biblical oratorios are certainly to be seen as godparents of *L'enfance du Christ*. The visionary grandeur of his two largest operas, *Ossian* (1804) and *La mort d'Adam* (1809) impressed Berlioz, even though they had long since passed out of the repertory. Reicha, unlike Lesueur, was a stranger to the French tradition, and concerned himself with instrumental media such as chamber music which Berlioz never cared for. But in his attitude to fugue at least Reicha's teaching rubbed off. In his *36 Fugues* (1803) Reicha displayed a wildly unconventional fugal technique, experimenting with chromatic entries, modulating stretti and a bewildering array of unorthodox procedures. When Berlioz does a similar thing in the *Judex crederis* of the *Te deum* and in 'Châtiment effroyable' in *Les Troyens*, Reicha's spirit shines through.

Two German composers, Weber and Beethoven, greatly enriched the brew. *Der Freischütz*, played in Paris in 1824, left its mark in *Les francs-juges*, both in dramatic and orchestral colour, and the Wolf's Glen scene closely influenced the *Course à l'abyme* in *La damnation de Faust* as well as the *Chasse royale et orage* in *Les Troyens* (another Reicha-influenced unconventional fugue, in its opening bars). The subtle scoring of *Oberon* was well appreciated by Berlioz, too. Beethoven's shadow over Berlioz was as considerable as over any of the Germans, Schumann, Brahms or Wagner, but it took a different course. Primarily it opened Berlioz's mind to the dramatic force of instrumental music and the possibilities of dramatic expression outside the theatre. But in details of style too we find many echoes of Beethoven in Berlioz's work. The *Eroica* and the Fifth Symphony both left a deep impression. The broken ending of *La captive* seems to come from the *Eroica*, the Fourth Symphony and *Coriolan*; the *Marche des pèlerins* in *Harold* echoes the Seventh Symphony, *Villanelle* the Eighth; and the *Pastoral* pictured real scenes in the eyes of a committed observer as Berlioz was frequently to do, especially in his first two symphonies. *Roméo et Juliette* is, partly, Berlioz's tribute to the Ninth with clear reference to the finale of the Eighth in the *Fête*.

Beethoven and Weber were the last composers to exercise any profound influence on Berlioz. He heard all the new music played in Paris but he very rarely adopted anything from his contemporaries. A debt to the grand style of Rossini and Meyerbeer must be acknowledged in the close of *Roméo et Juliette*, with its palpitating 9/8 pulse (in turn to influence *Tannhäuser*) and perhaps in Acts I and III of *Les Troyens*, but the Scribe dramaturgy in historical drama repelled him and his own inventiveness with new instruments was at least as advanced as theirs. He did not observe any special genius in Verdi, supposing him to be too enmeshed in the bad old Italian habits and too fond of historical drama, although for his personal qualities and his defiance of bureaucratic obstruction Verdi won Berlioz's admiration. Berlioz took no notice of Chopin's or Alkan's piano music; he admired Liszt and worked closely with him but never copied his style and in the end rejected it. Of Mendelssohn he admired most of the *Erste Walpurgisnacht* and conducted the Italian Symphony once in London. He seems to have known very little by Schubert or Schumann and never sought to learn more. Of Wagner's music he was unable to share its composer's view that it was the greatest since Beethoven, and though he would have liked to admire Wagner there were too many personal obstacles and too many differences in outlook and temperament. Wagner was essentially part of a younger generation whose ideas could only lead to the destruction of Berlioz's sacred notions of art, as they indeed did, and where Berlioz refused to follow. In sum Berlioz was simply not curious about contemporary developments in music, never sought to develop a school and never took pupils. Composition was for him too personal a matter to be transmitted except by deep instinct and intuitive love, the feeling he had always had towards Gluck.

For historical music, then being ardently revived by Fétis and others, he was largely contemptuous. He ridiculed the little Palestrina, Purcell and Handel he knew and was impatient with Bach. It is true that Palestrina, Allegri, Clari or Lully sometimes appeared in his concert programmes, but this was generally for his audiences' or singers' benefit. We are familiar with critics who have little appetite for music, old or new, yet he was strong enough in his genuine enthusiasms and discerning enough in his judgment of singers and performers to keep the reader delightedly on edge in all his *feuilletons*, humorous and passionate at the same time. Furthermore, although little modern music affected his own, he was often able to express his genuine admiration for it as a critic.

In Berlioz's style the traditional elements of melody, harmony, rhythm, counterpoint and form have distinctive features which we must observe at the heart of his music. First, melody: early debates about Berlioz's worth centred largely on the ridiculous question of whether his music had melody or not, and most Frenchmen were of the opinion that it did not. By the standards of Italian opera, *Hymns Ancient and Modern* or German folksong perhaps that is so, but by its own standards it is abundantly and unmistakably melodic. The vocal line or the top line is first in Berlioz's mind, as his sketches show, and it is designed to match the words or the expression. His melodies are not always regular, nor are they always irregular; usually they make play with regular phrases by curtailing and extending them or by filling out the gaps between phrases. The melody of *Villanelle*, for example, would mostly fall into four-bar units if the accompaniment did not keep subtly pressing the melody into more elongated shapes. Some early melodies are regular and balanced to the point of squareness, and these include the second subject of the *Francs-juges* overture (see Ex. 1, p. 3) and the recurrent theme of *Harold en Italie*. All Berlioz melodies repay analysis and study; here we can single out only two, one to a Latin text, from the *Te deum*, and one to a text of his own, from *Les Troyens*.

In the *Te ergo quaesumus* in the *Te Deum* we have an example of a melody which Berlioz seems to have written without words in mind, since it is played over first on the strings and then constrained to fit the words:

Ex. 56 a and b

(a)

(b)

Te er-go quae-su-mus, te quae-su-mus Do-mi-ne, fa-mu-lis___ tu - is

sub - ve - ni. quos_ pre - ti - o - so___ san-gui-ne re - de - mis - ti.

While the first phrase falls naturally over four bars the second does
not, preferring three-plus-five, if division is possible at all. His capacity for drawing further phrases out of an original simple phrase is
here well exemplified (and the bass line draws on the same figure
too). We should note the surprise F natural in bar 10, contradicting
the F sharp that precedes and follows it in a characteristically way-
ward fashion.

Later on the same melodic idea is applied to new words and the
span of the phrase is effortlessly reduced from twelve bars to eleven
without losing any of the music's natural flow:

Ex. 57

Fi - at su - per nos, su - per nos Do-mi-ne, mi - se - ri - cor - di - a tu - a

Do - mi-ne, quem ad-mo-dum spe - ra-vi-mus in te.

It is revealing, in this context, to study how the principal theme
of the *Marche des pèlerins* in *Harold en Italie* is treated to a process
of melodic variation so that each phrase reaches up to a higher note

of the scale, no two phrases being the same.

The length of Berlioz's melodies has often rightly been remarked upon. The opening theme of the *Grande symphonie funèbre et triomphale* is a splendid example, so too is the full *idée fixe* in the *Symphonie fantastique*. Very often a theme is not so much long as continually expanding to fill an entire scene or movement. The later music is particularly rich in these self-generating melodic spans, of which a good example is the passage in Act III of *Les Troyens* when Aeneas bids farewell to his son Ascanius before setting off to defend Carthage against the Numidians. There is no question of development since the scene is brief and self-contained. In a single span, with the resources of line, harmony, colour and rhymed verse, Berlioz creates one of the most moving and momentous episodes in the whole opera:

Ex. 58

Even without showing the harmony and orchestration, the strength of such a line is evident. Everything is simple, nothing is wasted, and the climax of 'gloire' is seemingly hewn out of granite, so overpowering is its solidity and strength. It is perhaps in melodies such as this, and in his melodic style in general, that Berlioz was least dependent on any music he ever heard or studied. Many other cases where long melodies have been built up in this way have already been noted in these pages.

Touches of chromaticism abound, usually for expressive effect, as in Ex. 56. Many of his lines fall chromatically from the fifth of the scale, such as the *Fête* music in *Roméo et Juliette*; many exploit the flattened sixth of the scale, with special poignancy in the major mode. Consider the bare viola line at the opening of *La damnation de Faust* and its haunting, expressive B flat in the tonality of D major:

Ex. 59

Other examples are found in Exx. 3 and 24 above (pp. 78 and 123). For major and minor sixths in alternation consider the solo horn at the end of the *Méditation religieuse*, or the second half of the *idée fixe* in the *Symphonie fantastique*. Chromaticism in Berlioz's line is as often for expression as for modulation.

The technique of transformation of themes, generally credited to Liszt for its main exploitation, in reality belongs already to Beethoven and Berlioz and indeed has ancient roots. In Berlioz we can see it used in pioneering fashion with the various apparitions of the *idée fixe*, in *La damnation de Faust* (when Mephistopheles's *Sérénade* is prefigured by the 'follets' on cavorting piccolos), in *Les Troyens* (when Narbal's solemn *Air* in Act IV appears first in confident strains as the first music of the act), at the opening of *L'arrivée à Saïs* and in many places where the observant ear will readily pick it up. A melody could have as many shapes as it could have characters and its musical elasticity provided a resource which even Berlioz did not fully draw upon.

In modality, which appears in pieces of naive or rustic character, Berlioz found a suggestion of charming old-world churchiness, not a direct ear to the soul of the people, as Bartók would have regarded it. In *La fuite en Égypte* he drew careful attention to his melodic flattened seventh, insisting that it is not an error. The Nubian slaves, in *Les Troyens*, chant on a curious modal scale; so, too, do the Trojan women in Act II (G to G in A flat major). But whereas the first is exotic, the second is intensely expressive and melancholy. So too is *Le roi de Thulé*, with its sharpened fourth.

Berlioz's harmony, like his melody, can only be imperfectly summed up in a short space, but its principal characteristics are clear: he was not an innovator in the vocabulary of harmonic combinations, and did not seek new chords and modulations from extended chromatic chords; he was not wedded to the four-part style seen most clearly in Spohr, Schumann and Wagner, not did he use the power of functional diatonic harmony in the manner of Chopin, Wagner and Brahms. Instead he was content with the basic vocabulary of Beethoven and Weber, and attributed a much looser obligation to individual chords than they or any others of his predecessors. Consider Ex. 8 (p. 88) for a surprisingly loose succession of chromatic harmonies. No chord in Berlioz inescapably determines the next one, even though for the most part the flow of his harmony is smooth and predictable enough. Ex. 30 (p. 133) might be taken as a good example of the smoothest harmonic style. When his harmony surprises us it does so by picking on the dark horse in the harmony, the note that does not obviously contain a modulating message. The fifth bar of Ex. 38 (p. 150) will serve as a good example, where the B sharp descends to B natural when all the harmonic implications are drawing it upwards to C sharp. Diminished sevenths, of which he was fond, here and elsewhere keep the listener guessing by offering four such alternative resolutions of which none is intrinsically more probable than any other.

As a full example of harmonic practice we may take the passage of recitative which follows the *Chant de la fête de Pâques* in Part II of *La damnation de Faust*. Faust breathes again after stepping close to the abyss of death and his mind can hardly yet be reconciled to the norms of life. Hence the fluidity of the harmony:

Ex. 60

There is much here to observe. The diminished sevenths are prominent (marked *x*) and they resolve in many different ways, if they
resolve at all. At *y* Berlioz doubles upper and lower notes of the
harmony in a way the textbooks forbid, though its use here seems
effective enough, and at the second *y* the F major chord is curiously

anticipated, weakening its actual arrival. Notice the falling chromatic line from the fifth of the scale at *z* and notice also the repose generated at that point by the music's unequivocal arrival in a settled tonic, that of F major. It is, of course, rudely shattered by the arrival of Mephistopheles at the next moment.

Berlioz's later music derives great harmonic subtlety from sevenths other than the simple dominants and diminisheds; one such chord is shown following a dominant seventh in Ex. 31 (p. 134). With his polarization of top and bottom lines, as melodically shaped as possible, harmony filling the space between, and chromatic notes always interjected, his later style is marvellously refined. The intimate scenes towards the end of *Les Troyens* provide numerous examples of this style, especially the *Quintette* and *Duo* in Act IV and Dido's farewell in Act V.

He liked to group the notes of a harmony high, isolating the bass line, and though he professed a distaste for enharmonic change he used it frequently, as for example in Exx. 38 and 60 (pp. 150 and 193). He disliked appoggiaturas which distort the melodic line, singling out the second theme of Hérold's *Zampa* overture for criticism; it was a predominantly Italian habit (a good example is found in Maddalena's line in the Quartet from *Rigoletto*) and avoidable for that reason. When he found Wagner vastly intensifying the force of appoggiaturas in the Prelude to *Tristan und Isolde* he was enraged, even though, perhaps because, all advanced harmony of the nineteenth century stemmed from just that kind of distortion of the inherited language. Yet Berlioz was none the less capable of complex modern harmony and we should note its occurrence. The final cadence of the *Chant de la fête de Pâques*, in *La damnation de Faust*, has a beautifully dense seven-part cadence:

Ex. 61

Similarly elegant is the seven-part writing of 'Tous pour goûter la vie' in the *Chœur de sylphes* a little later in the same work (Ex. 33, p. 139). There are bold sounds from Pantheus and his men when they storm in in Act V of *Les Troyens* (Ex. 49, p. 171) and some resonant clashes in the *Grande symphonie funèbre et triomphale* (Ex. 23, p. 122). One of the finest passages of all is the close of the *Hamlet* march, where after an overpowering climax the emptiness is broken by loose threads which gather themselves into a rich chromatic cadence:

Ex. 62

This is followed by the desolate close given above as Ex. 29 (p. 132).

A characteristic element of Berlioz's style is his fondness for harmonic variation, presenting a melody with new harmony on each appearance. *Villanelle*, in *Les nuits d'été*, does this, with orchestration also varied in each verse. The best example is the *Tibi omnes* in the *Te deum* where the three verses are sung respectively by the sopranos, tenors and basses with the accompaniment and harmony appropriately renewed in each verse. Furthermore the opening three-bar phrase is stated three times in each verse, reharmonized each time, giving a total of nine different harmonizations of the same four bars, a *tour de force* of harmonic inventiveness.

In rhythm Berlioz regarded himself, rightly, as an innovator, and he deplored the lack of a rhythm class at the Paris Conservatoire to provide for the study of metre, bar-subdivisions and rhythmic combinations. The predominant metre of the age was triple, with 9/8 and 12/8 being universally adopted for music of sentiment or solemnity, and the tendency in Meyerbeer and Wagner was to slow the pace. Berlioz did not escape the epidemic of triplets, using 9/8 and 12/8 for some grand scenes and often 3/4 for tenderness, but he resisted the growing fashion for rubato and loose pulse, and also the pervasive broadening of pace. His early music is, on the contrary, given to bouts of frantic speed and activity, as in *Le roi Lear* or the finale of the *Symphonie fantastique*. The carnival in *Benvenuto Cellini* and the Reine Mab scherzo of *Roméo et Juliette* have the speed of a cheetah. An obsessive preoccupation with rhythm is evident in the 1830s, particularly in *Harold en Italie* and *Benvenuto Cellini*, both of which make endless play of cross-rhythms, contrary rhythms and unusual time-signatures, taken to an alarming degree in the first drafts of Fieramosca's *Air* (in *Cellini*) and still provocative in the published version. The 7/4 cabalistic dance in *L'enfance du Christ* and the 5/8 *Combat de ceste* in *Les Troyens* are further examples. The three-layered superimposition of rhythms in the third movement of *Harold en Italie* is most poetic in its effect (see Ex. 15, p. 102), borrowed, as we noted before, from *Don Giovanni*.

This passage combines themes as well as rhythms in a fashion of which Berlioz was inordinately fond. Sometimes he was so proud of combining two themes that the words 'Réunion des deux thèmes' appear in the score. The most conspicuous other examples are found in the finale of the *Symphonie fantastique*, where the *Dies irae* combines with the main theme of the *ronde*, in the overture to *Benvenuto Cellini*, in the *Fête chez Capulet* in *Roméo et Juliette*, and in the scene for Anna and Narbal in Act IV of *Les Troyens*. The chorus of soldiers and students in Part II of *La damnation de Faust* is brilliantly effective, for the two groups are singing in different languages, metres and keys, finally climaxing in D flat, well away from the home key of either. In the carnival scene in *Benvenuto Cellini* three different layers of music are combined, the respective entry music of Balducci, Teresa, then Cellini with Ascanio, each heard as distinct and separate and then combined with choral elaboration.

This kind of contrapuntal technique Berlioz relished, for it also bore out his faith in the combination of opposites and the juxtaposition of deliberately different materials. For traditional contrapuntal skill he had only one use and that was to pour scorn on the technique of strict fugue. The Amen Chorus in *La damnation de Faust* is a parody choral fugue in which the most meaningless word in the dictionary is set to the most intricate music. It is difficult to judge whether Berlioz was trying to write a good or a bad piece of music, and the performance of it remains a challenging puzzle. The same applies to Somarone's ponderous *Epithalame grotesque* in *Béatrice et Bénédict*, a truly dreadful piece of music for which Berlioz hoped we would share his derision.

The unconventional fugues in the *Te deum* and *Les Troyens* derived from Reicha's teaching have already been mentioned. Techniques such as canon and inversion are occasionally to be found – the principal theme of the *Corsaire* overture is splendidly inverted at one point (see Ex. 27, p. 131) – but he greatly preferred the looser style of imitative writing in free fugato, a texture which he used frequently for atmospheric effect. The openings of *Harold en Italie*, *Roméo et Juliette* and both Parts I and II of *La damnation de Faust* are all of this type. The *Requiem* and the *Te deum* both contain more conventional choral counterpoint, and in *L'enfance du Christ* contrapuntal writing is pervasive throughout, culminating in the disarming skill of 'O mon âme' at the close, an exceptionally beautiful passage where simplicity and high technique join hands. In general his feeling for counterpoint is to be observed in the frequent polarization of upper and lower parts into separate expressive strands. His unusual progressions are often the result of thus treating the bass as a line, melodic in its own right, harnessed to the melody and moving by step wherever possible.

Berlioz's forms are much more elusive. Until recently, when the lost guitar studies of 1828 turned out, even though still lost, to be a set of variations on Mozart's 'Là ci darem la mano', it would have been reasonable to suggest that variations for their own sake played no part in his world. He would never write a sonata or an untitled symphony, relying always on the text or the poetic idea of a piece to provide him with its mood or shape. But clearly this is not enough, since the music always has its overwhelming demands of tonality and architecture which no nineteenth-century composer could gainsay. His music therefore does recapitulate, it does develop freely, it does rely on thematic reference and it does return to its tonal starting-point, but it does not employ the dominant or the relative key as a natural pole to the tonic, it does not give any special place to a subsidiary theme, and it does not obey any preconceived notion of formal balance, his codas often being abnormally long in instrumental movements. Two movements in *Les Troyens* do not even return to the tonic; the three movements of the *Symphonie funèbre et triomphale* are in three different keys; and *Sur les lagunes* (in *Les nuits d'été*) ends on the dominant. There are no large-scale tonal schemes in the operas, choral works, or miscellanies. Keys like D flat and G flat are used for colour, not for formal balance. Themes that are intended to be distinct are clearly contrasted, not secretly resemblant. To attach any importance to the structure of his music, therefore, without reference to its meaning and expression, is fallacious. He is as effective in music of very loose structural outline, such as the *Chasse royale et orage* in *Les Troyens* or the *Ronde du sabbat* in the *Symphonie fantastique*, as in the stricter framework of his overtures where he is generally prepared to approach nearer to the norm of instrumental sonata form. Something has already been said about individual works in this connection, enough perhaps to provide a warning that Berlioz presents a gruesome trap for unwary formalists who seek to explain too much.

Before considering his orchestral technique, we must note that his choral writing belongs to the French tradition, to the exasperation of British and German choral societies, in having a three-part basis of sopranos, tenors and basses, each divisible into two to make a six-part chorus where necessary. The French prefer to make greater demands on their tenors than to recognize the contralto voice, and only in his late music did Berlioz accept the four-part chorus. This change, which can be seen by comparing the three- or six-part textures of Exx. 4, 13, and 33 (pp. 79, 98 and 139) with the four-part writing of Ex. 38 (p. 150), probably came about as a result of his increasing experience with German and English choruses. His preferred solo voice was the mezzo-soprano, partly because he hated high coloratura, partly because it carried the seriousness that roles like Mary, Cassandra, Dido and Beatrice demand. Teresa is the only substantial role for soprano. His heroes were tenors and his villains basses, according to convention, the tenors being required to reach high C sharp on several occasions.

In his orchestration and sense of colour we have a much clearer view of his mastery than in his form, and he was proud of the expressive resource he had revealed in the modern orchestra. It was not wholly intuitive, for he saw instrumentation as a technique to be learned by the patient study of scores and by close understanding of how individual instruments sound and work. As a student he most prized his free pass to the Opéra for the chance to study what went on in the pit. His *Grand traité d'instrumentation*, of 1843, was the fruit of these labours, and though it offers insight into his attitudes and methods it leaves a great deal unsaid about his own orchestral practice. It does at least make plain his deep belief in the expressive function of orchestral colour and in the composer's obligation to match sonority to the music's purpose.

His own prowess on guitar and flute was probably of acceptable competence, but his lack of piano technique freed his mind from the tyranny of pianistic orchestration. His songs were written with piano accompaniment, but the best were all orchestrated later. His piano writing is neither awkward nor idiomatic, mostly neutral, and he made the piano reductions of his operas with considerable skill. The *Elégie* is the one case where his piano writing has been found inadequate for the conception of the music, and in this case there is alas no orchestral arrangement.

His sound is distinctive for the clarity of the wind writing, the sombre brilliance of the brass, and the original use of percussion. His string writing was not particularly adventurous except in using pizzicato and harmonics for special effects. The multiple divisi of *Lélio* was also an effective stroke; the divided double-bass chords in the *Symphonie fantastique* are more of an *idea* than an *effect*. The rolling pizzicatos of Mephistopheles's *Sérénade* (in its orchestral version) magnificently suggest a diabolic guitar, although on closer inspection the distribution of arpeggios in the second violins and violas is clumsy and impractical. Of all the strings he did most for the emancipation of the viola as a solo instrument. He liked to group the wind in a section, often in busy repeated chords as at the opening of *Villanelle* or Act I of *Les Troyens*; wind solos, like the oboe in *Le roi Lear* or the clarinet in Andromache's scene in *Les Troyens* are relatively rare, two or more instruments in combination, such as flute and clarinet an octave apart, being preferred. Piccolos have important parts in Satanic music (*Les francs-juges*, *La damnation de Faust*) and the cor anglais in music of resignation and sadness (Marguerite's *Romance*). The bass clarinet in *Benvenuto Cellini* was a brand new instrument, only used before in Meyerbeer's *Les Huguenots*; in *Les Troyens* (Dido's farewell) it sounds with the sadness of centuries. The contrabassoon makes rare appearances in *Les francs-juges* and the *Symphonie funèbre et triomphale*. His normal complement of bassoons, following French practice, is four, even when only two parts are given, though allowance should be made for the much weaker instruments of the time.

In the brass Berlioz welcomed the introduction of valve mechanisms even though he had devised a sophisticated technique, following Méhul, writing for four horns in as many as four different keys – a score-reader's nightmare. Only his late works use valve horns, but valve trumpets and cornets are found from the start, usually a pair of valved cornets alongside a pair of natural trumpets. He distrusted the vulgarity of the cornet, even though obbligato cornet solos were composed for *Les francs-juges* overture and *Un bal* in the *Symphonie fantastique*, probably for particular occasions. The trombone writing of Berlioz's later music is masterly in its controlled power, especially in *piano* entries. He had always used trombones for brilliance and force, as in *Le carnaval romain*, but he came later to explore their solemnity, as when Priam blesses Astyanax in *Les Troyens*. They give convincing profundity to Mephistopheles's 'Voici des roses', with assistance from one cornet. His bass brass instrument was the ophicleide, a French invention from the revolutionary period, combining woodwind fingering with brass embouchure. Its solo sound he used only in parody, in the *Dies irae* of the *Symphonie fantastique*, and to lampoon Balducci's awful taste in *Benvenuto Cellini*. But it was an essential member of the brass tutti and held its own in French orchestras against the incursion of the tuba from Germany, an instrument which Berlioz welcomed but used only alongside the ophicleide, not in its stead.

The harp was exclusively domestic or operatic before Berlioz brought it into the symphony, for *Un bal*. Even thereafter it was always used for pictorial and evocative purposes, for heaven, obviously, at the end of *La damnation de Faust*, for Lélio's Aeolian Harp, or for the Ishmaelites' house-music. Eight harps thrum the Trojans into the city, twelve harps parade the colour at the end of the *Te deum* – a glorious sound, as no one who has heard it can deny. Berlioz's orchestra also admitted the piano, four-hands, for the ethereal spirits of the *Tempête* music in *Lélio*, and in both *Benvenuto Cellini* and *Béatrice et Bénédict* he employed the guitar in strumming rhythm to evoke Italian sailors or Sicilian drinkers.

In the percussion section he extended the numbers of timpani to four in the *Symphonie fantastique*, and to sixteen in the *Requiem*, and specified the different types of sticks he required. He used reconstructions of ancient instruments for archaic effect. The little tuned cymbals used in *Roméo et Juliette* and *Les Troyens* he found in the museum at Pompeii, and the tarbuka and sistrum (in *Les Troyens*) were more fanciful. He has bells tolling in his *Ronde du sabbat*, a 'pavillon chinois' or 'Turkish crescent' in his military music, and a volley of musketry in the *Hamlet* march. The more regular percussion instruments, bass drum, cymbals, side drum and triangle, he used with great reserve and skill since he hated their over-use in operatic scoring and condemned it incessantly. The soft whoosh of cymbals and bass drum is wonderfully effective for the entries of the Pope and of Priam, solemnity made audible.

This is one case where Berlioz's command of expressive pianissimo is at least as striking as his fortissimo. His biggest climaxes, in the *Requiem* and the *Te deum* are shattering in their power and he knew well how to make an orchestra blaze with sound, as the caricaturists of his day were delighted to find. But he must be credited for extending dynamic range in both directions, to the soft as well as to the loud, to the fast as well as to the slow, to the high as well as to the low. The delicacy of the *Ballet de sylphes* corresponds to the elephantine grumbling of Narbal; the weight of the *Symphonie funèbre et triomphale* is off-set by the *Reine Mab* scherzo. 'Vulgar prejudice', he wrote, 'considers large orchestras *noisy*; if they are well constituted, well rehearsed, and well conducted, and if they play real music, the correct term is *powerful*. No two expressions are more dissimilar in meaning than these.'[3] He cared above all for the proper matching of music to its space as well as to its subject. He hated large orchestras in small theatres or tiny choirs in huge cathedrals. The building must serve the sonority, the forces must match the acoustics. In addition he specified the layout of his players and singers with great precision. His fondness for off-stage effects has been mentioned already; they are found not just in the operas but also in the *Scène aux champs*, in the finale of *Harold en Italie*, in *L'enfance du Christ* for the angels at the end of Part I, and in *Lélio*, the greater part of which is played behind a curtain. The foreword to *Roméo et Juliette* gives detailed instructions for the placing of the different groups of singers; the percussion in the *Symphonie funèbre et triomphale* is divided into two groups, left and right. This is not just the conductor in Berlioz speaking, it is the composer closely concerned with the actuality and presence of his music.

We must conclude with the centrepiece of Berlioz's artistic belief to which much reference has already been made: the notion of expression. It is a natural attitude for a literary musician to believe in the expressive power of music, especially in a country with such acute literary awareness as France where abstraction has always been regarded with suspicion. For Berlioz it was axiomatic that music had to express its subject. Strong subjects required strong music, restrained subjects required restrained music, and although the emotional meaning of the subject was expressed in the music, the music was not in itself expected to identify that subject. For that purpose a title or a programme was necessary and normally provided. At the same time the thrifty composer could frequently borrow his own music for more than one piece since there was much common ground between Juliet, Cleopatra and Hamlet, for example; Napoleonic material could be used for a *Te deum*; integrity of expression was not thereby broken. Musical expression was obviously applied to vocal music, but in instrumental music which carried only mime (as the *Chasse royale et orage*) or a title (the *Scène d'amour* from *Roméo et Juliette*), Berlioz found the expression could be all the more powerful since the imagination was free to respond. Expression included literal illustration, such as shepherds' pipes, the flapping wings of giant birds, a snore even, but it was primarily devoted to feeling, to the communication of the artist's feeling to the listener's feeling. Berlioz was unaware of any aesthetic problem in this; he had no wish to win the souls of those who had no feeling. As Lélio says: 'my advice would be useless for those who have any feeling and even more useless for those who have none.'

Yet feeling did not preclude technique, as many of his critics have imagined. Berlioz understood full well the role of technique in an artist's make-up and laboured to master it. His genius resides in his ample provision of both technique and feeling in felicitous balance and in the power of his musical invention. As much as any composer he has the capacity to surprise his listeners by the inventive force of his music and by the conviction of his utterance.

He was fond of misquoting *Macbeth*: 'Fair is not foul, foul is not fair', since good and bad art were absolutes which any sensitive person could recognize. One of the most pertinent passages in all his work is the scene in *Benvenuto Cellini* where Harlequin and Pasquarello perform their pieces to Balducci. It is a comic scene but it carries the deepest message. Harlequin's song is the soul of beauty, Pasquarello's (an ophicleide solo) the epitome of ugliness. Anyone in doubt about Berlioz's values might do well to begin here. If, like Balducci, they are bored by Harlequin and dazzled by Pasquarello, they should abandon hope of ever entering Berlioz's world.

Berlioz's reputation was so widely contested in the hundred years after his death that in most main lines of historical development his influence was of little or no moment. His works were only fragmentarily known, besides. Not until the 1880s did Paris respond with any fervour to their leading composer of the century, when *La damnation de Faust* was discovered anew. It became positively popular and has always remained so. The *Symphonie fantastique* and the overtures were always well loved, but only in the last twenty years has his music been cultivated with any true familiarity, especially in English-speaking countries. After the rapture of Berlioz's own visits the Germans have been guarded in their enthusiasm, while the French have persisted in a narrow choice of listening, preferring the image of a literary and artistic figure to that of a musician. Admiring Berlioz was for many years a mark of pioneering devotion, if not of eccentricity, and the virus of error and innuendo spread unchecked. Great labours by the French scholars Boschot, Tiersot and Prod'homme at the turn of the century did much to make literary and biographical material available but little to foster performance of his music, so that it was not until the 1950s that Barzun's comprehensive biographical study, the advent of long-playing records and the rediscovery of *Les Troyens* a hundred years after it was composed combined to ferment the wider dissemination given long before to many lesser figures but until that time denied to Berlioz. With long-term projects for the scholarly republication of his music (the *New Berlioz Edition*) and his letters (the *Correspondance générale*) in course, we come steadily nearer to a closer understanding of the man and his work. Yet at the same time his era recedes and the values which were taken for granted in the romantic period become ever more remote from our own: the task of exposition and understanding has to be constantly reanimated. The single great gap in our knowledge of Berlioz remains the huge corpus of critical writing in the *feuilletons*, of which only a fraction has been reprinted in his own anthologies and in modern publications. The great wealth of these articles, whatever their subject, is known only by very few.

Pleading Berlioz's cause is still necessary in certain quarters, but the wider battle is won, and it is correspondingly difficult to comprehend the curious place he occupies in nineteenth-century music. Although his inheritance, as we have seen, was predominantly French in origin, the tradition did not pass through him to the next generation. He might never have lived for all the direct influence he had on Gounod, Thomas, Bizet and Massenet, and both Debussy and Ravel rejected his music on technical grounds. His direct influence is to be seen only in minor composers like Félicien David and Peter Cornelius, and in the early works of Saint-Saëns; their music can on rare occasions sound like his. His style was too personal to be easily imitated. In the long term the impression he made on Liszt and Wagner was the most far-reaching, for his ideas infuse theirs, for all their individuality, and passed on from them to the Russians and the Czechs, and to Strauss and Mahler, both of whom admired and conducted his music.

In the twentieth century Berlioz is a symbol as well as a composer, standing for the ideal of the romantic artist, an individualist who lived passionately in his music against daunting odds. Reality is never simple, so that the picture has to be modified in innumerable details before the lines and edges in it become sharp. When we look at it closely, he is not after all the romantic artist through and through since the overriding demands of his profession and the harsh necessity of creating living music put the utopianism of our imagined romantic artist far out of reach. He turned his back on many causes we suppose to be dear to romantic hearts and his music is simply too dissimilar from that of other composers of his generation to be held up as an ideal or as a type. He was, essentially, a unique individual who found his ideas miraculously in tune (for the most part) with those of his age and whose thought and works flow as a tributary into the main flood of the romantic movement.

Cornelius summed up Berlioz's character and achievement with extraordinary insight in 1855:

> The musicians of Weimar greet him as the master of modern orchestration, the heir of Beethoven, a polyphonist of infinite resource and a polyrhythmist of the highest quality. They admire him as a musician who follows Beethoven and Schubert in sucking the nectar of his compositions only from the noblest flowers, who can fashion original forms out of poetic ideas and can give poetic shape to well-known forms, who is inspired not simply by Palestrina, Bach, Gluck, Mozart and Beethoven, but also by Shakespeare, Goethe, Byron, Moore, Hugo and Scott. As a critic he dispenses both enthusiasm and scorn with the keenest pen. But they acclaim him most as the hero who, out of love of his art, has had the strength to endure discredit, hatred and calumny in his own country, who has never written a note that was not offered in homage to the ideal of beauty ever present before his eyes, who has made no concession

to fashion nor ever sought to capture public favour by sensation, who has never bowed to public taste to gratify his vanity, and who waits proudly on the heights for the day when the public will rise to meet and greet him there.[4]

Notes to the text

CG: Berlioz, *Correspondance générale* (Paris, 1972-)
Memoirs: The Memoirs of Berlioz, trans. David Cairns (London, rev. ed.
1974).

1: Life, 1803–1830

1 *Memoirs*, p. 40; ch. 2.
2 CG 3, 4.
3 CG vol. I, p. 34n.
4 *Memoirs*, p. 53; ch. 5.
5 *Memoirs*, p. 73; ch. 10.
6 CG 41.
7 CG 48.
8 CG 48.
9 *Memoirs*, p. 79; ch. 12.
10 CG 77.
11 *Memoirs*, p. 109; ch. 18.
12 *Memoirs*, p. 120; ch. 20.
13 *Les grotesques de la musique*, p. 242.
14 *Memoirs*, p. 147; ch. 26.
15 CG 99.
16 CG vol. I, p. 248n.
17 *Journal des débats*, 8th June 1855.
18 CG 111.
19 CG 155.
20 CG 158.

2: Life, 1830–1848

1 CG 217.
2 The work's title in 1831 was *Le retour à la vie – Mélologue*. Berlioz
usually referred to it as his *mélologue* (a term borrowed from Thomas
Moore). For publication in 1855 it was retitled *Lélio – Monodrame*.
Since it has universally been known as *Lélio* it would be pedantic to
give it its original title in references earlier than 1855.
   The name Lélio may have been suggested by George Sand's story
La Marquise (first published on the same day as the first performance of
Le retour à la vie) in which a leading character is called Lélio, a name
taken from Goldoni and Italian comedy. Sand's novel *Lélia* appeared in
1833. Berlioz may also have been struck by the name's similarity to his
own.
3 *Memoirs*, p. 209; ch. 37.
4 CG 303.

5   *Memoirs*, p. 270; ch. 45.
6   *Memoirs*, p. 293; ch. 48.
7   *Memoirs*, p. 303; ch. 49.
8   CG 816.
9   *Memoirs*, p. 425; Travels in Germany, I, 10th letter.
10 *Memoirs*, p. 435; ch. 53.
11 *Memoirs*, p. 437; ch. 53.
12 CG 875.
13 CG 910.
14 V.V. Stasov, *Selected Essays on Music*, translated by Florence Jonas, London 1968, p. 23.
15 CG 1106.
16 Ganz, however, says she came over with Davison in December and returned soon after to Paris. (A.W. Ganz, *Berlioz in London*, London 1950, p. 25.)
17 CG 1131.
18 CG 1197.
19 CG 1158.

3: Life, 1848–1869

1   CG 1277.
2   CG 1279.
3   CG 1360.
4   *Memoirs*, p. 574; ch. 59.
5   CG 1664.
6   A.W. Ganz, *Berlioz in London*, London 1950, p. 171.
7   CG 1756.
8   CG 1783.
9   Peter Cornelius, *Literarische Werke*, Leipzig 1905, i. p. 223.
10 CG 2264.
11 Letter to Adèle, June 1856. Charavay Catalogue 697 (June 1957).
12 CG 2281.
13 Pauline Viardot to Julius Rietz, 22nd September 1859. *Musical Quarterly*, 2 (January 1916), p. 43.
14 *Memoirs*, p. 611; Postface.
15 *Memoirs*, p. 612; Travels in Dauphiné.
16 Letter to Princess Sayn-Wittgenstein, 30th August 1864. *Briefe an die Fürstin Carolyne Sayn-Wittgenstein*, p. 143.
17 *Memoirs*, p. 616; Travels in Dauphiné.
18 Letter to Louis, 13th November 1865. *Correspondance inédite*, p. 327.

4: Berlioz's character

1   Cited by David Cairns in *Memoirs*, p. 640.

2 Letter to Marie d'Agoult, 20th November 1866. Bibliothèque nationale, Paris, n.a.fr. 25186/41–2.

5: Music, 1818–1830

1 CG 412.
2 *Memoirs* p. 110; ch. 18.
3 *Revue musicale*, 30th October 1830, pp. 367–9.

6: Music 1831–1841

1 CG 1510.
2 *Memoirs* p. 297; ch. 48.
3 The Covent Garden production of 1966 and the Philips recording made a partial reconstruction of the 1838 version, and in addition used dialogue in place of recitative.

7: Music 1841–1849

1 CG 1265.
2 See *New Berlioz Edition*, vol. 10, p. 194.

8: Music 1850–1869

1 *Les grotesques de la musique*, p. 186.
2 CG 2207.
3 CG 2258.
4 See *New Berlioz Edition*, vol. 2c, p. 836.
5 CG 2277.
6 'Ah! When the time comes for the final farewell,
   Moment bathed in anguish and tears,
   How shall I bear the dreadful sight
   Of that undeserved grief?

   To struggle against both myself and you, Dido!
   To beg your forgiveness as I break your heart!
   Will I have the strength to do it?'
7 *Memoirs*, p. 602; Postface.
8 Letter to Louis, 4th May 1861. *Correspondance inédite*, p. 281.
9 It could be easily reconstructed in its original one-act form.

9: Berlioz's style

1 CG 2163.
2 See Jeffrey Langford, 'Berlioz, Cassandra and, the French Operatic Tradition', *Music & Letters*, July 1981.
3 *Grand traité d'instrumentation*, Paris 1843, p. 289.
4 *Revue et gazette musicale*, 27 May 1855.

Appendix A

Calendar

Year	Age	Life	Contemporary Composers
1803		Louis-Hector Berlioz born 11 Dec. at La Côte-St-André, Département de l'Isère.	Adam born, 24 July; Auber aged 21; Beethoven 23; Bellini 2; Berton 36; Boccherini 60; Boïeldieu 27; Catel 30; Cherubini 43; Clementi 51; Dalayrac 50; Donizetti 6; Dussek 42; Field 21; Gossec 69; Grétry 62; Halévy 4; Haydn 71; Hummel 25; Lesueur 43; Lortzing 2; Marschner 8; Méhul 40; Meyerbeer 12; Paer 32; Paganini 21; Paisiello 62; Reicha 33; Rossini 11; Salieri 53; Schubert 6; Spohr 19; Spontini 29; Weber 17.
1804	0		Glinka born, 1 June.
1805	1		Boccherini (62) dies, 28 May.
1806	2	Nanci Berlioz born, 17 Feb.	
1809	5		Mendelssohn born, 3 Feb.; Haydn (77) dies, 31 May; Dalayrac (56) dies, 27 Nov.
1810	6		Chopin born, 22 Feb.; Félicien David born, 13 April; Schumann born, 8 June; Nicolai born, 9 June.
1811	7		Liszt born, 22 Oct.
1812	8		Dussek (51) dies, 20 March.
1813	9		Dargomyzhsky born, 14 Feb.; Wagner born, 22 May; Grétry (72) dies, 24 Sept.; Verdi born, 10 Oct.; Alkan born, 30 Nov.
1814	10	Adèle Berlioz born, 8 May.	
1815	11		Heller born, 15 May.
1816	12	Learns the flageolet; falls in love with Estelle.	Paisiello (75) dies, 5 June.

Year	Age	Life	Contemporary Composers
1817	13	Plays the flute; first compositions, including the *Potpourri* for six instruments. Imbert engaged as music teacher.	Gade born, 22 Feb; Méhul (54) dies, 18 Oct.
1818	14	Two quintets for flute and strings.	Gounod born, 17 June.
1819	15	Some romances and other works offered to Paris publishers; *Le dépit de la bergère* (probably) accepted. Dorant becomes his music teacher.	Offenbach born, 21 June.
1821	17	*Bachelier ès lettres*, Grenoble. Leaves for Paris, end of Oct., and enters medical school. First visits to the Opéra.	Weber's *Der Freischütz*, Berlin, 18 June.
1822	18	Various romances published. Returns to La Côte for a visit, Oct. Becomes a pupil of Lesueur. Frequents the Conservatoire library.	Raff born, 27 May; Franck born, 10 Dec.
1823	19	More romances published. A second return visit to La Côte, April. First article in the press, August. *Estelle et Némorin, Le passage de la mer rouge* composed.	Lalo born, 27 Jan.; Reyer born, 1 Dec. Beethoven's *Choral Symphony* completed. Weber's *Euryanthe*, Vienna, 25 Oct.
1824	20	*Beverley* composed. *Bachelier ès sciences physiques*. Third return visit to La Côte, June. *Mass* composed and rehearsed. *Der Freischütz* heard in Paris. Abandons medicine.	Smetana born, 2 March; Bruckner born, 4 Sept.; Cornelius born, 24 Dec.
1825	21	*Mass* successfully performed, July. Fourth return visit to La Côte, Oct. *Scène héroïque* composed.	Salieri (75) dies, 7 May; J. Strauss born, 25 Oct.
1826	22	Opera *Les francs-juges* composed. Eliminated from preliminary round of the Prix de Rome. Enrols at the Conservatoire in classes of Lesueur and Reicha.	Weber's *Oberon*, London, 12 April; Weber (39) dies, 5 June.
1827	23	Sings in the chorus of the Théâtre des Nouveautés. Composes	Beethoven (56) dies, 26 March.

Year	Age	Life	Contemporary Composers
		Waverley overture. Passes preliminary round of the Prix de Rome and sets cantata *La mort d'Orphée*. Sees *Hamlet* and *Romeo and Juliet* at the Odéon, with Harriet Smithson in both plays.	
1828	24	Beethoven's Third and Fifth symphonies played at the Conservatoire. Gives his first orchestral concert (26 May). Second attempt at Prix de Rome, with cantata *Herminie*. Discovers Goethe's *Faust*. Publishes guitar pieces. Visits La Côte, Sept. Begins *Huit scènes de Faust*.	Schubert (31) dies, 19 Nov.; Auber's *La muette de Portici*, Opéra, 29 Feb.
1829	25	*Huit scènes de Faust* published as op. 1. *Le ballet des ombres* published as op. 2. Third attempt at Prix de Rome, with cantata *Cléopâtre*. Second public concert, 1 Nov. *Neuf mélodies irlandaises* composed.	Gossec (95) dies, 16 Feb.; Rossini's *Guillaume Tell*, Opéra, 3 Aug.
1830	26	Attends Hugo's *Hernani*. Composes *Symphonie fantastique*, Feb.–April. Liaison with Camille Moke. Fourth attempt at Prix de Rome, with cantata *Sardanapale*, this time successful. Arranges the *Marseillaise*. Overture on *La tempête*. First performance of the *Symphonie fantastique*, 5 Dec. Meets Liszt.	Catel (57) dies, 29 Nov.
1831	27	Travels to Rome, via La Côte, Marseilles and Florence. On news of Camille Moke's engagement to Pleyel, returns via Florence to Nice. Composes *Le roi Lear* and *Rob Roy*. Returns to Rome. Composes *Le retour à la vie (Lélio)*. Visits Naples and Pompeii.	Meyerbeer's *Robert le diable*, Opéra, 21 Nov.

Year	Age	Life	Contemporary Composers
1832	28	*La captive* composed at Subiaco. Returns to France, spending five months at La Côte. Plans Napoleonic work. On returning to Paris (Nov.) plans a concert, 9 Dec., and is introduced to Harriet Smithson.	Clementi (80) dies, 10 March.
1833	29	Courtship and marriage (3 Oct.) to Harriet Smithson. Revises *Les francs-juges*. Composes *Le jeune pâtre breton*. Writes for *Le Rénovateur*. First regular season of Paris concerts.	Brahms born, 7 May; Mendelssohn's *Italian Symphony* completed.
1834	30	Composes *Harold en Italie* in response to commission from Paganini. Move to Montmartre. Louis Berlioz born, 14 Aug. Libretto of *Benvenuto Cellini* refused by Opéra-comique. *Sara la baigneuse* composed.	Boieldieu (58) dies, 8 Oct.; Borodin born, 12 Nov.
1835	31	Becomes music critic of the *Journal des débats*. *Le cinq mai* composed. Takes over conducting of his own concerts.	Bellini (33) dies, 23 Sept.; Saint-Saëns born, 9 Oct.; Halévy's *La juive*, Opéra, 23 Feb.
1836	32	Composition of *Benvenuto Cellini*. Final stage appearance of Harriet Smithson.	Delibes born, 21 Feb.; Reicha (66) dies, 28 May; Meyerbeer's *Les Huguenots*. Opéra, 29 Feb.; Glinka's *A Life for the Tsar*, St Petersburg, 9 Dec.; Liszt's *Album d'un voyageur*.
1837	33	Composition and performance of the *Grande messe des morts*.	Balakirev born, 2 Jan.; Field (54) dies, 23 Jan.; Lesueur (77) dies, 6 Oct.; Hummel (58) dies, 17 Oct.
1838	34	Death of Berlioz's mother, 18 Feb. *Benvenuto Cellini* played at the Opéra, 10 Sep., but is a failure. After hearing *Harold en Italie*, Paganini gives Berlioz 20,000 francs.	Bruch born, 6 Jan.; Bizet born, 25 Oct.
1839	35	Composition and performance of *Roméo et Juliette*, dedicated to Paganini. Meets Wagner.	Mussorgsky born, 21 March; Paer (67) dies, 3 May.

Year	Age	Life	Contemporary Composers
1840	36	*Grande symphonie funèbre et triomphale* commissioned and played at tenth anniversary of the 1830 Revolution, 28 July.	Tchaikovsky born, 7 May; Paganini (57) dies, 27 May.
1841	37	*Les nuits d'été* completed and published. *La nonne sanglante* begun. Weber's *Freischütz* performed at the Opéra with recitatives by Berlioz. Beginning of liaison with Marie Recio.	Chabrier born, 18 Jan.; Dvořák born, 8 Sept.
1842	38	First concert tour abroad, to Brussels, Sept. Second tour in December, to Brussels, Frankfurt and Stuttgart. Marie Recio accompanies him on both tours.	Cherubini (81) dies, 15 March; Massenet born, 12 May; Sullivan born, 13 May; Verdi's *Nabucco*, Milan, 9 March; Glinka's *Ruslan and Lyudmila*, St Petersburg, 9 Dec.
1843	39	Tour continues through Karlsruhe, Mannheim, Weimar, Leipzig, Dresden, Brunswick, Hamburg, Berlin, Hanover and Darmstadt. Meets Schumann and Mendelssohn (again), Meyerbeer and Marschner. Returns to Paris, May. Publishes *Grand traité d'instrumentation et d'orchestration modernes*. *Carnaval romain* overture composed.	Grieg born, 15 June; Wagner's *Der fliegende Holländer*, Dresden, 2 Jan.
1844	40	*Voyage musical en Allemagne et en Italie* published. *Hymme à la France* composed for Industrial Exhibition concert, 1 Aug. Holiday in Nice, where he composes *Le corsaire* overture. Separation from Harriet. *Hamlet* march composed.	Rimsky-Korsakov born, 18 March; Berton (76) dies, 22 April; David's *Le désert*, Conservatoire, 8 Dec.
1845	41	Four concerts at the Cirque Olympique. Concert tour to Marseilles and Lyons, June–July. Attends inauguration of Beethoven's statue in Bonn, Aug. Begins *La damnation de Faust*. Leaves for Vienna, Oct, for three concerts	Fauré born, 12 May; Wagner's *Tannhäuser*, Dresden, 19 Oct.

Year	Age	Life	Contemporary Composers
		there. Composes *Zaïde* and *Le chasseur danois*.	
1846	42	Tour continues to Prague, back to Vienna, then Pest, Breslau, Prague again, Brunswick. Returns to Paris, May. Commission and performance of *Chant des chemins de fer* at Lille, June. Completion and performance (6 Dec.) of *La damnation de Faust*.	Mendelssohn's *Elijah*, Birmingham, 26 Aug.
1847	43	Concert tour to St Petersburg and Moscow. Concerts in Riga and Berlin on return journey. Returns to Paris, July. *La nonne sanglante* abandoned. Visit, with Louis, to La Côte, Sept. Departure for London, to conduct season at Drury Lane Theatre.	Mendelssohn (38) dies, 4 Nov.; Verdi's *Macbeth*, Florence, 14 March.
1848	44	February Revolution in Paris. Berlioz remains in London until July. Failure of Jullien's London season. Compilation of *Mémoires* begun. Death of Berlioz's father, 28 July. Visit to La Côte. Concert in Versailles, 29 Oct.	Duparc born, 21 Jan.; Parry born, 27 Feb.; Donizetti (50) dies, 8 April.
1849	45	Composed *Te deum*. Compiles *Tristia* and *Vox populi*.	Nicolai (38) dies, 11 May; Chopin (39) dies, 17 Oct; Meyerbeer's *Le prophète*, Opéra, 16 April.
1850	46	*Société philharmonique de Paris* launched. Succeeds as Librarian of the Conservatoire. Death of Berlioz's sister Nanci, 4 May. *La fuite en Egypte* composed.	Wagner's *Lohengrin*, Weimar, 28 Aug.
1851	47	Second and final season of *Société philharmonique*. Second visit to London, May – July, for Great Exhibition.	Lortzing (49) dies, 21 Jan.; Spontini (76) dies, 24 Jan.; d'Indy born, 27 March; Verdi's *Rigoletto*, Venice, 11 March.
1852	48	Third visit to London, Feb.–June, to conduct New Philharmonic Society. Revival of	Stanford born, 30 Sept.

Year	Age	Life	Contemporary Composers
		Benvenuto Cellini in Weimar, March. Berlioz visits Weimar for further performances in Nov. *Les soirées de l'orchestre* published.	
1853	49	Fourth visit to London, May – July, for *Benvenuto Cellini* at Covent Garden, withdrawn after one performance. First visit to Baden-Baden, Aug. Concert tour to Brunswick, Hanover, Bremen, Leipzig, Oct.–Dec.	Verdi's *Il Trovatore*, Rome, 19 Jan.; Verdi's *La Traviata*, Venice, 6 March; Liszt's Sonata in B minor.
1854	50	Death of Harriet, 3 March. Concert tour to Hanover, Brunswick and Dresden. Completion of *L'enfance du Christ*, July. *L'impériale* composed. *Mémoires* completed, 18 Oct. Marriage to Marie Recio, 19 Oct. First performance of *L'enfance du Christ*, Dec.	Janáček born, 4 July; Humperdinck born, 1 Sept; Liszt's *Faust Symphony* composed; Wagner's *Das Rheingold* completed.
1855	51	Visit to Weimar and Gotha, Jan. Visit to Brussels, March. First performance of *Te deum*, at St-Eustache, 30 April. Berlioz on jury of Exposition universelle. Fifth visit to London, June–July, to conduct the New Philharmonic Society. *L'art du chef d'orchestre* written and published. Three concerts in the Palais de l'Industrie, Nov., including first performance of *L'impériale*.	Chausson born, 21 Jan.; Verdi's *Les vêpres siciliennes*, Opéra, 13 June.
1856	52	Visit to Weimar and Gotha, Jan. Orchestration of *Les nuits d'été* completed. Moves to 4 Rue de Calais, April. *Les Troyens* begun, April. Succeeds to Adam's chair at the Institut, June. Visit to Plombières and Baden-Baden, July–Aug. Onset of intestinal illness.	Adam (52) dies, 3 May; Schumann (46) dies, 29 July; Wagner's *Die Walküre* completed; Liszt's *Dante Symphony* completed.
1857	53	Visit to Plombières and Baden-Baden, July–Aug.	Glinka (52) dies, 15 Feb.; Elgar born, 2 June.

Year	Age	Life	Contemporary Composers
1858	54	*Les Troyens* completed, April. Postscript to *Mémoires*, May. Visit to Baden-Baden, Aug., where Bénazet commissions a new opera. Serialization of *Mémoires* in *Le monde illustré*, Oct.	Puccini born, 22 Dec.
1859	55	*Les grotesques de la musique* published, March. Concert in Bordeaux, June. Visit to Baden-Baden, Aug. Gluck's *Orphée* revived by Berlioz at the Théâtre-lyrique, Nov. Acute illness. Baden-Baden commission abandoned.	Spohr (75) dies, 22 Oct.; Brahms' Piano Concerto No. 1, Hanover, 22 Jan.; Verdi's *Un Ballo in Maschera*, Rome, 17 Feb.; Gounod's *Faust*, Théâtre-lyrique, 19 March; Wagner's *Tristan und Isolde* completed.
1860	56	Wagner's concerts in Paris, Jan. *Les Troyens* accepted by Théâtre-lyrique, Jan. Death of Berlioz's sister Adèle, 2 March. Visit to Baden-Baden, Aug. Bénazet agrees to commission *Béatrice et Bénédict*. Private printing of *Les Troyens* begun, Sept.	Wolf born, 13 March; Charpentier born, 25 June; Mahler born, 7 July.
1861	57	Wagner's *Tannhäuser* fails at the Opéra, March. *Les Troyens* dropped by the Théâtre-lyrique but accepted by the Opéra, June. Visit to Baden-Baden, Aug.	Marschner (66) dies, 14 Dec.
1862	58	*Béatrice et Bénédict* completed, Feb. Berlioz's second wife, Marie, dies, 13 June. First performance of *Béatrice et Bénédict* at Baden-Baden, 9 Aug. *A travers chants* published, Sept.	Delius born, 29 Jan.; Halévy (62) dies, 17 March; Debussy born, 22 Aug.; Verdi's *La Forza del destino*, St Petersburg, 10 Nov.
1863	59	*Les Troyens* dropped by the Opéra but accepted by Carvalho at the Théâtre-lyrique, Feb. Berlioz conducts *Béatrice et Bénédict* in Weimar, April. Concert in Loewenberg, 19 April. Conducts *L'enfance du Christ* in Strasbourg, 22 June.	

217

Year	Age	Life	Contemporary Composers
		First two acts of *Les Troyens* abandoned, July. Visit to Baden-Baden, Aug., for revival of *Béatrice et Bénédict*. Last feuilleton in the *Journal des débats*, on Bizet's *Les pêcheurs de perles*, 8 Oct. First performance of *Les Troyens à Carthage*, Théâtre-lyrique, 4 Nov. Final performance, 20 Dec.	
1864	60	*Marche troyenne* arranged, Jan. Visits Dauphiné, Aug.–Sept., and meets Estelle again. Begins regular correspondence with her.	Meyerbeer (72) dies, 2 May. R. Strauss born, 11 June.
1865	61	Completes Postface of *Mémoires*, 1 Jan. *Mémoires* printed, July. Visits Estelle in Geneva and his relatives in Grenoble, Aug.	Nielsen born, 9 June; Glazunov born, 10 Aug.; Dukas born, 1 Oct.; Sibelius born, 8 Dec.; Meyerbeer's *L'africaine*, Opéra, 28 April.
1866	62	Liszt visits Paris, March. Visits Estelle in Geneva, Aug. Revival of *Alceste* at the Opéra, Oct. Conducts *La damnation de Faust* in Vienna, 16 Dec.	Satie born, 17 March; Busoni born, 1 April; Smetana's *The Bartered Bride*, Prague, 30 May.
1867	63	Two concerts in Cologne, Feb. Berlioz's son Louis dies in Havana, June. Visits Estelle in Vienne, near Lyons, Sept. Leaves for concert tour in Russia, Nov.	Granados born, 27 July; Verdi's *Don Carlos*, Opéra, 11 March.
1868	64	Returns from Russia exhausted, Feb. Visits Nice and falls twice, March. Visits Grenoble to address a choral festival, Aug.	Rossini (76) dies, 13 Nov.; Brahms' *Deutsches Requiem*, Bremen, 10 April; Wagner's *Die Meistersinger*, Munich, 21 June.
1869	65	Berlioz dies at 4 Rue de Calais, Paris, 8 March.	Dargomyzhsky (55) dies, 17 Jan. Alkan 55; Auber 87; Balakirev 32; Bizet 30; Borodin 34; Brahms 35; Bruch 31; Bruckner 44; Busoni 2; Chabrier 28; Charpentier 8; Chausson 14; Cornelius 44; David 58; Debussy 6; Delibes 33; Delius 7; Dukas 3; Duparc 21; Dvořak 27; Elgar 11; Fauré 23; Franck 46; Gade 52; Glazunov 3; Gounod 50;

Year	Age	Life	Contemporary Composers
			Granados 1; Grieg 25; Heller 53; Humperdinck 14; d'Indy 17; Janáček 14; Lalo 46; Liszt 57; Mahler 8; Massenet 26; Mussorgsky 29; Nielsen 3; Offenbach 49; Parry 21; Puccini 10; Raff 46; Reyer 45; Rimsky-Korsakov 24; Saint-Saëns 33; Satie 2; Sibelius 3; Smetana 45; Stanford 16; J. Strauss 43; R. Strauss 4; Sullivan 26; Tchaikovsky 28; Verdi 55; Wagner 55; Wolf 8.

Appendix B
List of works

In the following list all works except albumleaves and minor fragments have been included. The date of first performance is given only when it is known; the hall is identified for first performances in Paris, elsewhere only the city. Subtitles of works are separated from main titles by a colon. The abbreviations in the right-hand column give reference to, in turn:

H.   D. Kern Holoman, *A Catalogue of the Works of Hector Berlioz*, NBE vol. 25, (Kassel) 1987.

B&H   *Werke*, ed. C. Malherbe and F. Weingartner, Breitkopf & Härtel (Leipzig) 1900–7.

NBE   *New Berlioz Edition*, ed. Hugh Macdonald, Bärenreiter (Kassel), 1967– .

op.   Berlioz's own opus numbers.

I OPERAS

Les francs-juges, opera in three acts.
    Libretto by Humbert Ferrand.
    Composed 1826, revised 1829 and, in one
        act as *Le cri de guerre de Brisgau*, 1833.
    Overture and fragments survive.
    Overture first performed Conservatoire, 26
        May 1828.
    Overture published 1836.

H.23 A–C / – / NBE 4 / –

Overture:
H.23D / B&H 4 / NBE 4 / op.

Benvenuto Cellini, opera semiseria in two acts.
    Libretto by Auguste Barbier and Léon de
        Wailly.
    Composed 1836–8, revised in three acts
        1852.
    Overture and selections published 1838,
        vocal score 1856, full score 1886.
    First performed Opéra, 10 Sept. 1838.

H.76 / B&H 5 (overture) /
    NBE 1 / –

La nonne sanglante, opera in three acts.
    Libretto by Eugène Scribe.
    Composed 1841–7, unfinished.
    Fragments first performed London, 1968.

H.91 / – / NBE 4 / –

Les Troyens, grand opera in five acts. H.133 / – / NBE 2 / –
Libretto by Berlioz, after Virgil.
Composed 1856–8, divided 1863 into two
operas, *La prise de Troie* and *Les Troyens à
Carthage*.
First performance of *Les Troyens à Carthage*,
Théâtre-lyrique, 4 Nov. 1863, *La prise de
Troie* 1879 (concert), 1890 (stage).
Published 1863 (vocal scores), 1969 (full
score).
Béatrice et Bénédict, opéra-comique in two H.138 / B&H 19–20 / NBE 3 / –
acts.
Libretto by Berlioz, after Shakespeare.
Composed 1860–2.
First performed Baden-Baden, 9 Aug. 1862.
Published 1863 (vocal score), 1892 (overture
full score), 1907 (opera full score).

II SYMPHONIES

Symphonie fantastique: épisode de la vie d'un H.48 / B&H 1 / NBE 16 / op.14
artiste
Programme by Berlioz, revised 1855.
Composed 1830.
First performed Conservatoire, 5 Dec. 1830.
Published 1834 (piano reduction by Liszt),
1845 (full score).
Harold en Italie: symphonie, with viola solo. H.68 / B&H 2 / NBE 17 / op.16
Composed 1834.
First performed Conservatoire, 23 Nov.
1834.
Published 1848.
Roméo et Juliette: symphonie dramatique, for H.79 / B&H 3 / NBE 18 / op.17
alto, tenor and bass soloists, semi-chorus
(ATB), double chorus (STB–STB) and
orchestra.
Text by Emile Deschamps, after
Shakespeare.
Composed 1839.
First performed Conservatoire, 24 Nov.
1839.
Published 1847.
Grande symphonie funèbre et triomphale, for H.80 / B&H 1 / NBE 19 / op.15
military band, with strings and chorus
(SSTTBB) ad lib.
Text by Antoni Deschamps.

Composed 1840, strings and chorus parts
    added 1842. Last movement arranged
    1848 for chorus and piano (see WORKS
    FOR CHORUS).
First performed open-air, 28 July 1840.
Published 1843.

III OVERTURES

Les francs-juges, see OPERAS
Waverley: grande ouvertui e.　　　　　　H.26 / B&H 4 / NBE 20 / op.1
    Composed 1826–8.
    First performed Conservatoire, 26 May
    1828.
    Published 1839.
Le roi Lear: grande ouverture.　　　　　H.53 / B&H 4 / NBE 20 / op.4
    Composed 1831.
    First performed Conservatoire, 22 Dec.
    1833.
    Published 1839.
Intrata di Rob-Roy Macgregor　　　　　　H.54 / B&H 4 / NBE 20 / –
    Composed 1831.
    First performed Conservatoire, 14 April
    1833.
    Published 1900.
Benvenuto Cellini, see OPERAS
Le carnaval romain: ouverture caractéristique　H.95 / B&H 5 / NBE 20 / op.9
    Composed 1843, based on material from
      Benvenuto Cellini.
    First performed Salle Herz, 3 Feb. 1844.
    Published 1844.
Le corsaire: ouverture　　　　　　　　　H.101 / B&H 5 / NBE 20 /
    Composed, as *La tour de Nice*, 1844.　　op.21
    First performed Cirque Olympique, 19 Jan.
      1845 (as *La tour de Nice*), Brunswick, 8
      April 1854 (as *Le corsaire*).
    Published, as *Le corsaire*, 1852.
La fuite en Egypte, see WORKS FOR CHORUS.
Béatrice et Bénédict, see OPERAS.
Les Troyens à Carthage: Prologue, see OPERAS.

IV OTHER INSTRUMENTAL WORKS

Rêverie et caprice, for violin and orchestra.　H.88 / B&H 6 / NBE 21 / op.8
    Arranged 1841 from a cavatina withdrawn
      from *Benvenuto Cellini* (see OPERAS).
    Also for violin and piano.

First performed Salle Vivienne, 1 Feb. 1842.
Published 1841.

Marche funèbre pour la dernière scène d'Hamlet, for orchestra and wordless chorus (STB). Composed 1844. Published 1852 (as no.3 of *Tristia*).	H.103 / B&H 6 / NBE 12 / op.18 no.3
Sérénade agreste à la madone sur la thème des pifferari romains, for harmonium. Composed 1844. Published 1844.	H.98 / B&H 6 / NBE 21 / –
Toccata, for harmonium. Composed 1844. Published 1844.	H.99 / B&H 6 / NBE 21 / –
Hymne pour l'élévation, for harmonium. Composed 1844. Published 1844.	H.100 / B&H 6 / NBE 21 / –
Marche troyenne, for orchestra. Arranged 1864 from Act I of *Les Troyens* (see OPERAS). Published 1865.	H.133B / B&H 6 / NBE 21 / –

V PRIX DE ROME WORKS

Fugue, in four parts. Composed 1826.	H.22 / – / NBE 6 / –
La mort d'Orphée, cantata for tenor solo, chorus (SSSS) and orchestra. Text by Berton. Composed 1827. Published 1930.	H.25 / – / NBE 6 / –
Herminie, cantata for soprano and orchestra. Text by P.-A. Vieillard. Composed 1828. Published 1903.	H.29 / B&H 15 / NBE 6 / –
Fugue à 3 sujets. Composed 1829. Published 1902.	H.35 / B&H 6 / NBE 6 / –
Cléopâtre, scène lyrique, cantata for soprano and orchestra. Text by P.-A. Vieillard. Composed 1829. Published 1903.	H.36 / B&H 15 / NBE 6 / –
Sardanapale, cantata for tenor solo, chorus (TTBB) and orchestra. Text by J.-F. Gail.	H.50 / – / NBE 6 / –

Composed 1830. Only a fragment survives.
First performed Institut, 30 Oct. 1830.

VI WORKS FOR CHORUS

Resurrexit, STTB, with orchestra. H.20 / B&H 7 / NBE 12a / –
  Text of Latin Mass.
  Composed 1824, only surviving movement
  of the lost *Messe solennelle*.
  Revised 1828 and 1829 as *Le jugement
  dernier*.
  First performed St-Roch, 27 Dec. 1824.
  Published 1902.

La révolution grecque: scène héroïque, H.21 / B&H 10 / NBE 12a / –
  SSSTTBB, with two bass soloists and
  orchestra.
  Text by Humbert Ferrand.
  Composed 1825–6. Part arranged 1833 for
  chorus and military band.
  First performed Conservatoire, 26 May
  1828.
  Published 1903.

La mort d'Orphée, see PRIX DE ROME WORKS.

Huit scènes de Faust, SSTTBB, with soprano, H.33 / B&H 10 / NBE 5 / op.1
  tenor and bass soloists, six solo voices (in
  no.3), and orchestra.
  Text by Goethe, translated by Gérard de
  Nerval.
  Composed 1828–9, withdrawn.
    Incorporated in *La damnation de Faust*,
    1846.
  First performed Conservatoire, 1 Nov. 1829
  (no.3 only).
  Published 1829.

Le ballet des ombres: ronde nocturne, STTB, H.37 / B&H 16 / NBE 14 /
  with piano. op.2.
  Text by Albert du Boys, after Herder.
  Composed 1829, withdrawn.
  Published 1829.

Hélène, TTBB with orchestra, see SONGS.

Chant guerrier, TBB with tenor and bass H.41 / B&H 16 / NBE 14 / op.2
  soloists and piano. no.3
  No.3 of *Neuf mélodies irlandaises*.
  Text by Thomas Moore, translated by
  Thomas Gounet.
  Composed 1829.

Published 1830.

La belle voyageuse, SA with orchestra. H.42D / – / NBE 13 / op.2 no.4.

 Arranged 1851 from *La belle voyageuse* (see
 SONGS).

 First performed Salle Ste-Cécile, 25 March
 1851.

 Published 1975.

Chanson à boire, TBB with tenor soloist and H.43 / B&H 16 / NBE 14 / op.2
 piano. no.5

 Text by Thomas Moore, translated by
 Thomas Gounet.

 Composed 1829.

 Published 1830 (as no.5 of *Neuf mélodies*
 irlandaises).

Chant sacré, SSTTBB with tenor or soprano H.44 / B&H 16 / NBE 14 / op.2
 soloist and piano. no.6

 Text by Thomas Moore, translated by
 Thomas Gounet.

 Composed 1829. Arranged 1843 for chorus
 and orchestra, and 1844 for six solo wind
 instruments and orchestra (version lost).

 Published 1830 (as no.6 of *Neuf mélodies*
 irlandaises), 1844 (chorus and orchestra).

 First performed Athénée musical, 18 Feb.
 1830; Marseilles, Dec. 1843 (with
 orchestra); Salle Herz, 3 Feb. 1844 (with
 wind).

Sardanapale, see PRIX DE ROME WORKS.

Fantaisie dramatique sur la Tempête, drame de H.52 / B&H 13 / NBE 7 /
 Shakespeare, SSATT with orchestra. op.14bis

 Italian text by (?) Berlioz, after Shakespeare.

 Composed 1830. Incorporated in *Le retour à*
 la vie (Lélio) 1831.

 First performed Opéra, 7 Nov. 1830.

 Published 1855 (in *Lélio*).

Le retour à la vie: mélologue en six parties, later H.55 / B&H 13 / NBE 7 /
 called *Lélio, ou le retour à la vie*, op.14bis
 SSATTBB with reciter, two tenor soloists,
 baritone soloist, piano and orchestra.

 Text mostly by Berlioz.

 Composed 1831, revised 1855.

 First performed Conservatoire, 9 Dec. 1832.

 Published 1855 (nos.1, 3 and 4 in vocal score
 in 1833).

 The six movements have separate origins:

  1. *Le pêcheur, ballade*, tenor soloist and
   piano.

Text by A. Duboys, after Goethe.
Composed *c*. 1827.

2. *Choeur des ombres*, STB and orchestra.
Adapted from *Cléopâtre* (see PRIX DE
ROME WORKS).

3. *Chanson de brigands*, TTBB, baritone
soloist and orchestra.
Adapted from *Chanson de pirates* (see
LOST WORKS).

4. *Chant de bonheur*, tenor soloist and
orchestra.
Adapted from *La mort d'Orphée* (see
PRIX DE ROME WORKS).

5. *La harpe éolienne, souvenirs*, orchestra.
Adapted from *La mort d'Orphée* (see
PRIX DE ROME WORKS).

6. *Fantaisie sur la Tempête de
Shakespeare*, SSATT and orchestra.
(see above).

Méditation religieuse, SSTTBB with orchestra.   ⒤H.56 / B&H 14 / NBE 12b /
Text by Thomas Moore, translated by Louise   op.18 no.1
Sw. Belloc.
Composed 1831 for chorus and seven wind
instruments (version lost). Revised 1849.
Published 1849 (as no.1 of *Tristia*).

Quartetto e coro dei Maggi, SSTB with   ⒤H.59 / B&H 7 / NBE 12a / –
orchestra.
Italian text anonymous.
Composed 1832.
Published 1902.

Sara la baigneuse, ballade, three choruses   H.69 / B&H 14 / NBE 12a /
(STBB–SA–TTBB) with orchestra.   op.11
Text by Victor Hugo.
Composed 1834 for four male voices and
orchestra (version lost). Arranged 1838
for four soloists (STTB), chorus and
orchestra (version lost). Third version
1850, for three choruses and orchestra or
two soloists (SA or TB) and piano.
First performed Conservatoire, 7 Nov., 1834
(first version,) Conservatoire, 13 Dec.
1840 (second version), Salle Ste-Cécile, 22
Oct. 1850 (third version).
Published 1850.

Le chant des Bretons, TTBB (or tenor soloist)   H.71 / B&H 16 / NBE 14 /
with piano.   op.13 no.5.

Text by Auguste Brizeux.
Composed 1835, revised 1850.
First performed Ecole Chevé, March 1853.
Published 1835. Revised version 1850 (as
    no. 5 of *Fleurs des landes*).
See also SONGS.

Le cinq mai: chant sur la mort de l'Empereur   H.74 / B&H 13 / NBE 12a /
  Napoléon, SSTTBB, with bass soloist and   op.6.
  orchestra.
Text by Pierre-Jean de Béranger.
Composed 1831–5.
First performed Conservatoire, 22 Nov.
    1835.
Published 1840 (vocal score), 1844 (full
    score).

Grande messe des morts (Requiem), SSTTBB   H.75 / B&H 7 / NBE 9 / op.5
  with tenor soloist and orchestra.
Text from Latin Requiem Mass.
Composed 1837, revised 1852 and 1867.
First performed Invalides, 5 Dec. 1837.
Published 1838.

Roméo et Juliette, see SYMPHONIES.
Grande symphonie funèbre et triomphale, see
  SYMPHONIES.

L'apothéose, SSTTBB with mezzo-soprano or   H.80C / B&H 16 / NBE 14 / –
  tenor soloist and piano.
Text by Antoni Deschamps.
Arranged 1848 from *Grande symphonie*
  funèbre et triomphale.
Published 1848.

La mort d'Ophélie: ballade, SA with orchestra.   H.92B / B&H 14 / NBE 12b /
Text by Ernest Legouvé, after Shakespeare.   op.18 no.2
Composed 1842 (for voice and piano, see
  SONGS).
Arranged 1848 for chorus and orchestra.
Published 1852 (full score, as no.2 of *Tristia*),
  1863 (vocal score).

La belle Isabeau, see SONGS.

Hymne à la France, SSATTBB with orchestra.   H.97 / B&H 14 / NBE 12b /
Text by Auguste Barbier.   op.20 no.2.
Composed 1844.
First performed Festival de l'Industrie, 1 Aug.
  1844.
Published (as no.2 of *Vox populi*) 1849
  (vocal score), 1851 (full score).

Berlioz

Marche funèbre pour la dernière scène d'Hamlet, see OTHER INSTRUMENTAL WORKS.

Chant des chemins de fer, SSTTBB with tenor soloist and orchestra.
H.110 / B&H 14 / NBE 12b / op.19 no.3

Text by Jules Janin.
Composed 1846.
First performed Lille, 14 June 1846.
Published 1850 (vocal score, as no.3 of *Feuillets d'album*), 1903 (full score).

La damnation de Faust: légende dramatique, SSTTBB with mezzo-soprano, tenor, baritone or bass, bass soloists and orchestra.
H.111 / B&H 11–12 / NBE 8 / op.24

Text by Goethe, Almire Gandonnière and Berlioz, after Goethe.
Composed 1845–6, incorporating the *Huit scènes de Faust* and the *Marche de Rákóczy*.
First performed Opéra-comique, 6 Dec. 1846.
Published 1854.

Prière du matin: choeur d'enfants SS (children) with piano.
H.112 / B&H 16 / NBE 14 / –

Text by Alphonse de Lamartine.
Composed *c*.1846.
Published 1848.

La menace des Francs: marche et choeur, SSTTBB, with semichorus (TTBB or soloists) and orchestra.
H.117 / B&H 14 / NBE 12b / op.20 no.1

Text anonymous.
Composed before 1848.
First performed Salle Ste-Cécile, 25 March 1851.
Published (as no.1 of *Vox populi*) 1849 (vocal score), 1851 (full score).

Te deum, STB–STB–SS (children), with tenor soloist, organ and orchestra.
H.118 / B&H 8/ NBE 10 / op.22

Text of Latin hymn.
Composed 1849.
First performed St-Eustache, 30 April 1855.
Published 1855.

La fuite en Egypte: mystère en style ancien, SATB with tenor soloist and orchestra.
H.128 / B&H 9 / NBE 11 / –

Text by Berlioz.

Composed 1850. Incorporated in *L'enfance du Christ*.
First performed Salle Ste-Cécile, 12 Nov. 1850 (in part), Leipzig, 1 Dec. 1853 (complete).
Published 1852.

L'impériale: cantate, SATB–SATB with orchestra. H. 129 / B&H 13 / NBE 12b / op.26
Text by Captain Lafont.
Composed 1854.
First performed Palais de l'Industrie, 28 Nov. 1855.
Published 1856.

L'enfance du Christ: trilogie sacrée, SSAATTBB with soprano, two tenor, baritone, three bass soloists and orchestra. H.130 / B&H 9 / NBE 11 / op.25
Text by Berlioz.
Composed 1853–4, incorporating *La fuite en Egypte*.
First performed Salle Herz, 10 Dec. 1854.
Published 1855.

Hymne pour la consécration du nouveau tabernacle, SSATTBB, with organ or piano. H.135 / B&H 16 / NBE 14 / –
Text by (?) J.-H. Vries.
Composed 1859.
Published 1859.

Le temple universel, TTBB–TTBB with organ. H.137 / B&H 16 / NBE 14 / op.28
Text by Jean-François Vaudin.
Composed 1861. Revised *c.* 1867 for TTBB unaccompanied.
Published 1861, revised version 1868.

Veni creator: motet, SSA with SSA soloists. H.141 / B&H 7 / NBE 14 / –
Text from Latin hymn.
Composed *c.* 1860–8.
Published 1885.

Tantum ergo, SSA with SSA soloists and organ. H.142 / B&H 7 / NBE 14 / –
Text from Latin hymn.
Composed *c.* 1860–8.
Published 1885.

VII SONGS

La dépit de la bergère: romance, voice and piano. H.7 / B&H 17 / NBE 15 / –
Text anonymous.

Composed *c.* 1819.
Published *c.* 1819.

Le maure jaloux: romance, voice and piano.   H.9 / B&H 17 / NBE 15 / –
  Text by Florian.
  Composed *c.* 1819–21. Two versions exist,
    one entitled *L'arabe jaloux.*
  Published 1822.

Amitié reprends ton empire: romance, two   H.10 / B&H 16 / NBE 15 / –
    sopranos, baritone and piano.
  Text by Florian.
  Composed *c.* 1819–21. Two versions exist,
    one entitled *Invocation à l'amitié.*
  Published 1823.

Pleure, pauvre Colette: romance, two equal   H.11 / B&H 16 / NBE 15 / –
    voices and piano.
  Text by Bourgerie.
  Composed before 1822.
  Published 1822.

Canon libre à la quinte, alto, baritone and   H.14 / B&H 16 / NBE 15 / –
    piano.
  Text by Augustin de Pons.
  Composed before 1822
  Published 1822.

Le montagnard exilé: chant élégiaque, two   H.15 / B&H 16 / NBE 15 / –
    equal voices and piano or harp.
  Text by Albert du Boys.
  Composed before 1823.
  Published 1823.

Toi qui l'aimas, verse des pleurs: romance,   H.16 / B&H 17 / NBE 15 / –
    voice and piano.
  Text by Albert du Boys.
  Composed before 1823.
  Published 1823.

Nocturne, two voices and guitar.   H.31 / – / NBE 15 / –
  Text anonymous.
  Composed *c.* 1818–30.

Le pêcheur: ballade, tenor and piano.   H.55 / B&H 17 / NBE 7 /
  Text by Goethe, translated by Albert du   op.14bis
    Boys.
  Composed *c.* 1827. Incorporated in *Le
    retour à la vie* (see WORKS FOR CHORUS).
  Published 1833.

Le roi de Thulé: chanson gothique, soprano   H.33B / – / NBE 15 / op.1
    and piano.   no.6
  Text by Goethe, translated by Gérard de
    Nerval.

Composed 1828. Incorporated in *Huit scènes de Faust* and in *La damnation de Faust*.

Le coucher du soleil: rêverie, tenor and piano.   H.39 / B&H 17 / NBE 15 / op.2
   Text by Thomas Moore, translated by   no.1
     Thomas Gounet.
   Composed 1829.
   Published 1830 (as no.1 of *Neuf mélodies irlandaises*).

Hélène: ballade.
   Text by Thomas Moore, translated by
     Thomas Gounet.
   1. Composed 1829, for tenor and baritone   H.40A / B&H 16 / NBE 15 /
     (or soprano and contralto) and piano.   op.2 no.2
     Published 1830 (as no.2 of *Neuf mélodies irlandaises*).
   2. Revised 1844 for two tenors, two basses   H.40B / B&H 14 / NBE 12 / –
     (or TTBB chorus) and orchestra.
     First performed Salle Herz, 3 Feb. 1844.
     Published 1903.

La belle voyageuse: ballade
   Text by Thomas Moore, translated by
     Thomas Gounet.
   1. Composed 1829, for tenor and piano.   H.42A / B&H 17 / NBE 15 /
     Published 1830 (as no.4 of *Neuf mélodies*   op.2 no.4
     irlandaises).
   2. Arranged 1834 for two tenors, two   H.42B
     basses and piano (version lost).
     First performed Conservatoire, 9 Nov.
     1834.
   3. Arranged 1842 for mezzo-soprano and   H.42C / B&H 15 / NBE 13 / –
     orchestra.
     First performed Stuttgart, 29 Dec. 1842.
     Published 1844.
   4. Arranged 1851 for chorus and orchestra,
     see WORKS FOR CHORUS.

L'origine de la harpe: ballade, soprano or tenor   H.45 / B&H 17 / NBE 15 / op.2
   and piano.   no.7
   Text by Thomas Moore, translated by
     Thomas Gounet.
   Composed 1829.
   Published 1830 (as no.7 of *Neuf mélodies irlandaises*).

Adieu Bessy: romance anglaise et française,   H.46 / B&H 17 / NBE 15 / op.2
   tenor and piano.   no.8
   Text by Thomas Moore, translated by

Thomas Gounet.

Composed 1829, revised 1849.

Published 1830 (as no.8 of *Neuf mélodies
irlandaises*), revised version 1849 (as no.8
of *Irlande*).

Elégie en prose, tenor and piano.   H.47 / B&H 17 / NBE 15 /

Text by Thomas Moore, translated by Louise   op.2 no.9
Sw. Belloc.

Composed 1829.

Published 1830 (as no.9 of *Neuf mélodies
irlandaises*).

La captive: orientale

Text by Victor Hugo.

1. Composed 1832 for voice and piano.   H.60A-B / B&H 17 / NBE 15 /
   Published 1904.   op.12
2. Arranged 1832 for voice, cello and   H.60C / B&H 17 / NBE 15 /
   piano.   op.12
   First performed Conservatoire, 30 Dec.
   ~1832.
   Published 1833.

3. Arranged 1834 for soprano and   H.60D
   orchestra (version lost).
   First performed Conservatoire, 23 Nov.
   1834.
4. Arranged 1848 for soprano and   H.60E-F / B&H 15 / NBE 13 /
   orchestra.   op.12
   First performed London, 29 June 1848.
   Published 1849.

Le jeune pâtre breton (also entitled *Le jeune
paysan breton*)

Text by Auguste Brizeux.

1. Composed 1833, for voice and piano.   H.65A / B&H 17 / NBE 15 /
   First performed Conservatoire, 22 Dec.   op.13 no.4
   1833.
   Published 1904.

2. Arranged 1834 for soprano and   H.65B
   orchestra (version lost).
   First performed Conservatoire, 23 Nov.
   1834.
3. Arranged 1834 for voice, horn and piano. H.65C / – / NBE 15
   Published 1835.
4. Arranged 1835 for mezzo-soprano or   H.65D / B&H 15 / NBE 13
   tenor and orchestra.
   First performed Conservatoire, 22 Nov. 1835.
   Published *c.* 1839.

Les champs: romance, tenor and piano.　　　H.67 / B&H 17 / NBE 15 /
　　Text by P.-J. de Béranger.　　　　　　　　op.19 no.2
　　Composed 1834, revised 1850.
　　Published 1834, revised version 1850 (as
　　　no.2 of *Feuillets d'album*).
Sara la baigneuse: ballade, soprano and alto (or
　　tenor and bass) and piano, see WORKS FOR
　　CHORUS.
Je crois en vous: romance, voice and piano.　　H.70 / B&H 17 / NBE 15 / –
　　Text by Léon Guérin.
　　Composed 1834. Incorporated without
　　　words in *Benvenuto Cellini*.
　　Published 1834.
Le chant des Bretons, tenor (or TTBB chorus)　　H.71 / B&H 17 / NBE 14 /
　　and piano.　　　　　　　　　　　　　　op.13 no.5
　　Text by Auguste Brizeux.
　　Composed 1835, revised 1850.
　　Published 1835. Revised version 1850 (as
　　　no.5 of *Fleurs des landes*).
　　See also WORKS FOR CHORUS.
Chansonette, tenor or soprano and piano.　　H.73 / – / NBE 15 / –
　　Text by Léon de Wailly.
　　Composed 1835. Incorporated in *Benvenuto
　　　Cellini*.
　　Published 1974.
Aubade
　　Text by Alfred de Musset.
　　1. Composed 1839, for voice and two horns.　H.78A / – / NBE 15 / –
　　2. Revised later for tenor or soprano, four　　H.78B / – / NBE 13 / –
　　　horns and two cornets.
　　　Published 1975.
Villanelle (no.1 of *Les nuits d'été*)
　　Text by Théophile Gautier.
　　1. Composed 1840 for mezzo-soprano or　　H.82A / B&H 17 / NBE 15 /
　　　tenor and piano.　　　　　　　　　　op.7 no.1
　　　Published 1841.
　　2. Arranged 1856 for mezzo-soprano or　　H.82B / B&H 15 / NBE 13 /
　　　tenor and orchestra.　　　　　　　　op.7 no.1
　　　Published 1856.
Le spectre de la rose (no. 2 of *Les nuits d'été*)
　　Text by Théophile Gautier.
　　1. Composed 1840 for mezzo-soprano or　　H.83A / B&H 17 / NBE 15 /
　　　tenor and piano.　　　　　　　　　　op.7 no.2
　　　Published 1841.
　　2. Arranged 1856 for contralto and　　　H.83B / B&H 15 / NBE 13 /
　　　orchestra.　　　　　　　　　　　　op.7 no.2

First performed Gotha, 6 Feb. 1856.
Published 1856.

Sur les lagunes: lamento (no.3 of *Les nuits d'été*)

Text by Théophile Gautier.

1. Composed 1840–1 for mezzo-soprano or tenor and piano. Published 1841.

H.84A / B&H 17 / NBE 15 / op.7 no.3

2. Arranged 1856 for baritone or mezzo-soprano or contralto and orchestra. Published 1856.

H.84B / B&H 15 / NBE 13 / op.7 no.3

Absence (no.4 of *Les nuits d'été*)

Text by Théophile Gautier.

1. Composed 1840 for mezzo-soprano or tenor and piano. Published 1841.

H.85A / B&H 17 / NBE 15 / op.7 no.4

2. Arranged 1843 for mezzo-soprano or tenor and orchestra. First performed Leipzig, 23 Feb. 1843. Published 1844.

H.85B / B&H 15 / NBE 13 / op.7 no.4

Au cimetière: clair de lune (no.5 of *Les nuits d'été*)

Text by Théophile Gautier.

1. Composed 1840–1 for mezzo-soprano or tenor and piano. Published 1841.

H.86A / B&H 17 / NBE 15 / op.7 no.5

2. Arranged 1856 for tenor and orchestra. Published 1856.

H.86B / B&H 15 / NBE 13 / op.7 no.5

L'île inconnue: barcarolle (no.6 of *Les nuits d'été*)

Text by Théophile Gautier.

1. Composed 1840–1 for mezzo-soprano or tenor and piano. Published 1841.

H.87A / B&H 17 / NBE 15 / op.7 no.6

2. Arranged 1856 for mezzo-soprano or tenor and orchestra. Published 1856.

H.87B / B&H 15 / NBE 13 / op.7 no.2

La mort d'Ophélie: ballade, soprano or tenor and piano.

H.92A / B&H 17 / NBE 15 / op.18 no.2

Text by Ernest Legouvé, after Shakespeare.
Composed 1842. Arranged 1848 for female chorus and orchestra (see WORKS FOR CHORUS).
Published 1848. Reissued 1849 as no.2 of *Tristia*.

La belle Isabeau: conte pendant l'orage,   H.94 / B&H 17 / NBE 15 / –
    mezzo-soprano, chorus (SSTBB) ad lib.,
    and piano.
   Text by Alexandre Dumas, père.
   Composed 1843
   Published 1843.
Le chasseur danois
   Text by Adolphe de Leuven.
   Composed 1844.
   1. For bass and piano.   H.104A / B&H 17 / NBE 15 / –
     First performed Prague, April 1846.   -
     Published 1844.
   2. For bass and orchestra.   H.104B / B&H 15 / NBE 13 / –
     First performed Vienna, 29 Nov. 1845.
     Published 1903.
Zaïde: boléro
   Text by Roger de Beauvoir.
   Composed 1845.
   1. For soprano and piano.   H.108A / B&H 17 / NBE 15 /
     Published 1904.   op.19 no.1
   2. For soprano and orchestra.   H.108B / B&H 15 / NBE 13 /
     First performed Vienna, 29 Nov. 1845.   op.19 no.1
     Published 1845 (vocal score), 1903 (full
     score).
Le trébuchet: scherzo, two sopranos (or tenor   H.113 / B&H 16 / NBE 15 /
    and baritone) and piano.   op.13 no.3
   Text by Antoine de Bertin and Emile
    Deschamps,
   Composed *c.* 1846.
   Published 1850 (as no.3 of *Fleurs des landes*).
Nessun maggior piacere, voice and piano.   H.114 / B&H 17 / NBE 15 / –
   Text by Berlioz, after Dante.
   Composed 1847.
   Published 1904.
Le matin: romance, mezzo-soprano or tenor   H.124 / B&H 17 / NBE 15 /
    and piano.   op.13 no.1
   Text by Adolphe de Bouclon.
   Composed *c.* 1850.
   Published 1850 (as no.1 of *Fleurs des landes*).
Petit oiseau: chanson de paysan, tenor or   H.125 / B&H 17 / NBE 15 /
    mezzo-soprano or baritone and piano.   op.13 no.2
   Text by Adolphe de Bouclon.
   Composed *c.* 1850.
   Published 1850 (as no.2 of *Fleurs des landes*).

VIII ARRANGEMENTS

Fleuve du Tage (J.-J.-B. Pollet).　　　　　　H.5 / – / NBE 22 / –
　Arranged for voice and guitar, *c*. 1819.

Recueil de romances (various composers).　　H.8 / – / NBE 22 / –
　A volume of twenty-five romances by
　　different composers arranged for voice
　　and guitar, *c*. 1819–22.

Hymne des Marseillais (Rouget de Lisle)
　1. Arranged 1830 for chorus (TB–STB) and　H.51A / B&H 18 / NBE 22 / –
　　orchestra.
　　Published 1830.
　2. Arranged 1848 for tenor solo, chorus　　H.51B / – / NBE 22 / –
　　(SSTTBB) and piano.
　　Published 1848.

Chant du neuf Thermidor (Rouget de Lisle)　H.51 *bis* / – / NBE 22 / –
　Arranged 1830 (?) for solo (T/S),
　　chorus (SSTTBB) and orchestra.
　Published 1984.

Le chasseur des chamois (Félix Huber)　　　H.64 / – / NBE 22 / –
　1. Arranged for TTB chorus and (?) strings,
　　1833.
　　First performed Hôtel de l'Europe
　　littéraire, 6 June 1833.
　2. Arranged for voice and guitar.

Der Freischütz (Weber)　　　　　　　　　　H.89 / – / NBE 22 / –
　Recitatives composed 1841.
　First performed Opéra, 7 June 1841.
　Published 1842 (vocal score).

L'invitation à la valse (Weber)　　　　　　H.90 / B&H 18 / NBE 22 / –
　Arranged for orchestra, 1841.
　First performed Opéra, 7 June 1841.
　Published 1842.

Marche marocaine (Léopold de Meyer)　　　H.105 / – / NBE 22 / –
　Arranged for orchestra, 1845.
　First performed Cirque Olympique, 6 April
　　1845.
　Published 1846.

Marche de Rákóczy (traditional Hungarian)　H.109 / B&H 11 / NBE 8 /
　Arranged for orchestra, 1846. Incorporated　op.24
　　in *La damnation de Faust* (see WORKS FOR
　　CHORUS).
　First performed Budapest, 15 Feb. 1846.
　Published 1846 (piano reduction), 1854 (full
　　score).

Chant des Chérubins (Bortnyansky)　　　　　H.122 / B&H 18 / NBE 22 / –
　　Arranged 1850 for chorus (SSTB).
　　First performed Salle Ste-Cécile, 22 Oct.
　　1850.
　　Published 1851.
Pater noster (Bortnyansky)　　　　　　　　H.126 / B&H 18 / NBE 22 / –
　　Arranged 1850–1 for chorus (SATB).
　　First performed Salle Ste-Cécile, 28 Jan.
　　1851.
　　Published 1851.
Plaisir d'amour (Martini)　　　　　　　　H.134 / B&H 18 / NBE 22 / –
　　Arranged for voice and orchestra, 1859.
　　First performed Baden-Baden, 29 Aug. 1859.
　　Published 1859.
Le roi des aulnes (Der Erlkönig) (Schubert)　H.136 / B&H 18 / NBE 22 / –
　　Arranged for voice and orchestra, 1860.
　　First performed Baden-Baden, 27 Aug. 1860.
　　Published 1860.
Invitation à louer dieu (Couperin)　　　　H.143 / B&H 18 / NBE 22 / –
　　Soeur Monique: rondeau from the *18ᵉ ordre*
　　arranged for chorus (SSA) and piano.
　　Published 1885.

IX COLLECTIONS

Neuf mélodies irlandaises (1830), re-titled　　H.38 / op.2
　　Irlande in 1849.
　　1. *Le coucher du soleil.* See SONGS.
　　2. *Hélène.* See SONGS.
　　3. *Chant guerrier.* See WORKS FOR CHORUS.
　　4. *La belle voyageuse.* See SONGS.
　　5. *Chanson à boire.* See WORKS FOR CHORUS.
　　6. *Chant sacré.* See WORKS FOR CHORUS.
　　7. *L'origine de la harpe.* See SONGS.
　　8. *Adieu Bessy.* See SONGS.
　　9. *Elégie en prose.* See SONGS.
Les nuits d'été (1841). See SONGS.　　　　H.81 / op.7
　　1. *Villanelle.*
　　2. *Le spectre de la rose.*
　　3. *Sur les lagunes.*
　　4. *Absence.*
　　5. *Au cimetière.*
　　6. *L'île inconnue.*
Tristia (1849, revised 1851).　　　　　　　H.119 / op.18
　　1. *Méditation religieuse.* See WORKS FOR
　　CHORUS.

2. *La mort d'Ophélie.* See SONGS.
3. *Marche funèbre pour la dernière scène d'Hamlet.* See OTHER INSTRUMENTAL WORKS.

Vox populi (1849). See WORKS FOR CHORUS.   H.120 / op.20
1. *La menace des Francs.*
2. *Hymne à la France.*

Feuillets d'album (1850).   H.121 / op.19
1. *Zaïde.* See SONGS.
2. *Les champs.* See SONGS.
3. *Chant des chemins de fer.* See WORKS FOR CHORUS.

Fleurs des landes (1850).   H.124 / op.13
1. *Le matin.* See SONGS.
2. *Petit oiseau.* See SONGS.
3. *Le trébuchet.* See SONGS.
4. *Le jeune pâtre breton.* See SONGS.
5. *Le chant des Bretons.* See WORKS FOR CHORUS.

Collection de 32 mélodies (1863).   H.139
32 songs and choruses all previously published separately. With the addition of *Le cinq mai* it was re-issued as *Collection de 33 mélodies*.

X LOST WORKS (excluding lost versions of surviving works and incomplete projects of which nothing survives. Not all of the works listed here were certainly composed.)

Potpourri concertant sur des thèmes italiens,   H.1
for flute, horn and string quintet.
Composed *c.* 1818.

Two quintets, for flute and string quartet.   H.2–3
Composed *c.* 1818–19.

Le cheval arabe: cantate, for voice and   H.12
orchestra.
Text by Millevoye.
Composed 1822.

Canon à trois voix.   H.13
Composed 1822.

Estelle et Némorin, opera   H.17
Text by Gerono, after Florian.
Composed 1823.

Le passage de la mer rouge, oratorio.   H.18
Latin text.
Composed 1823–4.

Beverley, ou le joueur: scène dramatique, for H.19
    bass soloist and orchestra.
  Text by Saurin, after Edward Moore.
  Composed 1823–4.

Messe solennelle, for bass soloist, chorus and H.20
    orchestra.
  Latin text.
  Composed 1824. Resurrexit (see WORKS FOR
    CHORUS) survives.
  Performed St-Roch, 27 Dec. 1824.

Les francs-juges, opera in three acts. H.23
  Text by Humbert Ferrand.
  Composed 1826. Overture and fragments
    survive (see OPERAS).

Fugue H.24
  Composed 1827 for Prix de Rome.

Marche religieuse des mages H.27
  Composed *c*. 1828.
  Performed Conservatoire, 26 May 1828.

Fugue H.28
  Composed 1828 for Prix de Rome.

Là ci darem la mano, variations for guitar. H.30
  Composed *c*. 1828.
  Published 1828.

Salutaris, for three voices with organ or piano. H.32
  Composed 1828.

Chanson des pirates. H.34
  Text by Victor Hugo.
  Composed 1829. Probably the same music as
    the *Chanson de brigands* in *Le retour à la
    vie* (see WORKS FOR CHORUS).

Fugue H.49
  Composed 1830 for the Prix de Rome.

Sardanapale, cantata H.50
  Composed 1830. A fragment survives (see
    PRIX DE ROME WORKS).

Chœur H.57
  Text by Berlioz.
  Composed 1831.

Chœur d'anges H.58
  Text unknown.
  Composed 1831.

La chasse de Lutzow (Weber) H.63
  Text by Körner.
  Arranged 1833 for TTBB chorus, strings and
    piano.

Performed Hôtel de l'Europe littéraire, 6
  June 1833.
Romance de Marie Tudor, for bass and piano.   H.66
  Text by Victor Hugo.
  Composed 1833.
  Performed Conservatoire, 22 Dec. 1833.
Scène de la comédie (for *Hamlet*)   H.102
  Composed 1844.
Marche d'Isly (Léopold de Meyer)   H.108
  Arranged 1845 for orchestra.
Chant du départ (Méhul)   H.115
  Arranged 1848, probably for chorus and
    piano.
Mourons pour la patrie (Rouget de Lisle)   H.116
  Arranged 1848, probably for chorus and
    piano.

XI BOOKS

*Grand traité d'instrumentation et
  d'orchestration modernes* (Paris, [1843]);
  2nd ed. including *L'art du chef d'orchestre*
  (Paris, [1855]).
Voyage musical en Allemagne et en Italie
  (Paris, 1844).
Les soirées de l'orchestre (Paris, 1852).
Les grotesques de la musique (Paris, 1859).
A travers chants (Paris, 1862).
Mémoires de Hector Berlioz (Paris, 1870).

Appendix C

Personalia

Adam, Adolphe (1803–56). Though contemporary with Berlioz and with some background in common, Adam specialized in a type of opéra-comique Berlioz despised. His greatest successes were *Le postillon de Longjumeau* (1836) and the ballet *Giselle* (1841). He was elected to the Institut in 1844 and at his death in 1856 was succeeded by Berlioz. Berlioz's warm notice of *Le muletier de Tolède* in 1855 was in return for a favourable review by Adam of *L'enfance du Christ*, although in general neither composer could find much to admire in the other.

Alexandre, Edouard (1824–88). The son of Jacob Alexandre, founder of the firm which manufactured the 'orgue-mélodium', he became one of Berlioz's close friends and an executor of his will. Both Berlioz and Liszt gave public support to Alexandre instruments.

Auber, Daniel-François-Esprit (1782–1871). Most of Auber's considerable gifts were devoted to opéra-comique, some of which are still heard today. The work that most influenced Berlioz was *La muette de Portici*, also known as *Masaniello*, (1828), one of the leading serious operas of its time. He succeeded Cherubini as director of the Conservatoire in 1842, and was thus obliged to approve all Berlioz's absences abroad. Their relations appear to have been cordial.

Balfe, Michael (1808–70). Born in Ireland, Balfe spent much of his career as singer and composer abroad. Berlioz found him congenial company in Paris. He conducted his *Maid of Honour* at Drury Lane in 1848.

Balzac, Honoré de (1799–1850). Balzac dedicated stories both to Berlioz and to Harriet Smithson, and may have borrowed some of Berlioz's ideas for his *Gambara*. Berlioz appreciated Balzac's work without giving it the status of classic.

Barbier, Henri-Auguste (1805–82). Fashionable as a poet in his day, his friendship with Berlioz dates from Rome in 1831. Berlioz quoted him often. With Léon de Wailly he provided the libretto for *Benvenuto Cellini* and also the text of *Hymne à la France* (1844). Berlioz is warmly recalled in his later published recollections.

Bertin, Edouard (1797–1871) and **Armand** (1801–54). These two brothers were proprietors of the *Journal des débats*, founded by their father. Their influence in Paris was considerable and their support for Berlioz therefore invaluable. They employed him as music critic from 1834 to 1863 and supported performances of his works. Armand received the dedication of *Le roi Lear*.

Bertin, Louise (1805–77). Sister of the two preceding, and partially crippled from birth, she was poet, painter and composer. Her opera *Esmeralda* had a libretto fashioned by Victor Hugo from his own *Notre-Dame de Paris* and she had some support from Berlioz in its production at the Opéra in 1836, but it was not a success. He criticized its heavy orchestration and its irregular phrasing. The first version of *Les nuits d'été* was dedicated to her.

Berton, Henri-Montan (1767–1844). Widely regarded as outmoded in style after the 1820s, Berton's music found few admirers, and Berlioz treated him in his *Mémoires* with contempt. Nevertheless he belongs firmly to the tradition on which Berlioz based his own early style.

Carvalho, Léon (1825–97). Mauritian by birth, he brought numerous French operas to the Paris stage, with immense entrepreneurial energy and courage. His production of *Les Troyens à Carthage* in 1863 was highly creditable, although Berlioz was not alone among composers in complaining of his high-handed treatment of what the authors wrote and required.

Charton-Demeur, Madame Anne-Arsène (1824–92). She created the parts of Didon and Béatrice and was, in Berlioz's view, the finest mezzo-soprano of her day. She remained a close friend and was present at Berlioz's death-bed.

Châteaubriand, François-René, Vicomte de (1768–1848). His writings were avidly read by the Romantics, especially *René*, whose descriptions of indefinable longing are echoed in the programme of the *Symphonie fantastique*. Berlioz's request for 1500 francs in 1824 was the brave approach of a young student to a celebrity. The posthumous publication of the *Mémoires* was modelled on Châteaubriand's *Mémoires d'outre-tombe*.

Cherubini, Luigi (1760–1842). His many successful operas and his choral music impressed and influenced Berlioz profoundly, yet their personal relationship was poor. Cherubini's behaviour as director of the Conservatoire made him the butt of Berlioz's scorn.

Chopin, Frédéric (1810–49). He and Berlioz were close friends in the 1830s, but their music has virtually nothing in common. Berlioz seems only to have written admiringly of Chopin's music (the *Études*) in an obituary.

Damcke, Berthold (1812–75). Born in Germany, he was already familiar with Berlioz's music before settling in Paris in 1859; he and his wife were near-neighbours to Berlioz and supported him generously in his last years.

David, Félicien (1810–76). David was perhaps the only other French composer of Berlioz's generation to contribute to the widening outlook of romantic music. His success as a purveyor of near-eastern exoticism in *Le désert* (1844) appealed strongly to Berlioz at first, though this opinion was soon after retracted. They were not on close terms.

Deschamps, Emile (1791–1871) and **Antoni** (1800–69). Both brothers were well-known literary figures. Emile provided the text for *Roméo et*

Juliette and *Le trébuchet*, Antoni that for the *Grande symphonie funèbre et triomphale*.

Dorant, ? (dates unknown). He was music-teacher at La Côte-St-André from 1819 to 1821 during which time he taught Berlioz the guitar. In 1845 he played the violin in Berlioz's concert in Lyons.

Du Boys, Albert Marie (1804–89). Since his father was deputy for Isère, Berlioz's *département*, the two were probably friends when they went to Paris in 1821, Berlioz to study medicine, Du Boys to study law. Du Boys provided a number of texts for Berlioz's early songs, and later wrote on historical and political subjects as well as on law. It is curious that he is not mentioned in the *Mémoires*.

Duponchel, Charles-Edmond (1795–1863). He was director of the Opéra from 1835 to 1840 and from 1847 to 1849. Having presided over one Berlioz failure in 1838 his first act in 1847 was to stifle any chance of another (*La nonne sanglante*). Berlioz's contempt for him was total.

Ferrand, Humbert (1805–68). The series of letters addressed to Ferrand over a period of forty-three years is a remarkable source of information and is also testimony to a lasting friendship, formed in about 1823. They collaborated on the *Révolution grecque* and *Les francs-juges*. Ferrand published poetry under the pseudonym Georges Arandas.

Fétis, François-Joseph (1784–1871). Founder of the *Revue musicale*, Fétis was an influential music critic who published encouraging notices of Berlioz's first appearances in Paris. After 1832, when Berlioz lampooned him in *Lélio*, Fétis became hostile to his music. They were reconciled, out of mutual admiration, in later years.

Fornier, Estelle (*née* Duboeuf) (1797–1876). Dazzled by her beauty and her little pink boots, Berlioz fell in love with her at the age of twelve. Some of his juvenile works were inspired by her. She was already a widow in 1848 when Berlioz wrote to her and was sixty-seven when he visited her in 1864. He continued writing to her to the end of his life and left her an annuity in his will.

Girard, Narcisse (1797–1860). Conductor of some of Berlioz's early concerts, including the first performance of *Harold en Italie*. The overture to *Les francs-juges* was dedicated to him.

Gounet, Thomas (1801–69). A civil servant in the Ministry of Public Instruction, Gounet translated Thomas Moore for Berlioz in 1829 and also lent him money on occasions. Their friendship lasted about twenty years.

Habeneck, François-Antoine (1781–1849). As conductor of both the Opéra and the Conservatoire concerts he was the most influential musician in Paris for twenty years. He conducted the first performances of the *Symphonie fantastique*, *Lélio*, the *Requiem* and *Benvenuto Cellini*. His relations with Berlioz were variable, and their methods of conducting quite different, yet he must have had some faith in the music to undertake it at all.

Hallé, Charles (1819–95). Coming to Paris in 1836 from Germany, Hallé joined the wide circle of foreign musicians and became one of Berlioz's admirers. This friendship continued in London in 1848 where Hallé moved next before his final residence in Manchester. His reminiscences include many references to Berlioz.

Heine, Heinrich (1799–1856). The German poet lived in Paris for twenty years and followed musical events closely, reporting on them in the German press. His friendship with Berlioz was particularly close at the end of his life. Heine called Berlioz a 'colossal nightingale, a lark the size of an eagle' and first used the words 'Babylonian' and 'Ninevitish' of his music.

Heller, Stephen (1815–88). Heller reached Paris from Hungary in 1838 and published many piano works, mostly didactic in nature. He was very close to Berlioz in his last years.

Hiller, Ferdinand (1811–85). Hiller lived in Paris from 1828 to 1834. His friendship with Berlioz lasted nearly forty years, with extensive correspondence between them. The affair with Camille Moke in 1830 seems not to have damaged the friendship and mutual admiration of the two men.

Hugo, Victor (1802–85). Berlioz set three of his poems, *La captive*, *Sara la baigneuse* and the *Romance* from *Marie Tudor*. Berlioz admired him enormously as a writer but never penetrated Hugo's somewhat haughty treatment of musicians.

Jullien, Louis (1812–60). His spectacular concerts in Paris and London won enormous audiences, and his showmanship set a new style. He was an eccentric who eventually lost his money and his wits, and Berlioz fell foul of his promises in 1848, having conducted a season for him in London.

Legouvé, Ernest (1807–1903). One of the many minor literary figures whom Berlioz counted as close friends. Legouvé provided the text of *La mort d'Ophélie* and lent Berlioz money during the composition of *Benvenuto Cellini*. He may have advised about the libretto of *Les Troyens* and *Béatrice et Bénédict*. His reminiscences (1886) devote extensive space to Berlioz.

Lesueur, Jean-François (1760–1837). A fortunate choice as Berlioz's teacher, since he was in many ways a kindred spirit. A composer with a restless, searching mind, he had enjoyed great success under Napoleon, but his operas were only briefly influential.

Liszt, Franz (1811–86). One of the few people Berlioz addressed as 'tu', Liszt joined Berlioz's circle of friends in 1830. He transcribed the *Symphonie fantastique* and certain overtures for piano. In the 1850s he promoted many Berlioz performances in Weimar, but his admiration for Wagner drew the two composers apart. *La damnation de Faust* was dedicated to Liszt, and the *Faust Symphony*, in return, was dedicated to Berlioz. In 1855 he published a long essay on *Harold en Italie*.

Massart, Lambert (1811–92). Although he was active in Paris as a violinist and teacher all his life, Berlioz's intimate friendship with him and his wife, the pianist Louise Masson, dates mainly from the 1860s. Massart played a leading part in the Société Philharmonique in 1850–1.

Mendelssohn (-Bartholdy), Felix (1809–47). The two composers met in Rome in 1831 and again in Leipzig in 1843. Berlioz's admiration for Mendelssohn's music was not reciprocated, even though their relations were always cordial.

Meyerbeer, Giacomo (1791–1864). As an influential critic and an inventive composer Berlioz could not escape Meyerbeer's insistent friendship. Meyerbeer genuinely admired Berlioz's music and attended many performances of *Les Troyens à Carthage* at the very end of his life, and Berlioz saw the virtues of Meyerbeer's music, even if he resented his domination of the Opéra throughout his working life.

Moke, Camille (1811–75). Berlioz was probably lucky to escape marriage to Camille, since she soon established a reputation for persistent infidelity. She was undoubtedly a very able pianist: Berlioz said her talent had 'something miraculous about it'. She appears, thinly disguised, in his futuristic novel *Euphonia*.

Morel, Auguste (1809–80). He came to Paris from Marseilles in 1836 and returned there in 1850 as director of its conservatoire. His correspondence with Berlioz between 1838 and 1868 is second only to that with Ferrand for its source value. A number of Morel's compositions are dedicated to Berlioz.

d'Ortigue, Joseph (1802–66). As a critic he supported Berlioz's works ardently and published numerous articles on them. They were very close friends for many years despite Berlioz's failure to share d'Ortigue's admiration for plainsong and the traditional music of the Catholic church.

Paganini, Nicolo (1782–1840). Berlioz never heard him play (except once in chamber music) but wrote *Harold en Italie* at his request. There is no reason to doubt the genuineness of Paganini's admiration expressed in the gift of 20,000 francs in 1838. The dedication of *Roméo et Juliette* was a heartfelt expression of thanks.

Recio, Marie (*née* Martin) (1814–62). Berlioz's second wife. Her career as a singer was brief and undistinguished; she sang in some of his concerts in the early 1840s, and the orchestration of *Absence* was written for her. She was the subject of, and probably also the originator of, much spiteful gossip and she undoubtedly made Berlioz's life difficult in some respects. On the other hand she provided twenty years' companionship of inestimable value to him.

Reicha, Anton (1770–1836). He was born in Bohemia and had lived in Bonn for some years, where he knew Beethoven. Despite his tireless academic labours at the Paris Conservatoire, where he taught from 1818 until his death, he was a curious mixture of accomplished composer and experimental theoretician, whose work and influence is still not well understood.

Ritter, Théodore (1838–86). Berlioz predicted, wrongly, a great future for this young pianist in the mid-1850s, and praised him lavishly in the press. Ritter helped with the piano score of *L'enfance du Christ* and arranged parts of the *Te deum*. He composed some variations on a theme provided by Berlioz (now lost), but his career vanished into obscurity.

Rossini, Gioacchino (1792–1868). Rossini resided for many years in Paris, but his regular soirées seem never to have included Berlioz, doubtless because there was little admiration on either side, except by Berlioz for the more ambitious and dramatic later operas. Rossini's jokes at Berlioz's expense were characteristically mordent.

Saint-Saëns, Camille (1835–1921). As a young man Saint-Saëns came under Berlioz's spell. He prepared the piano score of *Lélio* in 1855 and betrayed some Berliozian influence in his early symphonies. He left an interesting portrait of Berlioz in his *Portraits et Souvenirs* (1900).

Sax, Adolphe (1814–94). Berlioz was a vociferous supporter of Sax's new wind instruments and his improvements to existing families. He was the first to write for the saxophone (the *Chant sacré* arranged for wind in 1844) and considered using the instrument in the closing scene of *La damnation de Faust*. The soprano saxhorn, now obsolete, has prominent parts in the *Te deum* and *Les Troyens*.

Sayn-Wittgenstein, Princess Carolyne (1819–87). Of aristocratic Polish birth, she settled with Liszt in Weimar in 1847 and dominated his life for many years. Her immense intellectual willpower generated great undertakings in others, notably in persuading Berlioz to compose *Les Troyens*, a task for which she was justly rewarded with its dedication.

Schumann, Robert (1810–56). Their personal acquaintance was brief and superficial, and Berlioz showed no interest in Schumann's music. He probably knew none of it. But Schumann's perceptive essay on the *Symphonie fantastique*, written in 1835, laid the ground for Berlioz's success in Germany.

Scribe, Eugène (1791–1861). As successful librettist for Auber, Meyerbeer and Halévy, Scribe's influence at the Opéra was even more powerful than theirs. Berlioz's fruitless attempts to set his *La nonne sanglante* were bedevilled with mistrust on both sides and doomed to failure.

Smithson, Harriet (1800–54). Berlioz's first wife. She was brought up in Ireland and first played in London in 1818. Her moderate success there was overshadowed by her overwhelming, but brief, success in Paris, which made the rapid end to her career all the harder to bear. Berlioz always adored the Ophelia and the Juliet in her however difficult their daily life became.

Spontini, Gasparo (1774–1851). Admiration for Spontini's music already animated Berlioz and had influenced his own when he met the older master and found some degree of admiration reciprocated. Berlioz consciously based his early style on the three most successful Spontini operas, *La Vestale*, *Fernand Cortez* and *Olympie*.

Stasov, Vladimir (1824–1906). His extensive intellectual interests and forceful character gave him great influence over the new Russian school of composers, and it was largely his faith in Berlioz's music that brought it to the notice of his compatriots. Berlioz corresponded with him until the end of his life.

Urhan, Chrétien (1790–1845). A violinist, he was also an outstanding viola player. He gave the first performance of *Harold en Italie* and played it subsequently on many occasions.

Verdi, Giuseppe (1813–1901). Contact between the two men was disappointingly brief and intermittent, perhaps because neither composer after the 1850s was very curious about the other's work. Verdi acknowledged the influence of Berlioz's *Requiem* on his own, but with severe qualifications.

Viardot, Pauline (1821–1910). One of the great mezzo-sopranos of her time, Berlioz would certainly have wished her to sing Didon if *Les Troyens* had been staged four or five years earlier. She sang *La captive* in London in 1848 with Berlioz conducting, and their friendship was deep and lasting, with more than a hint of passion on Berlioz's side at times.

Wagner, Richard (1813–83). Much has been written on the ebb and flow of friendship and influence between Berlioz and Wagner, and their interaction was complex. Berlioz's music was the most striking of any Wagner heard during his stay in Paris from 1839 to 1841 and it affected his own. But despite moments of closer understanding their natures were fundamentally different. Wagner eventually rejected Berlioz as a relic of traditional French values, and Berlioz regarded *Tristan* with horrified dismay.

Appendix D

Select bibliography

A SCORES

The most scholarly and complete texts are those of the *New Berlioz Edition* (Kassel, 1967–   ) whose volumes published to date are:

2   *Les Troyens*
3   *Béatrice et Bénédict*
5   *Huit scènes de Faust*
8   *La damnation de Faust*
9   *Grande messe des morts*
10   *Te deum*
13   Songs for solo voice and orchestra
16   *Symphonie fantastique*
18   *Roméo et Juliette*
19   *Grande symphonie funèbre et triomphale*
25   D. Kern Holoman, *Catalogue of the Works of Hector Berlioz*

Nos. 2, 10, 16 and 19 of this series are also reprinted in Eulenburg miniature scores. Many other Berlioz works, including symphonies, overtures and vocal works are to be had in Eulenburg edition, which is in general more correct than the Kalmus miniature scores. These are mostly reprinted from the Breitkopf & Härtel edition of Berlioz's works published in 1900–7. For smaller choral works, and for a full score of *Benvenuto Cellini*, the Kalmus edition is the best currently available.

B WRITINGS BY BERLIOZ

Mémoires: David Cairns's admirable translation is indispensable reading for any student of Berlioz, and it contains much additional information of value (Panther Arts, London). The French text is available in the Garnier Flammarion edition, but without annotation.

Criticism: Berlioz's three collections, *Les soirées de l'orchestre* (1852), *Les grotesques de la musique* (1859) and *A travers chants* (1862) have been copiously edited by Léon Guichard and published by Grund, Paris (1968, 1969 and 1971). For English readers there exist translations of *Les soirées de l'orchestre* by Roche (1929), Barzun (1956), and Fortescue (1963), and of *A travers chants*, translated by Edwin Evans and published as three books: *Mozart, Weber and Wagner, Gluck and his Operas* and *Beethoven's Symphonies* (1913–18).

Of the remaining hundreds of feuilletons, the only modern selection is Gérard Condé's *Cauchemars et Passions* (Paris, 1981), which provides, in French, a precious treasure for the enquiring reader. An earlier collection, *Les musiciens et la musique,* was edited by A. Hallays in 1903. The *Grand traité d'instrumentation* (1844) and the *Art du chef d'orchestre* (1855) were translated in 1856 by Mary Cowden Clarke under the title *Modern Instrumentation and Orchestration* (London, 1856).

Letters: The *Correspondance générale* (Paris, 1972–   ) is an essential adjunct for a closer study of Berlioz's life. The volumes to date are:

1   1803–1832
2   1832–1842
3   1842–1850
4   1851–1855
5   1855–1859

Two more volumes are anticipated. Meanwhile, the later years' letters can be gleaned from the following:

Correspondance inédite (Paris, 1879).

'Vingt lettres inédites . . . adressées à M. Adolphe Samuel', *Le ménestrel*, xlv (1879), 217–59.

Lettres intimes (Paris, 1882).

Briefe von Hector Berlioz an die Fürstin Carolyne Sayn-Wittgenstein (Leipzig, 1903).

'Une page d'amour romantique: lettres à Mme Estelle F.' (1903).

Tiersot, Julien, ed.: 'Lettres de musiciens écrites en français: du XVe au XXe siècle (Turin, 1936).

Barzun, Jacques, ed.: *Nouvelles lettres de Berlioz* (New York, 1954).

A useful selection of letters in English was published by Humphrey Searle in 1966 under the title: *Hector Berlioz: a Selection from his Letters*.

C BIOGRAPHIES

Berlioz's own writings – the *Mémoires*, the letters and the critical writings – provide the basis for any biographical study. The fullest biographies to date are:

Jullien, Adolphe. *Hector Berlioz, sa vie et ses œuvres* (Paris, 1888).

Hippeau, Edmond. *Berlioz et son temps* (Paris, 1890).

Prod'homme, J.-G. *Hector Berlioz (1803–1869): sa vie et ses œuvres* (Paris, 1904).

Tiersot, Julien. *Hector Berlioz et la société de son temps* (Paris, 1904).

Boschot, Adolphe. *Hector Berlioz, une vie romantique*, 3 vols. (Paris, 1906–13).

Masson, P.-M. *Berlioz* (Paris, 1923).

Barraud, Henri. *Hector Berlioz* (Paris, 1955).

Ballif, Claude. *Berlioz* (Paris, 1968).

For English readers, the most important biographies are:

Barzun, Jacques. *Berlioz and the Romantic Century*, 2 vols. (Boston, 1950).

Cairns, David. *Berlioz, the Making of an Artist* (London, 1989).

Holoman, D. Kern. *Berlioz* (Cambridge, Mass., 1989).

Other general studies in English are:

Bennett, Joseph. *Hector Berlioz* (London, 1883).

Turner, W.J. *Berlioz, the Man and his Work* (London, 1934).

Wotton, Tom S. *Hector Berlioz* (London, 1935).

Of particular value is *Berlioz and the Romantic Imagination*, Arts Council Exhibition Catalogue, London, 1969.

More specialised studies and articles:

Fouque, O. *Les révolutionnaires de la musique* (Paris, 1882).

Tiersot, Julien. 'Berlioziana', *Le ménestrel*, lxx–lxxii (1904–6) [series of articles].

Pohl, Richard. Hector Berlioz: *Studien und Erinnerungen* (Leipzig, 1884/R1974).

Ganz, A.W. *Berlioz in London* (London, 1950).

Dickinson, A.E.F. 'The Revisions for "The Damnation of Faust" ', *The Monthly Musical Record*, lxxxix (1959), 180.

Friedheim, Philip. 'Radical Harmonic Procedures in Berlioz', *The Music Review*, xxi (1960), 282.

Hartnoll, Phyllis, ed. *Shakespeare in Music* (London, 1964).

Macdonald, Hugh. 'Berlioz's Self-borrowings', *Proceedings of the Royal Musical Association*, xcii (1965–66), 27.

Cairns, David. 'Hector Berlioz (1803–69)', *The Symphony*, ed. R. Simpson, i (London, 1966), 201–31.

—— 'Berlioz and Virgil', *Proceedings of the Royal Musical Association*, xcv (1968–9), 97.

Macdonald, Hugh. *Berlioz Orchestral Music* (London, 1969).

Klein, J.W. 'Berlioz's Personality', *Music and Letters*, l (1969), 15.

Cone, Edward T. 'Inside the Saint's Head: the Music of Berlioz', *Musical Newsletter*, i (1971), 3, 16; ii (1972), 19.

Bailbé, J.-M. *Berlioz: artiste et écrivain dans les Mémoires* (Paris, 1972).

Primmer, Brian. *The Berlioz Style* (London, 1973).

Holoman, D. Kern. 'The Present State of Berlioz Research', *Acta musicologica*, xlvii (1975), 31–67).

Rushton, Julian. 'The Genesis of Berlioz's "La damnation de Faust" ', *Music and Letters* , lvi (1975), 129.

Holoman, D. Kern. *The Creative Process in the Autograph Musical Documents of Hector Berlioz, c. 1818–1840* (Ann Arbor, 1980).

Crabbe, John. *Hector Berlioz, Rational Romantic* (London, 1980).

Rushton, Julian. *The Musical Language of Berlioz* (Cambridge, 1983)

Kemp, Ian. *Hector Berlioz: Les Troyens* (Cambridge, 1988).

A fuller list of books and articles is found in *The New Grove*, (London, 1980), article 'Berlioz'.

D BIBLIOGRAPHIES

The most complete list of works and writings is found in the *Catalogue of the Works of Hector Berlioz*, by D. Kern Holoman, New Berlioz Edition, volume 25 (Kassel, 1987).

Previous catalogues are found as follows:

Music and books:
Hopkinson, Cecil. *A Bibliography of the Musical and Literary Works of Hector Berlioz, 1803–1869* (Edinburgh, 1951) (2nd rev. edition, 1980).

Feuilletons:
Prod'homme, J.-G. 'Bibliographie Berliozienne', *Revue Musicale*, 1956, no.233, pp.97–147.

Writings on Berlioz:
Wright, Michael G. H. *A Berlioz Bibliography* (Farnborough, n.d.)
Langford, Jeffrey and Graves, Jane Denker, *Hector Berlioz: A Guide to Research* (New York, 1989).

Index

252

Printed in the United States
72850LV00001B/76

9 780198 164838